ISHUN
DZHANKOI
AIBAR
KARASU R.
SALGIR RIVER
BURULCHA R.
ZUYA R.
BIYUK R.
KUCHUK R.
BULGANAK R.
INDOL R.
EVPATORIA
SAKI
KARASUBAZAR
FEODOSIYA
SIMFEROPOL
SUDAK
BAKHCHISARAI
KAGA R.
ALUSHTA
BLACK SEA
SEVASTOPOL
BALAKLAVA
YALTA
LIVADIA
KOREIS
ALUPKA
CRIMEA
GERMANY
U. S. S. R.
FRANCE
HUNGARY
ITALY
YUGOSLAVIA
ROMANIA
CRIMEA
SPAIN
BLACK SEA
BULGARIA
ROME
NAPLES
GREECE
ANKARA
TURKEY
ALGIERS
TUNIS
SYRIA
MALTA
MEDITERRANEAN SEA
ALGERIA
TRIPOLI
ALEXANDRIA
SUEZ CANAL
LIBYA
CAIRO
palacios

St. Francis College

Roosevelt and the Russians

EDWARD R. STETTINIUS, JR.

Roosevelt and the Russians

THE YALTA CONFERENCE

Edited by Walter Johnson

DOUBLEDAY & COMPANY, INC., 1949

GARDEN CITY, NEW YORK

Copyright, 1949, by The Stettinius Fund, Inc.
All Rights Reserved

Printed in the United States at The Country Life Press, Garden City, N. Y.

TO VIRGINIA WALLACE STETTINIUS

Acknowledgments

Many of my friends read the next to final draft of this book and offered helpful suggestions. Above all I am deeply grateful to Dr. Leo Pasvolsky, of the Brookings Institution, for his critical reading of different drafts and for making invaluable recommendations.

W. F. Richmond and Norman Portenoy kindly supplied information about the trip to and from Yalta, and Dr. T. L. Tyson's personal diary furnished interesting material.

A not inconsiderable contribution—in the form of typing the various drafts of the manuscript and other details—was made by Constance Myers, Lucy Stockwell, Carol Tanner, Betty Jane Swan, Fred T. Lininger, Jean Facey, Leona Lusin, Sara Morgan, and Lois Holmes.

The staff of the Alderman Library, the University of Virginia—particularly Harry Clemons, Francis L. Berkeley, Jr., and William Gaines—have been most co-operative.

ACKNOWLEDGMENTS

Ivan von Auw, Jr., of the Harold Ober Agency, too, was helpful at all times.

Our great indebtedness to Lilburn F. Wallace for his untiring efforts cannot be adequately expressed.

Foreword

A deep respect for the memory of President Roosevelt and unshaken faith in the rightness of his foreign policy have impelled me to write this book about the Yalta Conference.

The American people have encountered grave disappointments in our relations with the Soviet Union since 1945. These have resulted in widespread acceptance of the idea that at Yalta vital interests of the United States were sacrificed to appeasement of the Soviet Union.

This idea is false. It is not Yalta that is the trouble with the world today, but subsequent failures to adhere to the policies Yalta stood for and to carry out agreements that were reached there. Difficulties have developed, not from the agreements reached at Yalta, but from the failure of the Soviet Union to honor those agreements.

The Conference itself was an honest effort on the part of Great Britain and the United States to determine whether or not long-range co-operation with the Soviet Union could be

FOREWORD

attained. Had such an effort not been made the world would quite rightly be in doubt as to where the blame lies for the present world situation.

I firmly believe that when all the evidence is in and when the Conference is seen in its proper perspective Yalta will become a symbol—not of appeasement, but of a wise and courageous attempt by President Roosevelt and Prime Minister Churchill to set the world on the road to lasting peace.

It is important for the public to know exactly what took place in the Crimea and, almost equally important, what did not take place. I was present at Yalta as Secretary of State, and there are certain facts that may be known to me alone since the deaths of President Roosevelt and Harry Hopkins. There were also other participants who could help clear the record. I hope they will come forward.

In the writing of this book I have associated myself with Walter Johnson, a member of the History Department of the University of Chicago and author of *William Allen White's America*. Mr. Johnson, a trained historian, who brings a fresh insight to the Yalta story, has assisted me in placing this Conference in its proper perspective in the unfolding of American foreign policy and in filling an important gap that has hitherto existed in the history of the war period.

Mr. Johnson and I, working together, have condensed and rearranged my notes on Yalta for this present book. I have had access to copies of official documents covering this period. In addition we have discussed this manuscript with a number of individuals who were active in various aspects of the Conference.

I also have had the privilege of conversations over a period of time with President Harry S. Truman, and he has wholeheartedly supported me in my effort to clarify the record and

FOREWORD

to write a truthful, factual account of this important Conference.

The royalties from this book will go to an educational and charitable foundation.

EDWARD R. STETTINIUS, JR.

The Horseshoe
Rapidan, Virginia

Contents

ACKNOWLEDGMENTS vii

FOREWORD ix

PART ONE: TRYING TO BUILD A BETTER WORLD

1 Background of the Yalta Conference 3
2 Meetings at Marrakech and Naples 27
3 Rendezvous at Malta 59

PART TWO: AT THE CONFERENCE

4 Argonaut 79
5 The Big Three Meet (February 4) 99
6 The German Question (February 5) 117
7 The Big Three Veto Power (February 6) 135
8 "Captain of Her Soul" (February 6) 151
9 "A Step Forward" (February 7) 161

CONTENTS

10	Planning the World Security Conference (February 8)	189
11	"The Glories of Future Possibilities Stretching Before Us" (February 8)	209
12	The Sixth Day of the Conference (February 9)	223
13	The High Tide of Allied Unity (February 10)	251
14	The End of the Conference (February 11)	279

PART THREE: THE BALANCE SHEET

| 15 | Appeasement or Realism? | 295 |
| 16 | The Breakdown after Yalta | 309 |

| APPENDIX | 327 |
| INDEX | 353 |

Illustrations

	Facing page
Winston Churchill, Franklin D. Roosevelt, and Joseph Stalin at Livadia Palace	64
The Yalta Conference in session	65
Ambassador Gromyko, Mr. Stettinius, and Sir Alexander Cadogan at Saki airfield	80
The three foreign ministers sign the Protocol of the Yalta Conference	80
President Roosevelt, Prime Minister Churchill, Molotov, Stettinius, Vishinsky, and Harriman	81
Livadia Palace, the official headquarters of the Yalta Conference, and the American residence	128
The courtyard at Livadia Palace	128

ILLUSTRATIONS

	Facing page
President Roosevelt's study in Livadia Palace	129
Russian maids making President Roosevelt's bed	129
Secretary of State Hull, Edward R. Stettinius, Jr., and Assistant Secretary of State Dean Acheson	144
Mr. Stettinius with Alger Hiss of the State Department delegation	145
Marshal Stalin and Prime Minister Churchill	240
Marshal Stalin confers with Mr. Roosevelt at Livadia Palace	241
Winston Churchill with Secretary Stettinius	256
Marshal Stalin, Foreign Minister Molotov, and Deputy Foreign Minister Vishinsky	257
President Roosevelt with King Farouk of Egypt	288
Ibn Saud of Saudi Arabia and the President	288
Emperor Haile Selassie and the President	288
Ambassador John G. Winant, Anna Roosevelt Boettiger, and Harry Hopkins	289
Molotov, Eden, and Stettinius	304
President Roosevelt with Secretary of State Stettinius and Marshal Stalin	305
The Prime Minister and the President aboard the U.S.S. Quincy in Malta Harbor	305

PART ONE

Trying to Build a Better World

CHAPTER 1

Background of the Yalta Conference

The Yalta Conference—February 4–11, 1945—was the most important wartime meeting of the leaders of Great Britain, the Soviet Union, and the United States. It was not only the longest meeting of President Roosevelt with Prime Minister Churchill and Marshal Stalin; it was also the first time that the three leaders reached fundamental agreements on postwar problems as distinct from mere statements of aims and purposes. Many problems of a non-military nature had been discussed at Teheran, but basic agreements were not reached or even attempted.

This was the second time the three war leaders had met, but it was the first occasion on which they had met with all their foreign ministers. Although Anthony Eden and V. M. Molotov had participated in the Teheran Conference—November 28–December 1, 1943—Cordell Hull had not.

The Yalta Conference, too, was the first real occasion on which the Chiefs of Staff of the three countries conducted an exhaustive examination of the respective military positions of the Allied forces and discussed in detail their future plans. The timing of the second front and related military questions had been discussed at Teheran, but it was not until Yalta that sufficient confidence existed among the three nations for a free and open examination of future operational plans.

Thus the Yalta Conference marked the high tide of British, Russian, and American co-operation on the war and on the postwar settlement. In the days immediately after the Conference most American newspapers gave high praise to what had been accomplished in the Crimea.

On February 13, 1945, the New York *Times* wrote:

> *The long and detailed agreements announced at the end of the second conference between President Roosevelt, Prime Minister Churchill and Marshal Stalin and now submitted to the judgment of the world are so broad and sweeping that it will take a detailed analysis and a demonstration of their application in actual practice to measure their full scope and final implications. But even the first glance gives assurance that, though they may disappoint some individual expectations, they justify and surpass most of the hopes placed on this fateful meeting, and in their aims and purposes they show the way to an early victory in Europe, to a secure peace, and to a brighter world. . . .*
>
> *The alliance of the Big Three stands firm. Progress has been made. The hope of further gains is high. This conference marks a milestone on the road to victory and peace.*

The New York *Herald Tribune* called the Yalta communiqué a "remarkable document." "The over-riding fact," this paper observed, "is that the conference has produced another great proof of allied unity, strength and power of decision." The Philadelphia *Record* termed the Conference the "greatest United Nations victory of this war."

Congressional leaders like Senators Barkley, Vandenberg, White, Kilgore, and Connally praised the results of the meeting. A survey of public reaction, conducted for the State Department during the last week of February, revealed that the American people considered the Yalta Conference a success. This survey reported that the Conference had raised hopes for a long-time peace; it had increased satisfaction with the way the Big Three were co-operating, and with the way the President and the State Department were handling American interests abroad.

Although the public reaction to the Yalta communiqué was overwhelmingly favorable, there was a critical minority who singled out a variety of aspects for attack. The voting formula in the Security Council was challenged by some on the basis that the Great Power veto left the proposed world organization without sufficient power. Some bitterly attacked the communiqué for failing to spell out what was involved in the unconditional surrender of Germany. The greater portion of the minority criticism centered on the Polish boundary arrangement and on the new agreement on the Polish Government. In spite of all these attacks, the over-all reaction of the country was favorable to the solution of the Polish—as well as to the other—questions.

Three years after the meeting in the Crimea, however, the Yalta Conference was under bitter attack. "High Tide of Appeasement Was Reached at the Yalta Conference . . . ," *Life* declared in its caption to a picture of the Conference. In the same issue of September 6, 1948, William C. Bullitt charged:

> At Yalta in the Crimea, on Feb. 4, 1945, the Soviet dictator welcomed the weary President. Roosevelt, indeed, was more than tired. He was ill. Little was left of the physical and mental

vigor that had been his when he entered the White House in 1933. Frequently he had difficulty in formulating his thoughts, and greater difficulty in expressing them consecutively. But he still held to his determination to appease Stalin.

Many more bitter statements have been made in recent criticism of the Yalta Conference. Some of them have been based on misunderstanding, others on prejudice. The following pages of this book reveal how unjust they are. The Yalta record, in spite of these attacks, reveals that the Soviet Union made more concessions to the United States and Great Britain than were made to the Soviet Union by either the United States or Great Britain. On certain issues, of course, each of the three Great Powers modified its original position in order to reach agreement. Although it is sometimes alleged that there is something evil in compromise, actually, of course, compromise is necessary for progress as any sensible man knows. Compromise, when reached honorably and in a spirit of honesty by all concerned, is the only fair and rational way of reaching a reasonable agreement between two differing points of view. We should not be led by our dislike and rightful rejection of appeasement in the Munich sense into an irrational and untenable refusal to compromise.

The attacks on the Yalta Conference, excluding those which are motivated by a blind hatred of Franklin D. Roosevelt, really result from bitter disappointment over subsequent failures to carry out the agreements reached at Yalta rather than over the agreements themselves.

The Yalta Conference was the culmination, in many respects, of long and patient efforts, dating back to President Roosevelt's first term, to find some basis for a new international understanding with Russia. It was not until eight years after diplomatic relations had been restored, and after the Soviet Union had been attacked by Germany on June 22, 1941, that important steps toward effective co-operation took place between the two nations.

Although some American isolationists tried to bar Lend-Lease appropriations for the Soviet Union, Congress affirmed such aid in October by a strong majority. As Walter Lippmann wisely remarked, the United States and the Soviet Union were "separated by an ideological gulf and joined by the bridge of national interest."

It is a human frailty to forget too soon the circumstances of past events, and the American people should remember that they were on the brink of disaster in 1942. If the Soviet Union had failed to hold on its front, the Germans would have been in a position to conquer Great Britain. They would have been able to overrun Africa, too, and in this event they could have established a foothold in Latin America. This impending danger was constantly in President Roosevelt's mind.

Lend-Lease proved to be a powerful cementing force between the two nations. During 1942 the Soviet Union and the United States were just beginning to learn to work together as allies. We did not receive from the Soviet Union the detailed information about its army or about economic conditions within the country which we expected from other Lend-Lease countries. Nor, it must be said, did we give the Russians as much information as the British, for example, received from us. Although this policy has since been criticized, such complete pooling of secret information as took place between the British and the United States was hardly possible in the face of the history of our relations with Russia in the preceding twenty-five years.

The exigencies of war also brought about somewhat closer collaboration between the Soviet Union and the United States. In June 1942, President Roosevelt, Secretary Hull, and Foreign Minister Molotov discussed in Washington not only co-operation in the war, but also the question of maintaining peace, freedom, and security after the war. President Roosevelt told me that Molotov was cold and restrained during the early portion of his visit, but that before his departure he had become friendlier and more co-operative.

Either through diplomatic channels or at the Teheran Conference, Roosevelt, Churchill, and Stalin had already raised most of the questions that were to be discussed at Yalta. At Teheran, although no agreements had been reached, the three leaders had discussed in a preliminary way such problems as the treatment of Germany, the future of Poland, General de Gaulle and France, Russian participation in the Far Eastern war, a warm-water port for the Soviet Union, colonial empires, Turkey's entrance into the war, and the founding of an organization of nations.

Actual progress on these and related issues did not occur, however, until Yalta, when a high degree of frankness and co-operation developed among Roosevelt, Churchill, and Stalin. Although Anglo-American co-operation had developed to a noteworthy degree during the war, diplomatic relations of the two Western powers with the Soviet Union had been far from satisfactory most of the time. Russian disappointment over the unavoidable delay in opening a second front across the Channel was undoubtedly real, and even at the end of 1944 some highly placed Russians were still suspicious of both British and American motives in regard to the future of liberated Europe. All three powers faced, in the months before Yalta, not only the need to push forward plans for a world organization, but a more immediate and urgent need to reach decisions which could be applied as soon as the fighting ended.

As early as 1941 some of the Russian demands in the Balkans and elsewhere were known to us. Shortly after June 22, 1941, Anthony Eden had gone to Moscow to determine what aid the Soviet Union wanted. At this time, even though the Russian armies were in retreat, Stalin indicated that he was less interested in military assistance than in a political alliance and in a territorial settlement affecting Russia's borders. Then in the months just before Pearl Harbor the Russians became excessively suspicious of British and American intentions toward their postwar claims. Eden, as a consequence, prepared to leave for Moscow again on December 7. He was informed that the American attitude—and it remained the same to the eve of the Yalta Conference—on the postwar settlement was contained in the Atlantic Charter. We would continue to discuss in general terms problems of a territorial nature, but we would delay any commitments as to specific terms until the end of the war.

At his conference with Eden, following Pearl Harbor, Stalin indicated that he wanted a Soviet-Polish boundary based on the Curzon Line, parts of Finland and Hungary were to be incorporated into the Soviet Union, while the Baltic States were to be absorbed. In addition "Stalin also proposed the restoration of Austria as an independent state; the detachment of the Rhineland from Germany as an independent state or protectorate; possibly the constitution of an independent state of Bavaria; the transfer of East Prussia to Poland; the return of the Sudetenland to Czechoslovakia; Yugoslavia should be restored and receive certain additional

9

territory from Italy; Albania should be reconstituted as an independent state; Turkey should receive the Dodecanese Islands, with possible readjustments of Aegean islands in favor of Greece; Turkey might also receive some territory from Bulgaria and in Northern Syria; Germany should pay reparations in kind, particularly in machine tools, but not in money. . . .

"Stalin said he was willing to support any arrangements Britain might make for securing bases in the Western European countries, France, Belgium, The Netherlands, Norway, and Denmark.

"Eden parried these demands by saying that for many reasons it was impossible for him to enter into a secret agreement, one of which was that he was pledged to the United States Government not to do so. Stalin and he agreed that Eden should take these provisions back to London for discussion with the British Cabinet, and they should be communicated to the United States."[1]

Our position after this meeting of Stalin and Eden was unchanged: we did not favor territorial settlements until the end of the war. The British, when they signed a treaty of alliance with the Soviet Union on May 26, 1942, also refused to agree to territorial changes at that time. By 1944, however, the progress of the war, particularly in the Balkans, made it clear that some agreement on specific details regarding Europe's postwar problems had to be made.

On May 30, 1944, British Ambassador Halifax had asked Secretary Hull how the United States would feel about an arrangement between the British and the Russians whereby Russia would have principal military responsibility in Ro-

---

[1] *The Memoirs of Cordell Hull* (New York: The Macmillan Company, 1948), Vol. II, p. 1167. Copyright, 1948, by Cordell Hull. Used by permission of The Macmillan Company.

mania and Britain principal military responsibility in Greece. The advance of the Russian armies into the Balkans in April 1944 had brought the relationship between the Soviet Union and the Balkans to the forefront, and Halifax said that difficulties had developed between Russia and the British over the Balkans, particularly with regard to Romania. He explained that the proposed arrangement would apply only to war conditions and would not affect the rights and responsibilities which each of the three Great Powers would exercise at the peace settlement.

Hull expressed opposition to this proposal. The following day Churchill sent a cable to the President urging approval of the proposed arrangement and emphasizing that it applied only to war conditions. Churchill added that he had proposed the arrangement to the Russians and they were willing to accept it but wanted to know whether the United States was in agreement. While the State Department was preparing a reply, Halifax on June 8 brought Hull another message from the Prime Minister. Churchill argued that no question of spheres of influence was involved. He added that it seemed reasonable to him that the Russians should deal with the Romanians and Bulgarians and that the British should deal with the Greeks and the Yugoslavs, who were in Britain's theater of operations and were Britain's old allies.

The President sent our reply on June 10, pointing out that the government responsible for military actions in any country would make decisions which the military situation required. On the other hand, the proposed arrangement, he said, might allow these military decisions to extend into political and economic matters. Such a situation, he pointed out, would surely lead to a division of the Balkans into spheres of influence. The United States preferred, he added, to see some consultative machinery to deal with the Balkans.

The Prime Minister cabled back the next day that such machinery would delay action, and he could not see why the President and he could not keep the matter in their own hands. He then suggested that the arrangement be given a three months' trial.

The President, without consulting the State Department, cabled back acceptance of the three months' condition. He stressed that by this action he was not agreeing to any postwar arrangement for spheres of influence.

Even with this qualification, I felt then and still believe that this agreement was a serious mistake. I also felt that this lack of proper co-ordination between the White House and the State Department in the determination and execution of foreign policy was a serious weakness. One of the first steps that I took as Secretary of State was to establish a closer liaison between the White House and the Department by appointing Charles E. Bohlen as liaison officer. He was extremely effective in helping develop the co-ordination and integration of the diplomatic decisions made by the White House and the State Department.

When Ambassador Gromyko asked the State Department on July 1 our views on the Balkans, he was informed that the United States had agreed to the arrangement for a three months' trial period, but we wanted it to be made clear that we did not favor the extension of the arrangement into spheres of influence.

Churchill and Stalin at Moscow in October 1944 did, however, extend the arrangement by reducing to percentages the degree of influence each would have in the Balkans. Our embassies in Moscow and Ankara informed us that the

Soviet Union would have 75/25 or 80/20 predominance in Bulgaria, Hungary, and Romania; Britain and Russia would share influence in Yugoslavia 50/50; and the British would have full responsibility in Greece.

This (Russian-British agreement) made it evident that the United States could no longer adhere to the position it had adopted on the eve of Pearl Harbor. Agreements regarding Europe's postwar problems would have to be worked out at a conference of the three leaders. We specifically desired a pledge by the Soviet Union and Great Britain that in liberated Europe free elections would be held and governments representative of the people would be established.

This was only one of many immediate problems which required an effort to reach agreement at the end of 1944. It was President Roosevelt's belief, and he expressed it to me many times, that if he and the Prime Minister could sit around a conference table again with Marshal Stalin, not only would the war be brought to a speedier conclusion, but plans could also be laid to solve these problems and to create the basis for an enduring peace. Plans for this enduring peace, to be sought through a world organization after the war, had been worked on for years by the State Department. President Roosevelt contributed greatly to this effort by his speech on January 6, 1941, advocating a world based on the Four Freedoms—freedom of speech and expression, freedom to worship God, freedom from want, and freedom from fear.

Then in August 1941 the President and Prime Minister Churchill, when they met aboard a battleship for the Argentia Conference, outlined in the Atlantic Charter a more specific declaration of principles. On January 1, 1942, while Churchill was in Washington, the nations then at war with the Axis signed the United Nations Declaration, which had originated in the State Department, and pledged themselves to construct a postwar system of peace and security.

In October 1943, Cordell Hull flew to Moscow, the first flight he had made in his seventy-two years, to win the support of the Soviet Union for a postwar organization of nations. It was partly because the Four-Power Declaration of October 30, 1943, was signed at Moscow that it became the subject of general rejoicing throughout the United States. Russia, too, had seemingly recognized the necessity of a world organization.

At Moscow the foreign ministers of Great Britain, the Soviet Union, and the United States not only pledged closer military co-operation for the future, but also agreed that "it was essential in their own national interests and in the interests of all peace-loving nations to continue the present close collaboration and co-operation in the conduct of the war into the period following the end of hostilities. . . ."

They furthermore recognized "the necessity of establishing at the earliest practicable date a general international organization, based on the principle of the sovereign equality of all peace-loving states, and open to membership by all such states, large and small, for the maintenance of international peace and security."

On his return from Moscow Mr. Hull told a joint session of Congress: "Of supreme importance is the fact that at the conference the whole spirit of international co-operation, now and after the war, was revitalized and given practical expression. The conference thus launched a forward movement which, I am firmly convinced, will steadily extend in scope and effectiveness. Within the framework of that movement, in the atmosphere of mutual understanding and confi-

BACKGROUND OF THE YALTA CONFERENCE

dence which made possible its beginning in Moscow, many of the problems which are difficult today will, as time goes on, undoubtedly become more possible of satisfactory solution through frank and friendly discussion."

The great ovation from the public, press, and members of Congress which the Secretary received on his return did not turn his head. At a meeting in the Secretary's office shortly after his return someone remarked that a current question depended upon political considerations. Turning to Hull, this person had said: "Mr. Secretary, what's your view? You're a politician." Hull replied, "Oh no. I used to be a politician. But since I came back from Moscow I've been a statesman."

It was less than a month after the Moscow Conference that Roosevelt, Churchill, and Stalin met at Teheran and reaffirmed the pledge made at Moscow that the three countries would work together in the postwar world.

"We shall seek," the three great war leaders pledged, "the co-operation and active participation of all nations, large and small, whose peoples in heart and mind are dedicated, as are our own peoples, to the elimination of tyranny and slavery, oppression and intolerance. We will welcome them, as they may choose to come, into a world family of Democratic Nations."

Back in Washington, in the State Department, on December 9, 1943, Leo Pasvolsky, special assistant to the Secretary of State, at Mr. Hull's request, organized an informal Political Agenda Group for discussions on international organization—carrying forward work which had been under way since February 1942. The regular members of this group were Dr. Isaiah Bowman, the Hon. Myron C. Taylor, Benjamin V. Cohen, James C. Dunn, Stanley K. Hornbeck, Green H. Hackworth, Leo Pasvolsky, and Harley Notter.

President Roosevelt sent me to Great Britain on a special mission in April 1944. In the group that accompanied me was Dr. Bowman, who was my adviser on a number of matters including those pertaining to international organization. I reached an agreement with Anthony Eden that the two countries should participate in conversations that summer in the United States on the world security organization. I advised Russian Ambassador Gusev of this agreement before I left London. On my return to Washington, Mr. Hull asked me to take charge of the preparations for the coming Conference.

It was apparent from my conversations in London that the United States would have to assume the initiative on the question of a world organization. I am convinced that if the United States had not continually pushed the plans there would have been no United Nations by the end of the war.

As the result of our initiative we held exploratory talks on world organization at Dumbarton Oaks with the British and the Russians from August 21 to September 28, 1944, and with the British and the Chinese from September 29 to October 7. (The Russians would not sit with the Chinese because of possible complications which might develop with the Japanese.)

The American proposals on world organization were accepted by the other powers as the basic documents of the conversations. At this conference the representatives of the major powers drafted the document that was to be the basis of discussion at San Francisco the following spring. We agreed on a statement of principles and purposes, a General Assembly, a Security Council, a Secretariat, an International Court of Justice, and an Economic and Social Council. It was only the insistence of the United States that secured a provision for an Economic and Social Council. The Soviet Union, and to a lesser extent Churchill, did not seem to understand the American concern for an organization that was broader than just a security organization.

Although we had agreed at Dumbarton Oaks that Great Britain, the Soviet Union, China, the United States, and even finally France should be permanent members of the Security Council, we had come to no agreement as to the voting procedure. There was also complete disagreement with the Russians over their proposal that all sixteen Soviet Republics be admitted as members of the world organization. When I told Mr. Hull of the impossible request which the Soviet Union had placed before the conference, he remarked, "Are these Russians going to break up our hope of a world organization?"

The crucial voting problem at Dumbarton Oaks and after concerned the voting procedure in the Security Council that should be adopted for making the necessary decisions in maintaining peace and security. There was no disagreement at Dumbarton Oaks regarding the desirability of having the Security Council function on the basis of a qualified majority vote, or of the necessity of having all *procedural* questions decided by a majority vote with no distinction made between the permanent and non-permanent members of the Security Council.

On procedural questions the British favored a two-thirds majority vote while the Russians preferred a simple majority. We originally favored a simple majority but were willing to accept the British proposal provided the Russians agreed. There was, however, no agreement on this question. The President told Gromyko at a meeting in the White House on

September 8, 1944, that we would accept a simple majority of the eleven members of the Security Council on decisions of procedure. At Dumbarton Oaks we suggested that the number be seven, and this was included in a cable from the President to Stalin on December 5 and later adopted at Yalta.

The sharpest disagreement on voting in the Security Council related to the vote to decide substantive questions. Great Britain, the Soviet Union, China, and the United States had to decide whether or not they would accept as binding all the decisions made by a majority of the Council. A straight majority vote on substantive as well as as on procedural matters would mean that the armed forces of any major nation could be used without its consent, quite likely as the result of a vote cast largely by nations which had few armed forces to contribute.

At Dumbarton Oaks none of the four major powers was willing to accept this situation. They all agreed that the only way each of them could be safeguarded was by adding the requirement that any majority of the Security Council had to include the concurring votes of the permanent members— or, in other words, the right of each major power to veto decisions.

The military and naval staffs working with the State Department—including Admirals Russell Willson, Harold Train, and Arthur Hepburn and Generals Stanley D. Embick, George V. Strong, and Muir Fairchild—had insisted on the right of the United States to veto decisions involving the use of American military forces. The armed forces would not recommend to the Senate a world organization that permitted American forces to be used without the express permission of the United States.

Most of the civilian experts in the State Department and advisers, too, agreed on the need of the veto in all matters involving the use of economic sanctions and armed forces. The fact, for instance, that a major argument against American participation in the League of Nations had been that membership would commit us in vital matters was of real significance in determining American support of the veto power by the permanent members.

With the agreement that the permanent members of the Security Council had to be unanimous for any action involving sanctions, the unsettled question at Dumbarton Oaks was what the voting procedure should be on other substantive questions in case one of the permanent members was a party to a dispute—such a dispute having been brought before the Security Council under the peaceful settlement provisions of our proposals. The Soviet Union insisted that the right of veto should apply, and we disagreed with this position. We recommended instead that a special procedure be developed for dealing with these cases where one of the permanent members was a party to a dispute.

Throughout the discussions on the world organization at Dumbarton Oaks, Yalta, and San Francisco it was constantly emphasized by the representatives of the three major nations that—regardless of the voting formula—unanimity of the major powers was in the final analysis vital for the functioning of the organization. It was obvious to all of us that the United Nations would collapse and peace would be endangered if any of the major powers failed to co-operate. Regardless of the voting formula adopted by the Security Council, no world organization could succeed without the co-operation of the Soviet Union, Great Britain, and the United States.

At 9:30 A.M. on September 8, 1944, I took Gromyko to the President's bedroom for a thirty-five-minute discussion of the disagreements that had developed at Dumbarton Oaks between the Soviet Union and the United States.

At the beginning the President warmed the atmosphere by telling Gromyko some of his plans for his forthcoming meeting at Quebec with Churchill. Roosevelt emphasized that these discussions would be on military matters only. He added that he felt it was desirable to have another conference of the three Chiefs of State as early as possible. He also spoke briefly of the war, commenting that our forces in the west as well as the Soviets in the east had gone beyond their respective supply lines and that this was a period of pause for consolidation on the part of both. The President told Gromyko how delighted he was with the way things had gone on both fronts. He then read to him a wire from General Patrick Hurley, in which Hurley had said that Molotov had told him that the Soviet Union was not interested in the Chinese Communists, that they were not really Communists anyway.

After this preliminary friendly exchange of comments on the several subjects mentioned, the President finally came around to Dumbarton Oaks and said that he understood there was only one fundamental point remaining open. Gromyko said that there were others, but when I asked him about the others it turned out that only one point, other than our refusal to agree to the proposal for sixteen Soviet votes, was really difficult. Gromyko stated that he could not yield on the voting question and the request for sixteen votes, but he did say that he could approve our proposal for an Economic and Social Council.

The President opened the discussion on the question of

whether one of the Great Powers should have the veto power when it was a party to a dispute not involving the use of sanctions by saying that traditionally in this country, when husband and wife brought a disagreement to the courts, both had the right to state their case but neither had the right to serve on the jury. The President traced the development of this American concept of fair play back to the days of our founding fathers. He then stressed the difficulty which we would have in our Senate with the Soviet proposal, adding, however, that he felt the issue of the quick and immediate use of armed force could be met successfully in the Senate.

Gromyko did not seem at all depressed by what the President said. He accepted the remarks gracefully, asked a number of questions, and discussed the way in which he could explain our position clearly to Moscow.

At this point I asked if it would be helpful to him if President Roosevelt sent a message on the question to Marshal Stalin. The President added that we did not desire to send such a message unless it would be helpful to him. Gromyko said he would leave that to our judgment. I then handed to the President a draft which Bohlen had prepared. This outlined the difficulty we faced on the voting question, referred to the traditional American concept that parties to a dispute never vote on their own case, and said that American public opinion would neither understand nor support a plan of international organization in which this principle was violated. It also indicated that we felt that other nations, particularly the smaller nations, would feel as we did. It ended with an expression of hope that Stalin would be able to instruct his delegation to meet our point on this issue. The President thought the cable was excellent but wanted us to add a reference to his husband-and-wife simile and put more stress on the probably adverse reaction of the Soviet proposal on the smaller nations and the difficulty we would have in getting their plan through our Senate. The President asked that the cable be redrafted to incorporate his suggestions and be sent to Miss Grace Tully, the President's private secretary, for transmission immediately.

Stalin sent a generally negative reply on September 14, reiterating his belief that the unanimity of the Great Powers must be maintained on all questions. He did, however, say that he would not object to an effort to work out a special formula for disputes not involving sanctions which involved one of the major powers. This left the door open and Pasvolsky and his staff worked out a formula which was sent to Stalin and Churchill on December 5 and later accepted at Yalta.

I am convinced that the President's discussion with Gromyko was an important step in winning the co-operation of the Soviet Union for a world organization. President Roosevelt's handling of Gromyko was only one of the many examples of the way he could work with the Russians in a spirit of patience and calmness, at the same time presenting the American position with firmness and clarity.

When the Dumbarton Oaks conversations were concluded, as head of the American delegation and chairman of the conference, I recommended that steps be taken promptly to obtain an agreement on the unsettled voting question.

For months Roosevelt had been convinced of the paramount importance of another meeting with Churchill and Stalin to plan military strategy for the final phases of the war. By late 1944 the course of the war had undergone drastic changes since the three leaders had met at Teheran. The second front was now a reality. The Red Army had driven the Germans from Russian soil and were now well into the fortress of Europe. Planning was vital for the final attack on Germany and to bring the Soviet Union into the Far Eastern war. In addition the liberation of France, Belgium, Greece, and parts of the Netherlands, Norway, Poland, Yugoslavia, and Czechoslovakia, as well as the surrender of Romania and Bulgaria, required decisions by the three leaders.

The President took advantage of this pending Russian, British, and American Conference to add to the agenda the questions which had not been settled at Dumbarton Oaks. A strong world organization, created before the end of the war, he felt, would help the world to deal with the inevitable difficulties that would arise over the control of liberated territories and would make spheres of influence of less importance than in the past.

There had been considerable discussion of the location of this Big Three Conference. Stalin had informed both the President and the Prime Minister that, while the Soviet winter offensive was on, because of the many decisions he personally had to make, he could not leave Soviet territory. While we were at the Yalta Conference we had many opportunities to see the immense amount of time the Marshal devoted to top military strategy. We then better understood his refusal to leave the Soviet Union for these meetings of the three leaders.

President Roosevelt, who was a keen geographer in his own right, studied maps to find a possible location for the next conference at a warm-weather port in Russian territory. He had exchanges with Ambassador Harriman on this question. Finally, after his re-election to his fourth term, Harry Hopkins, at the President's request, raised the possibility of the Crimea with Gromyko as the location of the forthcoming Conference. Although there was objection to the President's traveling that far, Hopkins wrote, "I was sure the President would wind up by going to the Crimea, the primary reason being that it was a part of the world he had never visited and his adventurous spirit was forever leading him to go to unusual places and, on his part, the election being over, he would no longer be disturbed about it for political reasons."[2]

I remember clearly the day in mid-December when the President in a whisper informed me that we were going to Yalta. "You had better look at a map," he remarked, "but with no one else present when you do."

Although some of the President's advisers tried to dissuade him from going to the Crimea, he knew that a conference was essential and that the prize of world peace was too great to lose over the location of the meeting. Churchill was as bitterly opposed to the Crimea as some of the President's advisers. He remarked at Malta that no one could have selected a more inconvenient location for a conference. On the other hand, he, like the President, wanted to achieve a stable world. When I visited Churchill in England in April 1944 he had remarked, "The world is a wounded animal." A few days later, in the midst of a discussion of the days ahead when we all hoped that there would be a world security organization, the Prime Minister had declared:

"You young fellows will have to make it work. I may not be here. It will not work if there is no will to make it work. . . . Tennyson's line is apposite. We must 'faintly cling to the larger hope.'"

[2] Robert E. Sherwood, *Roosevelt and Hopkins: An Intimate History* (New York: Harper & Brothers, 1948) p. 845.

BACKGROUND OF THE YALTA CONFERENCE

While the President was aboard the U.S.S. *Quincy* en route to Malta to meet the British, our intelligence services discovered that the enemy knew of the location of the Conference. The President was immediately informed of this but, mindful of the difficulties of arranging any meeting with Stalin at that time, he was determined to go through with the original plans.

It was not that President Roosevelt believed that he had a hypnotic influence or that he had a liking for personal diplomacy, but his attitude was based on the solid fact that it was only Marshal Stalin who could make decisions. We had found out over a period of years that when we thought Stalin had been informed as to the American position this was not always true. When he then learned what our position was he frequently overruled his advisers.

The President believed that peace depended upon developing and maintaining unity of the three Great Powers. If the Soviet Union, through patience and understanding, could be brought into a functioning world organization, it might become a constructive force in world affairs. If, on the other hand, the world were divided into two armed camps, then the Soviet Union would become a disruptive force in world affairs. Although the President did not desire to travel as far as the Crimea for his second conference with Stalin, the attainment of world peace was above everything else in his mind. The prospect of peace, to the President, was a prize well worth traveling half around the globe as often as was necessary.

The President had no illusions about the Russians before or at the Yalta Conference. He was well aware of the dangers and difficulties that confronted him in dealing with the Soviet Union. He worked in the hope and faith that a stable world order could be achieved. He did not have the illusion, as his enemies have charged, that world peace could be achieved easily or by appeasing the Soviet Union. Hopes and illusions are two different things, and the President was well aware of the difference.

CHAPTER 2

Meetings at Marrakech and Naples

Yalta, on the eastern shore of the Crimea, was within a three-hundred-mile radius of Turkey, Romania, and Bulgaria. It was approximately 900 miles south of Moscow, 5700 miles east of Washington, and 3000 miles southeast of London. The line of communications was a masterpiece of organization and was a tribute to the communications services of the armed forces. The President had to be in constant touch with developments in Congress, with members of the Cabinet, and with the changing situation in the various theaters of action. The State Department and the Chiefs of Staff, too, had to be in constant communication with their offices in Washington. Permission was secured well in advance from Turkey to allow United States ships to pass through the Dardanelles, and the U.S.S. *Catoctin* was sent to Sevastopol as the communications ship. The *Catoctin* was based at Sevastopol, eighty miles from the Conference, because all the German mines had not as yet been cleared from the harbor at Yalta. Signal Corps men set up the communications equipment at Livadia Palace—the American headquarters—to afford direct communication from Yalta via the *Catoctin* to Washington.

Although President Roosevelt went as far as Malta by ship, most of the military, and all of the State Department delegation, flew across the Atlantic Ocean. In the week just before the combined British and American delegations assembled on the island of Malta, the United States Navy made the most careful arrangements to safeguard the lives of those flying to the Conference. Each plane was required to fly a course laid out by the Navy, and destroyers were stationed at 300- to 500-mile intervals from Bermuda to the Azores to assist any plane in distress. After the intelligence agencies had reported that the enemy had been alerted on the Conference, all of our planes were required, as an additional safety measure, to maintain radio silence across the Atlantic. The only time that the radio could be used was to flash a signal of distress. In addition to the destroyers the Navy also had a number of planes with rescue equipment on the alert in Bermuda.

The hazardous flight from Malta across the Mediterranean and the Black Sea to Saki airfield in the Crimea required the most extreme care and preparation. Approximately twenty C-54s and five British Yorks carried the President and his military, naval, and diplomatic staff and the Prime Minister and his staff on this seven-hour flight.

The flight plan from Malta required the planes to leave at ten-minute intervals. All the planes were to fly at a constant air speed, each plane at a different altitude. The planes were to fly without lights and their radios were to be silent. In case any plane was attacked there was an agreed-upon radio frequency to be used to warn the other planes. If an attack did occur all the planes had directions to fly to bases in Africa.

Not only was there great concern over the danger of German fighter-plane interception, but a most unfortunate plane accident made everybody at Malta extremely uneasy over the safety of President Roosevelt and Prime Minister Churchill. A British plane, carrying Foreign Office personnel, had crashed on its way to Malta, killing several members of the British delegation.

The flight plans for the trip from Malta to the Crimea required a three-and-a-half-hour flight due east and then a ninety-degree turn to the left just before reaching the island of Crete, still held by the Germans. When the planes reached the coast of Greece they were to fly along the coast and then over the Aegean Sea to the Dardanelles and Turkey and across the Black Sea. A security code had been put into effect whereby each plane, on reaching Saki, had to execute a ninety-degree turn at a radio transmitter so that the Russians would know it was not an enemy plane.

Fear for the safety of the planes was greatly increased by an incident that occurred the day before the combined delegations left Malta. A plane with equipment for the Conference was sent on a test run of the flight corridor that had been projected by the British and American staffs. The tail wind was so strong during the first three and a half hours that the plane was carried faster and farther than the flight chart had planned. The plane actually reached Crete, and German anti-aircraft opened up and made two direct hits before it was able to fly out of range.

In the days just before the President sailed for the island of Malta, he talked with me many times about such problems as voting in the Security Council, French participation in the control of Germany, Soviet views on reparations, Poland, Iran, the Balkans, and the question of spheres of influence in Europe.

The President was greatly impressed by the thoroughness of the material prepared by the State Department staff on all these questions. It had been placed in a loose-leaf binder for him. After he had thumbed through it, he said, "I want this binder in my cabin aboard ship," and I handed it to Miss Tully.

In the many conferences that I had with the President as Secretary of State, as Under Secretary of State, and as Lend-Lease administrator, I was constantly impressed by his grasp of complex world problems. The facts I presented might be new, but this world statesman, like Churchill, seemed to have an instinctive comprehension of the problem even before I had finished my explanation. Sir Alexander Cadogan, British Permanent Under Secretary of State for Foreign Affairs, once agreed with me that he knew few men who possessed this rare ability in such measure as President Roosevelt and Prime Minister Churchill.

At the President's suggestion the State Department delegation flew to North Africa to spend a few days reviewing the American position on the various problems to be discussed in the Crimea, and then flew to Malta to conduct discussions with the British before he arrived.

The State Department experts who traveled with me to the Conference were H. Freeman Matthews, director of the Office of European Affairs; Alger Hiss, deputy director of the Office of Special Political Affairs; and Wilder Foote, assistant to the Secretary of State. At Malta and Yalta Ambassador Harriman and Charles Bohlen were also part of the State

Department delegation. While I was in London in April 1944, Hiss had been transferred from the Office of Far Eastern Affairs to the Office of Special Political Affairs to serve under Edwin C. Wilson, a foreign service officer who had been called back from his post as United States representative to the French Committee of National Liberation to take charge of this division to plan for the Dumbarton Oaks Conference. Shortly after I became Under Secretary of State—October 1943—with the approval of the President and Mr. Hull I called in the FBI to conduct a security examination of the State Department. Assistant Secretary of State G. Howland Shaw served as liaison with the FBI during this examination. I never heard of any questioning of Mr. Hiss's loyalty from anyone inside or outside of the State Department or from the FBI during my time of service in the Department.

Hiss performed brilliantly throughout the Dumbarton Oaks conversations, the Yalta Conference, the San Francisco Conference, and the first meeting of the United Nations Assembly in London. I always had reason to believe that Hiss acted honorably and patriotically in the performance of his duties at these conferences. The following pages of this book reveal his contribution at the Yalta Conference.

In addition to the State Department experts who went with me to the Crimean Conference there was a secretariat composed of Lee Blanchard, George T. Conn, and Ralph L. Graham. Major Terence Lloyd Tyson was assigned by the United States Army to accompany us as the medical officer to the American delegation.

It was a bitterly cold morning that January 25, 1945, when we left the National Airport in Washington for the trip to the Crimea. Our plane, a C-54, took off at nine o'clock, and just over three hours later we dropped through the clouds, caught our first glimpse of coral reefs, and landed at Kindley Field, Bermuda, in a 70-degree temperature.

We had an unusually fine crew on this trip to Yalta. Major William F. Richmond, the commanding officer, had flown me from London the previous spring. He had been Eddie Rickenbacker's pilot to Russia in 1943 and had flown Lieutenant General G. C. Kenney all over the South and Southwest Pacific. Major Richmond was top-notch, both as a man and as a pilot. He was quiet, steady as a rock, and evidently one of the half-dozen key pilots in the Army Transport Command, since he was assigned exclusively to VIPs.[1]

Being classified as a VIP reminded me that when Hull was being shown the airfield at Cairo on his trip to Moscow his pilot had said to him, "This is the VIP house; you know what that stands for." Hull replied, "I don't know what it stands for, but I know what some of them are."

We left Bermuda at 7 P.M. and flew all night across the South Atlantic. Just before our party retired I asked Major Richmond whether it was his desire that we undress that night. He replied, "Yes, Boss, you'd better undress, because when you hit the water you'll freeze over quicker."

It was about daybreak when we sighted the Azores. After a few minutes we began to descend over Lagens Airport on Terceira, a beautiful island seen from the air. The coast line of Terceira consisted of steep cliffs dropping precipitously into the ocean, while the island itself was quite hilly with

---

[1] In addition to Major Richmond, the three other key members of our crew were the senior pilot, Lieutenant Norman S. Portenoy; the junior pilot, Lieutenant Kenneth J. Stevens, a six-foot-three, heavily built man called "Junior" by the other three; and the navigator, Captain William F. Finney, Jr. Master Sergeant Jess J. Kerekes, Staff Sergeant David T. Kenneth, Staff Sergeant Raymond J. Godschalx, and Staff Sergeant Day U. Moser, the other four members of the crew, were an outstanding, efficient group.

quaint fields surrounded by stone walls as far as the eye could see.

The Azores were of particular interest to me on this trip because President Roosevelt had told me that he had been to the Azores when he was Assistant Secretary of the Navy and thought that they would be ideal as the permanent headquarters of the world organization.

I had passed through Terceira nine months before, on my way home from London, and the change in the airport was immense. Then there had been no buildings, the Air Corps personnel were all housed in tents, and the runway was a metal strip. Now a concrete runway was in use, there was a huge hangar, fifteen or twenty semipermanent barracks, and many other buildings.

After a hearty American breakfast General Marshall, whose plane had landed twenty minutes after ours, joined me on a terrace overlooking the airfield and the hills across the valley. As we watched the sun come up over the hills on this lonely island we discussed our hopes for the future and for the new age that was dawning.

A few weeks before, President Roosevelt had called me to his upstairs study one day after lunch at the White House and had told me in the utmost secrecy that he must take me into his confidence on a far-reaching experiment that might revolutionize the world. He told me that he was not sure how long it would take to perfect a new bomb—the atomic bomb—but that before too long it might be possible to drop this bomb in New York City at Forty-second Street and Broadway. The resulting explosion, the President said, would lay New York low. His description seemed like a fantastic dream.

The time had been reached, the President added, for the State Department to come into the atomic picture. Up to now only the very top military men and key scientists had been aware of the atomic program, and I was the first civilian in the State Department to be informed. The secrecy surrounding the entire program was so tight, said the President, that appropriations could not be specified from Congress in the usual way because of the danger of a leak from Capitol Hill.

After my talk with the President I went to see Secretary of War Stimson, at his request, to establish liaison on this question with the military. Stimson, in the presence of his assistant, Harvey Bundy, described something of the history of the atomic project and of the way in which the scientists had brought the question to the President and to the War Department. At this conference I said that I would appoint James C. Dunn, Assistant Secretary of State, to take charge of liaison with the military on all matters pertaining to the atomic question.

During the weeks just before the Big Three Conference at Yalta considerable Soviet intelligence activity was reported to be taking place on our West Coast. From these reports it was my definite impression that the Russians certainly had an indication of what was taking place. At no time, however, did the Russians ever raise with the State Department the question of our atomic research.

I had the feeling, however, that at the Crimea Conference the Russians might ask the President, General Marshall, or me about atomic development, and thought we should be prepared for the question.

There in the Azores in the early morning of January 26, 1945, General Marshall and I discussed this possibility. It was his feeling that we could not plan ahead for such an eventuality and that the matter therefore would have to be handled, depending upon the circumstances and the conditions, as and if it arose. Actually the Russians never raised the question at Yalta, and it was reported to me that when President Truman officially told the Russians about the bomb at the Potsdam Conference the Russians, outwardly at least, appeared to be unimpressed.

After my talk with Marshall in the Azores the State Department group and I boarded our plane and took off for Marrakech in French Morocco. General Marshall flew, at the same time, to a secret rendezvous with General Eisenhower at Marseilles. He rejoined us later at Malta.

For the next few hours we worked over our papers for the Yalta meeting. At approximately 1 P.M. Major Richmond called me to the nose of the plane to catch the first view of the African coast. Within six minutes we were over the coast line. The land below reminded me of Arizona. The brown and yellow desert was dotted with bright clean squares of new wheat where the land was irrigated, and here and there could be seen mud-walled Arab villages, some of them brown in color and some of them whitewashed. The Atlas Mountains, with snow visible on some of the peaks, were hazy in the distance.

We soon picked up a paved highway leading straight to our destination at Marrakech. As we landed at the Marrakech Airport at 1:48 P.M. Azores time we saw at least a hundred new four-engine bombers on their way to the battle front.

While we were at Marrakech, from Friday, January 26, through Monday, January 29, we had long discussions over the problems to be raised at the coming conference. There were many incoming telegrams from Acting Secretary of State Joseph C. Grew, in Washington, informing us of the latest developments on all these questions. In addition to this constant flow of information from Washington we had brought with us excellent material for any conceivable question that might be raised at Yalta.

Among the questions reserved for subsequent discussion with the President at Malta, which I reviewed at Marrakech with Matthews, Hiss, and Foote, were:

1. The Establishment of a European High Commission Composed of Great Britain, the Soviet Union, France, and the United States.

The proposed commission was to assist in the establishment of popular governments and in facilitating the solution of emergency economic problems in the former occupied and satellite states of Europe. The commission was to have no responsibilities in regard to the conduct of the war or the postwar control of Germany. Questions regarding Germany were to be left to the European Advisory Commission which had been created at the Moscow Conference. It was the State Department's feeling that the establishment of the European High Commission "would reassure public opinion in the United States and elsewhere that these four nations will work together in the solution of pressing problems while further steps are being taken toward the establishment of the General International Organization."

An integral part of the proposal for this commission was a "Declaration on Liberated Europe." With some changes, the "Declaration on Liberated Europe" was accepted at Yalta, but President Roosevelt decided against presenting the European High Commission to the Conference. I disagreed with the President on this question and was greatly disappointed that he did not present the proposal for a European

High Commission to the Conference. The State Department had worked hard preparing this proposal, and the establishment of such a commission, I believe, might have forestalled some of the difficulties which arose in eastern Europe.

2. *The Treatment of Germany.*

The State Department recommended the approval of the draft agreement on the zones of occupation and the control machinery worked out by the European Advisory Commission in London. Our representative on that body, Ambassador John G. Winant, and Philip E. Moseley, Winant's political adviser and alternate, had to share responsibility for American decisions with the military. In September and November 1944 the representatives of Great Britain, the United States, and the Soviet Union on the E.A.C. signed agreements on zones of occupation dividing Germany into three zones and establishing "Greater Berlin" as a fourth joint zone.[2] At Yalta, it was decided to assign a zone to France, and thus Germany was divided into four zones with Berlin as the fifth or joint zone. Berlin, however, was not a part of the Soviet zone. As a result of the 1944 agreements—plus the subsequent agreement to include France—British, French, and American forces were stationed in Berlin by exactly the same right as the Soviet forces. The right of Allied access to Berlin was not, however, made specific in these agreements signed in 1944.

The right of access to Berlin was not spelled out in 1944 because at that time it was not possible to predict just what railroads, bridges, roads, and canals around Berlin would be

---

[2] General Eisenhower in *Crusade in Europe* (New York: Doubleday & Co., Inc., 1948), p. 474, remarks that the United States at Yalta should have insisted upon the Elbe as the boundary line dividing the eastern and western occupation areas. The boundaries were *not* drawn at Yalta. They were agreed to in London, in September and November 1944. The Yalta Conference merely approved these previous agreements.

usable after Germany's surrender. It was agreed, therefore, that the European Advisory Commission should leave to the military authorities the arrangement of the details for Allied access to Berlin. In June 1945 the high commands conducted these negotiations. The resulting agreements assured access and egress to Berlin. Since these arrangements seemed satisfactory, the military felt that it was not necessary to negotiate an elaborate agreement to guard against contingencies which might never arise.[3]

The State Department also recommended that the three leaders at the Yalta Conference agree to the disbandment and future prohibition of all German military forces, the destruction of existing German war equipment and the prohibition of the future manufacture of such equipment, and the destruction of industrial plants and machinery incapable of being converted to peaceful use. In addition it was recommended that the National Socialist party be destroyed, Nazi laws, institutions, cultural and educational activities be eliminated, and active Nazis be removed from public office and from positions of importance in private enterprise.

In the case of the transfer of population required by the proposed German-Polish boundary changes, it was recommended that although this government should not oppose some transfer of the German minorities from neighboring states, it should, wherever possible, favor a selective transfer. Such action, if carried out gradually, in an orderly manner, and under international supervision, would contribute to better relations between the states concerned.

With respect to the economic treatment of Germany, the State Department recommended that the eventual objectives

[3] See Philip E. Moseley, "The Berlin Deadlock," *American Perspective*, Vol. II, No. 7, December, 1948, p. 334. See also the New York *Times*, October 12, 1948, for British support of this position.

should be to abolish German autarchy and eliminate the instruments for German economic aggression. For the immediate future, we recommended that the objectives be to reduce Germany's war potential and assist the economic reconstruction of the victorious countries. In order to accomplish these objectives the State Department suggested that the following points be discussed with the British and the Russians:

>   a. We should advocate allied acceptance of large responsibilities for guidance and reorientation of German economic life, including prevention of an unmanageably chaotic economic situation in the initial period after defeat.

>   b. Economic disarmament should include prohibition of the manufacture of land and naval armament and all types of aircraft; destruction of specialized facilities for their manufacture; establishment of controls to detect any forms of surreptitious preparation for war.

>   c. Consideration should be given to selective prohibitions upon the manufacture of key industrial items and of broader restraints on exports within the field of metals, metal products and chemicals.

>   d. During the early post-defeat period, the occupation authorities should take no steps to provide a higher living standard than is required for prevention of disease and disorder. Agreement should be sought on definition of this minimum and the measures to be taken, if necessary, to assure such a minimum.

>   e. We should favor conversion of remainder of German industry to peacetime production, particularly reparation goods for rehabilitation of European countries.

>   f. Payment for such current imports as are allowed by control authorities should be a first charge on German exports.

>   g. We favor full restitution of identifiable looted property.

h. We advocate establishment of machinery to assure interzonal exchange of essential goods.

i. We should seek agreement with Britain and Russia regarding policies for control of large industrial firms and elimination of active Nazis from influential positions in industry and finance.

Reparations and long-range economic policies for Germany had been the subject of long discussion in the State Department and in other government departments. Although we firmly adhered to the policy of unconditional surrender, we had helped the President prepare the following statement made on December 24, 1943: "The United Nations have no intention to enslave the German people. We wish them to have a normal chance to develop, in peace, as useful and respectable members of the European family. . . ."

At the Quebec Conference in September 1944, Secretary of the Treasury Henry Morgenthau, Jr., had persuaded the President and the Prime Minister to initial a drastic program for Germany. Secretaries Hull and Stimson both went to the President and protested against the Morgenthau Plan. The State Department also understood that Anthony Eden had had a heated discussion with the Prime Minister over his initialing of the agreement. Hull and Stimson were convinced, as the result of their separate conversations with the President, that he had not realized the extent to which he had committed himself at Quebec.

Although Morgenthau continued to press his plan, the President, by October 1944, had decided not to accept it. In a memorandum to the State Department on October 20 he made it clear that he agreed with the Department's economic objectives. Our policy as we expressed it in a memorandum to the President at Yalta on February 4, 1945, was:

"We should favor abolition of German self-sufficiency and its position of economic domination of Europe, elimination of certain key industries, prohibition of manufacture of arms and of all types of aircraft, and continuing control to achieve these aims."[4]

3. *The Polish Question.*

It was decided on the territorial settlement to recommend that every effort be made to secure a Polish frontier which, in the north and central areas, would run along the Curzon Line, and in the south generally follow the eastern frontier of Lwow Province. This frontier, we pointed out, would correspond closely with the Curzon Line and would leave the Polish city of Lwow and the oil fields to Poland.

The Curzon Line had been drawn on December 8, 1919, by an Allied Commission and had been recommended by Lord Curzon of Great Britain in an attempt to define an eastern frontier of the indisputably Polish area. To the east of the Curzon Line the population was extremely mixed, with the Poles forming an important minority. The Line ran, however, somewhat farther west than the line that had been reached by Polish troops in 1919 or the boundary which was accepted by Soviet Russia in the Treaty of Riga of 1921. We opposed extending the Polish boundary to the Oder or the Oder–Neisse line. In regard to German territory to be turned over to Poland, we favored limiting this compensation to East Prussia (except for Königsberg, which we expected the Soviet Union to request), a small salient of Pomerania, which would include an area of roughly one hundred miles west along the Baltic coast to the Polish Corridor, and Upper Silesia.

[4] By the "abolition of German self-sufficiency," the State Department meant the abolition of German autarchy for warmaking purposes.

On the political problem in Poland, we recommended that:

We should make every effort to resolve the Polish political differences by the creation of a government of national unity which would be composed of representative members of the five Polish political parties (Peasant party, National Democratic party, Socialist party, Christian Democratic Labor party, and Polish Workers party [Communist party]). We should insist that Mikolajczyk and other representative moderate Poles in London representing various parties be included in the provisional government. Representative Poles now in the Lublin Government should also be included in the government of national unity. It would be inadvisable for us to agree to an amalgamation of the Polish Government in London and the Polish Government in Lublin per se.

The question of who should occupy the presidency of the Polish Government should be held in abeyance until free elections had been held and the entire constitutional question settled by the Polish people themselves.

We should insist on the untrammeled right of the Polish people freely to choose their own government and if necessary we should be prepared to assist in the supervision of these elections.

4. Relations between UNRRA and the Soviet Government.

We recommended that the Soviet Union agree to permit UNRRA to carry out the distribution and supervision of relief supplies in areas liberated by the Soviet armies. Full co-operation on the part of the Soviet Government with UNRRA had not occurred in eastern Europe. On January 18, 1945, UNRRA had at last been notified officially by Soviet authorities that two Black Sea ports were available and that the transit of supplies through Soviet territory would be permitted, but no developments had taken place on the transit of UNRRA personnel through Soviet territory.

5. The Rights of American Representatives on the Allied Control Commissions for Bulgaria, Romania, and Hungary.

The status and responsibilities of the American representatives in these countries, which had surrendered to the Soviet armies, needed clarification. We recommended that our representatives be assured of the right to be consulted on policy directives to be issued in the name of the Control Commissions sufficiently in advance to enable them to communicate with Washington whenever a directive seemed to be in conflict with the general policies of the United States; of the right to determine the size of our delegation on the Control Commissions and to bring in and send out personnel with rapid and automatic clearance by the Soviet authorities on the spot; of the right of courier communication in addition to the right to communicate with Washington and other places outside the country; and of the right, if it were desired, to travel freely within the countries unaccompanied by Soviet officers. Molotov, who was Commissar of Foreign Affairs, had been unwilling to stipulate these points in statutes governing the Control Commission for Hungary. He had told Ambassador Harriman, however, that he agreed with all these rights except the right to have time enough to consult Washington.

6. Iran.

We recommended that Soviet agreement be secured (in accordance with the spirit of the "Declaration of Iran" of December 1, 1943—when the Big Three expressed "their desire for the maintenance of the independence, sovereignty, and integrity of Iran") to respect the decision of the Iranian Government to postpone negotiations with foreign powers or companies regarding oil concessions until the termination of hostilities and the withdrawal of Allied troops now on Iranian soil.

7. *China.*

We recommended that the Soviet and British agree to the desirability of securing the maximum degree of unity in China. The Soviet Union should be urged to use its influence with the Chinese Communists to further an agreement between them and the Nationalist Government. Genuine unity, we believed, would not only shorten the war, but would also save American lives and possibly prevent a disastrous civil war and foreign intervention. General Hurley had been working in China since September 1944, in an attempt to co-ordinate all Chinese military forces for the defeat of Japan.

8. *The Turkish Straits Question.*

We had material ready for the President in case this question were raised at Yalta. We described the history of the Russian desire to have access through the Dardanelles to the Mediterranean. We favored holding a conference of the signatories to the Montreux Convention for revision of Turkish control of the straits.

9. *International Trusteeships.*

We favored the inclusion of provisions for international trusteeships in the world organization. We believed that this should include League of Nations mandates established after the First World War, territories taken from the enemy during the present war, and any territories which might be voluntarily placed under trusteeships.

Our State Department staff also had two lengthy discussions at Marrakech over the question, left unsolved at Dumbarton Oaks, of the voting procedure to be followed in the Security Council. At the suggestion of the State Department, Roosevelt had sent personal messages on December 5, 1944, to Churchill and Stalin setting forth the American formula for solving the deadlock on voting in the Security Council. It was, however, more than a Russian-American disagreement. We had received word that the Prime Minister now favored complete unanimity among the permanent members even in cases where one of the permanent members was involved in a dispute.

In essence, and this was to be adopted at Yalta, the American formula proposed that any member of the Council that was a party to a dispute should abstain from voting on decisions relating to that dispute as long as the decisions referred to proceedings of pacific settlement or peaceful adjustment. On the other hand, decisions relating to the determination of the existence of a threat to the peace or a breach of the peace and decisions to use enforcement measures would, in all cases, require the unanimous agreement of the permanent members. This formula was sent only after a most thorough consideration and after it had been discussed with congressional leaders of the Republican and Democratic parties.

The text of the formula in the President's message to Stalin on December 5 read:

PROPOSAL FOR SECTION C OF THE CHAPTER ON THE SECURITY COUNCIL

C. VOTING

1. Each member of the Security Council should have one vote.

2. Decisions of the Security Council on procedural matters should be made by an affirmative vote of seven members.

3. Decisions of the Security Council on all other matters should be made by an affirmative vote of seven members including the concurring votes of the permanent members; provided that, in decisions under Chapter VIII, Section A, and under paragraph 1 of Chapter VIII, Section C, a party to a dispute should abstain from voting.

You will note that this calls for the unanimity of the permanent members in all decisions of the Council which relate to a determination of a threat to the peace and to action for the removal of such a threat or for the suppression of aggression or other breaches of the peace. I can see, as a practical matter, that this is necessary if action of this kind is to be feasible, and I am, therefore, prepared to accept in this respect the view expressed by your Government in its memorandum on an international security organization presented at the Dumbarton Oaks meeting. This means, of course, that in decisions of this character each permanent member would always have a vote.

At the same time, the Dumbarton Oaks proposals also provide in Chapter VIII, Section A, for judicial or other procedures of a recommendatory character which the Security Council may employ in promoting voluntary peaceful settlement of disputes. Here, too, I am satisfied that recommendations of the Security Council will carry far greater weight if they are concurred in by the permanent members. But I am also convinced that such procedures will be effective only if the Great Powers exercise moral leadership by demonstrating their fidelity to the principles of justice, and, therefore, by *accepting a provision under which, with regard to such procedures, all parties to a dispute should abstain from voting. I firmly believe that willingness on the part of the permanent members not to claim for themselves a special position in this respect would greatly enhance their moral prestige and would strengthen their own position as the principal guardians of the future peace, without in any way jeopardizing their vital interests or impairing the essential principle that in all decisions of the Council which affect such interests the Great Powers must act unanimously. It would certainly make the whole plan, which must necessarily assign a special position to the Great Powers in the enforcement of peace, far more acceptable to all nations. . . .*

The State Department group and I agreed, in our discussions at Marrakech, that we would bolster the American formula by emphasizing to the Russian delegation and to Churchill that we thoroughly agreed that unanimity of thought and action on the part of the Great Powers was of the greatest importance to peace and security. An atmosphere of harmony among the Great Powers and a willingness to employ measures of enforcement in behalf of peace and security should result in more stable conditions in international relations. Furthermore, there could be no more effective justification of the special position of the Great Powers as the chief guardians of peace than the voluntary willingness by each of them to abstain in any controversy in which it was a party. This step would make it evident that the leadership of the Great Powers was to be based not only upon size, strength, and resources, but also on the enduring qualities of moral leadership.

After our busy conferences at Villa Taylor we rested in the warm African sunshine or visited the city of Marrakech. The city had a population of 300,000, including an average of 30,000 transients a day as the result of its activity as a caravan trading center and, of course, because of its usefulness to the American Army as a key center for the Air Transport Command and a ferry point for our bombers.

Hopkins, accompanied by Bohlen, had left Washington a few days ahead of our party to visit London, Paris, and Rome. He had thought that such a trip might prove to be valuable to the President, and Roosevelt had allowed him to go to sound out the general situation. I personally felt that this w s a great mistake. Hopkins had neither the strength nor the vitality to undertake the strain of both this trip and the Yalta Conference. It would have been far wiser for him to have been on the battleship with the President, resting and reviewing with the President the questions to be discussed at the conference.

In spite of Hopkins' chronic ill-health he was a most invaluable adviser to President Roosevelt. He was his devoted friend and confidant. He had an uncanny knowledge of the President's moods. He knew when to suggest a given policy and when to remain quiet. Many of my friends from my business days—if not the public at large—had a complete misconception of Hopkins. Although many people who hated the New Deal expressed their rage by attacking Hopkins, he was an able, honorable, intelligent, hard-working individual who left an enviable record of public service.

While we were working at Marrakech, I received a radio message from Bohlen naming Naples as the rendezvous where I was to meet Hopkins as had previously been arranged. We left Marrakech on Tuesday morning, January 30, and after two hours of flying we reached the Mediterranean and then flew along the coast toward Algiers. The mountain country of Tunisia, where so much of the North

African campaigns of 1942–43 took place, looked from the air much as it had been described in Ernie Pyle's vivid dispatches. By midafternoon we had reached the coast of Sicily; and at 4 P.M. we sighted the steep cliffs of the Isle of Capri on our left, and on our right Vesuvius, with her usual plume of smoke, soon came into sight.

We were met at the Marchionese airfield at Caserta by Lieutenant General Joseph T. McNarney, deputy commander in chief of the Allied forces in the Mediterranean Theater, Lieutenant General Ira C. Eaker, commander of the United States Mediterranean Air Force, Alexander Kirk, American Ambassador to Italy, Bohlen, and Hopkins.

I had not been in Italy since 1931. As Hopkins, Kirk, and I drove from the airport to the center of Naples, I was appalled at the hungry and dispirited-looking people. I had never seen a more depressing sight.

Before dinner Hopkins, Bohlen, Kirk, Matthews, Hiss, and I had a discussion of the political and economic situation in Italy. Hopkins informed me that the Prime Minister was extremely irritated over the divergent views of the United States and Great Britain on Italy. The British had blocked Count Carlo Sforza from becoming Italy's Foreign Secretary a few months before. From the time of the surrender of Marshal Badoglio to General Eisenhower on September 3, 1943, there had been disagreements between Great Britain and the United States over the government of Italy. We did not favor keeping Victor Emmanuel on the throne, unless the Italian people wanted him, and we did not consider Badoglio adequate for the purpose of governing Italy. Churchill, on the other hand, would have been happy to see the Italian royal family continue its rule, and he did succeed temporarily in keeping the King in power.

When the Badoglio government declared war on Germany on October 13, 1943, Badoglio promised that his government would soon include representatives of all political parties. These parties, however, did not approve of serving under the King nor did they consider Badoglio to be a representative of democracy. Sforza, who had been Italian Foreign Minister before Mussolini came to power, headed the opposition to the King.

The United States had aided the return of Sforza to Italy in 1943, and he had told Churchill as well as Assistant Secretary of State Adolf Berle that he would support Badoglio or any other Italian Government acceptable to the Allied powers in fighting against Germany.

When he reached Italy and talked with other anti-Fascist leaders, however, he refused to enter the Badoglio government as long as Victor Emmanuel was on the throne. Instead he suggested that the King abdicate.

We in Washington favored Sforza's suggestion. On January 25, 1944, after the Allied landing at Anzio, twenty-five miles south of Rome, Hull had cabled our representative on the Advisory Council for Italy that there should be no further delay in reorganizing the Italian Government on a more liberal basis. He also stated that we did not favor the retention of the King, although it was for the Italian people to decide whether or not they wanted to retain a monarchy.

Churchill objected and urged that both the King and Badoglio should remain. Action on this matter, however, was delayed by stiff German resistance to the Allied advance: they established a strong defensive line between Naples and Rome and contained our landing at Anzio.

Finally, in April, our representative on the Advisory Council for Italy, Robert D. Murphy, discussed with the British representative on the council our belief that the King should abdicate. London soon instructed its representative to accept our position. The King then promised Murphy to retire in favor of the Crown Prince when Rome was occupied. A few days later the anti-Fascist parties joined the Italian Cabinet. After the fall of Rome in June, the Crown Prince replaced the King and a new Cabinet was formed with the prominent anti-Fascist leader, Ivanoe Bonomi, as Premier.

Not only did Churchill object to the installation of the Bonomi Cabinet, but his representative in Italy told Bonomi that Sforza should not be appointed Foreign Minister. The Prime Minister eventually agreed to the new Cabinet, but he was adamant on Sforza. We, on the other hand, told Bonomi that the appointment of Sforza was agreeable to the United States.

Late in November a political crisis forced the resignation of the Bonomi government. The British Embassy, without consulting us, again intervened and warned that it would not approve any Cabinet which included Sforza. There was immediately great criticism in the United States of this arbitrary action on the part of the British. In a cable to the State Department on December 4, 1944, Churchill declared that Sforza was not only intriguing against the monarchy but that he was a mischief-maker in general. The following day I issued the following public statement:

> ... This Government has not in any way intimated to the Italian Government that there would be any opposition on its part to Count Sforza. Since Italy is an area of combined responsibility, we have affirmed to both the British and Italian Governments that we expect the Italians to work out their problems of government along democratic lines without influence from outside. ...

The Prime Minister immediately dispatched a violent cable to the President, and in a speech to the House of Commons declared:

"We have to assume the burden of the most thankless tasks, and in undertaking them to be scoffed at, criticized and opposed from every quarter; but at least we know where we are making for, know the end of the road, know what is our objective. . . . We have not attempted to put our veto on the appointment of Count Sforza. If tomorrow the Italians were to make him Prime Minister or Foreign Secretary, we have no power to stop it, except with the agreement of the Allies. All that we should have to say about it is that we do not trust the man, we do not think he is a true and trustworthy man, nor do we put the slightest confidence in any government of which he is a dominating member. I think we should have to put a great deal of responsibility for what might happen on those who called him to power."

Hopkins said at Naples that Churchill "would beat us all up" when we arrived at Malta, and that I, therefore, had better brief the President before the Prime Minister raised the Italian question with him. Hopkins added that by early 1945 many Italian problems were of a non-military nature. He remarked that political questions were beyond the competence of Naval and Army officials. Yet, added Hopkins, the State Department was still not in charge of American policy in Italy. He pointed out that the British military authorities in Italy, as elsewhere, took their orders from the Foreign Office, whereas American military officials did not hesitate to take a position quite independent of that of the State Department. That same evening Ambassador Kirk, a seasoned State Department career officer, told me with great force that he believed the time had arrived when the civilian agencies' viewpoint must be taken into consideration by the military in Italy.

It was most essential, furthermore, Hopkins said, for the United States Government to stop being merely a silent partner of the British in Italy. Instead of automatically acquiescing in British decisions, the United States should insist that the Allies give the Italians greater political responsibility. The Italian Government, Hopkins stated, could not take action on even the most inconsequential matter without Allied military approval. In view of the fact that the United States was participating in a military fashion in Italy, Hopkins insisted that we could not escape responsibility for military decisions on political matters, even though it was the British who were really making these decisions.

We also gave considerable time to a discussion of the need of increasing the Italian food ration with particular emphasis on importing wheat immediately. The Supreme Allied commander in Italy, Sir Harold Alexander, was, however, opposed to such an increase. The British, with their extreme sensitivity to the shortage of shipping—as well as to the short food supply in the United Kingdom itself—felt that the necessary shipping could not be spared to bring wheat to Italy from halfway around the world.

Hopkins remarked that for political reasons the bread ration had to be increased promptly. The shipping requirements necessary to meet this increase, he observed, would be "a mere drop in the bucket." We all agreed that there could be no recovery, no peace, and no democracy in Italy and Europe unless the people had enough to eat and the tools and materials with which to go back to work.

The following morning, Wednesday, January 31, before taking off for Malta, we met again to discuss a wide variety of topics. Hopkins reported that he had had several talks with Churchill and Eden on the question of the voting procedure in the proposed Security Council. Hopkins said that the Foreign Office was in entire agreement as to the advisability of the American position. The Prime Minister, however, had made it plain that he himself was not committed to the American proposal. This struck me as rather strange, since before we left Washington the British Embassy had officially informed us that the British Government approved of the American formula. I knew that Field Marshal Smuts had cabled Churchill that he favored granting an absolute right of veto on all questions, and this position of the leader of the Union of South Africa apparently was affecting the Prime Minister's views when he talked to Hopkins, for Smuts had great influence with the Prime Minister. Churchill had also told Hopkins that he felt there had to be agreement on this question at the Yalta Conference. If the British and the Americans were unable to persuade the Russians to accept the American formula, he thought that some other alternative would have to be found.

Eden had told Hopkins that Lord Halifax, British Ambassador in Washington, had cabled the Foreign Office that the President himself said that he was not unalterably committed to the American proposal. From these discussions in London, Hopkins observed that it was clear that the Foreign Office and the State Department were in precisely the same situation. Although both realized the importance of securing Russian agreement to the American proposal, Roosevelt and Churchill were not yet convinced that the difference with the Russians on the voting question was a matter of major importance.

Both Hopkins' statement and the reference to Halifax's

cable were a bit bewildering to me. The President had worked with the State Department on the voting formula and he had sent the cables to Marshal Stalin and the Prime Minister on December 5, 1944, making his position entirely clear. The proposal described in the December 5 message continued to be the President's position. It was this proposal that Stalin and Churchill accepted at the conference table at Yalta.

The British situation, Hopkins added, was complicated by the fact that the Cabinet was not in unanimous agreement with the Foreign Office. He said that the Prime Minister had shown him a copy of a memorandum from Sir Stafford Cripps, arguing that the Soviet voting formula of complete unanimity was more desirable from the standpoint of British interests. I was told at Yalta that Eden had been extremely irritated with Churchill for having shown Hopkins this memorandum, since it revealed a lack of unanimity within the British Government.

It was no surprise to me that the Prime Minister had revealed this type of information to Hopkins. He had complete confidence in Hopkins, as well as great affection for him. When I had visited Churchill the previous April, both he and Mrs. Churchill were most solicitous over Harry's ill-health.

Hopkins and Bohlen had also discussed with the British the explosive Russian proposal, made at Dumbarton Oaks, that all sixteen Soviet Republics be granted a vote in the world organization. The British, they reported, were in complete agreement with us that the Soviet suggestion was preposterous. The fact that each of the British dominions—including India, which was not then self-governing—was to have a separate vote, however, made the British decide that for reasons of tactics the primary burden of opposition had to be carried by the United States.

Then Hopkins reported that Ambassador Winant was greatly disturbed because, although the British and American representatives on the European Advisory Commission had signed the agreement on the German zones of occupation, no agreement had been concluded between the governments. Winant feared, Hopkins observed, that the Russians might reach the border of their zone and then keep on going.

I explained to Hopkins that the State Department was also concerned over this delay, and that Assistant Secretary Dunn had been in constant communication with our Joint Chiefs of Staff, urging their approval. The issue between the United States Chiefs of Staff and the British Chiefs of Staff was the degree of American control over the port of Bremerhaven in the British zone. Hopkins and I agreed that it was of the utmost urgency that the President and the Prime Minister reach an agreement on this at Malta.

Hopkins also reported at our Naples conference on the talks he had had with General de Gaulle in Paris. The general had not been too cordial, and was particularly irritated that he had not been invited to attend the Yalta Conference. Hopkins also reported on the talks he had with French Foreign Minister Georges Bidault. Bidault had been definite, Hopkins said, about the French wanting some special kind of control over the Ruhr and the west bank of the Rhine. Although Bidault had explicitly said that the French did not desire to acquire German territory, he had spoken in general terms about internationalization of this area with French predominance in the occupying military forces.

When we concluded this talk on January 31 we lunched with General Eaker and his staff, and then took off from Naples to join the British and American delegations gathering at the island of Malta for discussions prior to our meeting with the Russians at Yalta. Hopkins was so sick that we put him to bed on the plane even during this three-hour flight. He was so weak that it was remarkable that he could be as active as he was. He fought his way through difficult and trying conferences on coffee, cigarettes, an amazingly small amount of food, paregoric, and sheer fortitude. He was so exhausted by the time we reached Yalta, for instance, that he was confined to bed almost all of the time except when Roosevelt, Churchill, and Stalin were in session. He was to be active with us, however, in our talks at Malta with the British.

CHAPTER 3

Rendezvous at Malta

The sun was just setting as we sighted the hills of Malta and its capital city, Valletta. It has been written:

> There is a Mohammedan saying that certain sentiments can be adequately expressed only "if written in golden ink." That appears to me to be the medium for writing about Valletta, for only in shining letters could one perhaps convey the luminous golden beauty of the Maltese City.[1]

From the air as we first viewed it this was a perfect description, but as we circled to land we could see everywhere the heavy damage caused by the Germans during the long siege of Malta.

Anthony Eden, Sir Alexander Cadogan, and Sarah Churchill Oliver met us at the airport on our arrival from Naples and drove us through the heavily bombed city to the harbor. Many of the forts, watchtowers, and intricate defense works,

[1] Bella Sidney Woolf, "The 'Golden City' of Valletta," *The Crown Colonist*, June 1948, p. 299.

done in glorious color and form, dated back centuries ago to the Knights of Malta, who lived, fought, and died here to maintain this island as a small outpost of Christian Europe against Islam.

We were escorted aboard the British light cruiser, H.M.S. *Sirius*, where my cabin was just opposite one occupied by Eden. Some of the State Department staff were billeted on the *Eastern Prince*, a Furness Withy Line passenger vessel which was being used as a transport. The *Eastern Prince* was tied up at the dock directly below the *Sirius*. Just across the bight the Prime Minister and Harriman were aboard another British light cruiser, the H.M.S. *Orion*. General Marshall, Admiral E. J. King, General B. B. Somervell, and other members of the Army and Navy staff were staying at Montgomery House in Valletta. So many buildings had been demolished by aerial bombardment, in the early days of the war, that there was not room enough ashore for all the visitors who had converged on Malta.

On the evening of our arrival there was a large formal dinner at Government House given by the governor in honor of the visiting British and American delegations. The Prime Minister was aroused over the sharp differences between the British and American positions on the political situation in Italy. He told me in blunt language that I had made the Italian situation extremely difficult for him.

He was still incensed over my public statement of December 5, 1944. He was magnificent when his fighting temperament was aroused, and there was nothing he loved more dearly than to hurl himself into the fray. Although I had worked with the Prime Minister when I was Lend-Lease administrator and Under Secretary of State, in both Washington and London, Malta was my first meeting with him in the role of Secretary of State. In pungent English he expressed his distress over my attitude on the Italian question and told me that he considered Sforza to be untrustworthy.

I made our position clear to the Prime Minister, stating that even if we had been consulted in advance by the British we would have been unable to say anything which would not have caused him resentment. I told him that I took full responsibility for the statement of December 5. I was subsequently to learn that two days later the Prime Minister complained to the President that his new Secretary of State did not have a helpful attitude on Italy.

The situation in the Balkans and particularly in Greece, the Prime Minister told me that night, was also causing him great concern. On December 5, 1944, the Prime Minister had told the House of Commons:

". . . Greece is faced with the most desperate economic and financial problems apart from the civil war which we are trying to stop. . . . The main burden falls on us, and the responsibility is within our sphere—that is the military sphere agreed upon with our principal Allies."

Churchill had flown to Athens on Christmas Day with Eden. He brought an end to hostilities, established a temporary regency under Archbishop Damaskinos, and secured from King George the promise that he would not attempt to return to the country "unless summoned by a free and fair expression of the national will."

Churchill explained to me at Malta that his position was that, if the British had not had troops in Greece, the Greek Communists would have taken over the government. The British, he declared, had a definite responsibility not to allow this to happen.

I also mentioned briefly to Churchill that evening the

question of our formula for voting in the Security Council. It was apparent to me that the Prime Minister had not as yet applied his mind to this difficult problem. He then emphasized to me that he felt the world organization should concentrate its efforts on just keeping the peace. Churchill clearly believed that the world organization should be restricted to enforcing the peace and that economic and social matters, as in the past, should be handled by direct governmental agreements. Both Eden and I argued with him about this, and I told him how disappointed we would be if the Economic and Social Council which we had proposed at Dumbarton Oaks did not have an important function.

The morning after this conversation with Churchill, Eden and I discussed some of the problems to be raised at Yalta. The President had asked me to begin these talks before his own arrival at Malta. Churchill had suggested to Roosevelt that Eden and I hold a preparatory meeting even before Malta, but the President had refused. The President knew how overly suspicious the Russians were—a Russian trait that antedated the Communist regime. He feared that too many Anglo-American meetings before Yalta would merely feed the traditional Russian suspicion of a combined front being formed against them by the West.

The President was always careful to keep the Russians informed of diplomatic negotiations between the British and our government. At the Teheran Conference, although the Prime Minister was quite irritated at the time, the President had declined to have lunch with him alone just before a plenary session. At Yalta, too, the President and the Prime Minister did not hold a private luncheon until five days after the Conference had been in session.[2]

[2]Sherwood, op. cit., furnishes many examples of how the President kept Marshal Stalin informed of negotiations with the British.

During the slightly more than two days spent at Malta, Eden and I saw a great deal of each other. Eden's courageous break with the Chamberlain government over the prewar appeasement policy and his fine intellectual capacity had won him the respect of the Foreign Office personnel and of the average British citizen.

On February 1, as we walked off the British battleship at Malta, he was recognized by the shipyard workers and given a great ovation. When we returned to the ship Eden was accorded a genuine, although unintentional, compliment. One of the British non-commissioned officers did not recognize him and asked the bugler, who had just piped him aboard, who that was. A member of our group overheard the bugler reply that he was the Foreign Secretary. The noncommissioned officer remarked, "You're crazy. He's too bloody British to be a foreign secretary."

After our walk, Matthews, the rest of my staff and I met with Eden, Cadogan, and other representatives of the Foreign Office to canvass many outstanding issues. We agreed that we would join forces to urge the Combined Chiefs of Staff to reach a decision before leaving Malta on the protocol on the German zones of occupation and recommend that the technicality over Bremerhaven be settled at a later date. General Marshall and Field Marshal Sir Alan Brooke lunched with Eden and me that day aboard the *Sirius*. The two Chiefs of Staff, after a thorough discussion of the question with us, authorized us to cable our representatives on the European Advisory Commission in London that the two governments now approved the zones.

I next pointed out to Eden that the President attached great importance to giving the French a zone of occupation in Germany. Eden agreed with me that the two governments might give France portions of their respective zones.

We also discussed the Polish question at great length. I told Eden that recognition of the Lublin National Liberation Committee as the government of Poland would cause great resentment in the United States. I explained that we had hoped for some kind of a coalition government with Mikolajczyk, former head of the London Polish Government, invited to join. Eden made it plain that the British could not recognize the Lublin Government either. We both agreed to present a joint memorandum to the President and to the Prime Minister urging the formation of a new Polish Government.

Eden wondered whether the Russians might give assurances to Great Britain and the United States of really free elections in Poland. He realized, he added, that this would be asking "rather a lot." I am not sure just what prompted this remark. It may have been merely an expression of apprehension, but at Yalta the British certainly joined wholeheartedly with us in insisting on and securing such an agreement. I pointed out that the whole unsatisfactory Polish situation jeopardized the participation of the United States in a world organization. Then I said that Mr. Roosevelt and Mr. Churchill *simply had to get* this fact across to Marshal Stalin. Eden remarked that if the Russians did not agree to our approach to the Polish problem we would have to announce to the world a deadlock on the question.

On the question of the Polish-German frontier, Eden said that he was worried over the clamors of the Lublin Poles for more German territory. He remarked that he thought the proper western boundary of Poland should recognize the cession to Poland of East Prussia, Silesia, and a coastal sector of Pomerania. He pointed out that this would include eight million Germans and would be all that the Poles could swal-

Winston Churchill, Franklin D. Roosevelt, and Joseph Stalin with their foreign ministers, Anthony Eden, Edward R. Stettinius, Jr., and V. M. Molotov, at Livadia Palace, headquarters of the Yalta Conference. Charles E. Bohlen, Lord Leathers, Sir Alexander Cadogan, and W. Averell Harriman are in the rear. (Sovfoto)

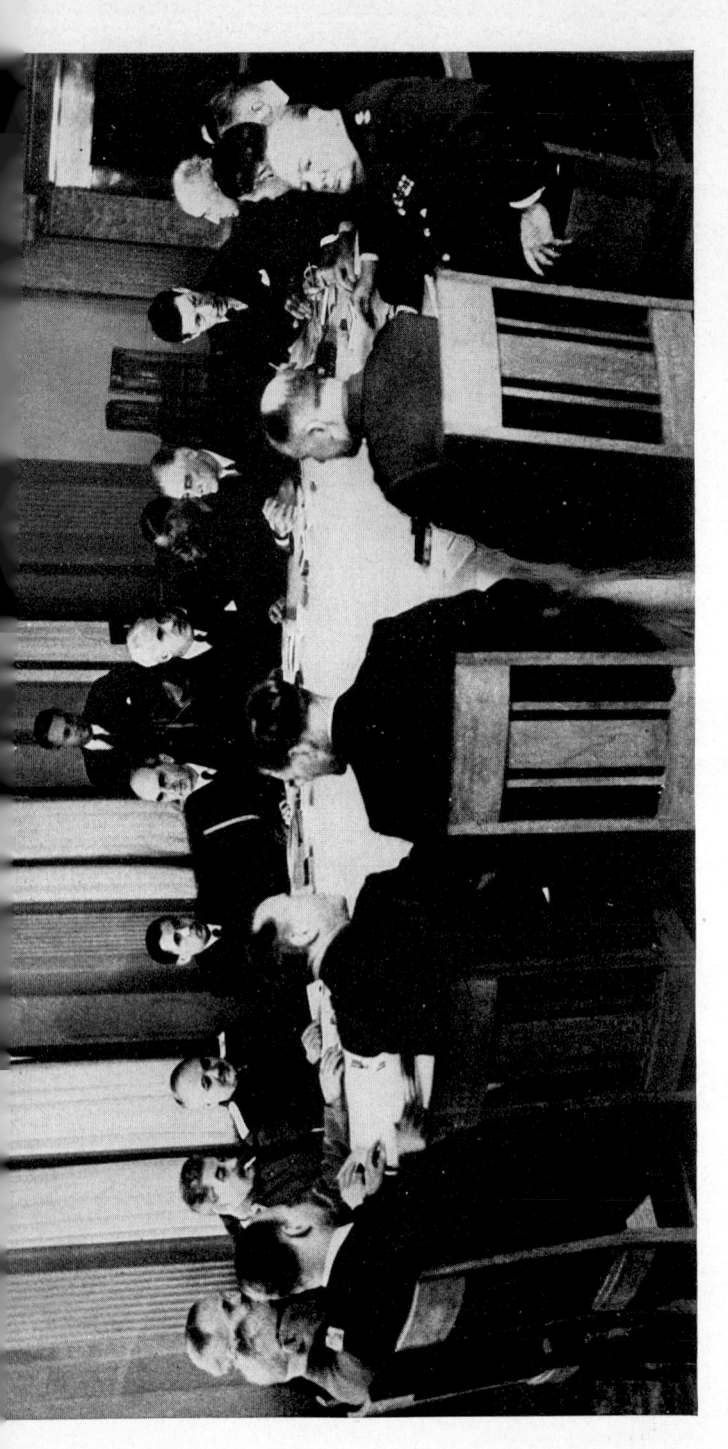

The Yalta Conference in session. Reading clockwise from the President are Charles E. Bohlen, James F. Byrnes, Sir Alexander Cadogan, Anthony Eden, Winston Churchill, Major Birse, Sir Edward Bridges, Sir Archibald Clark Kerr, F. T. Gusev, Andrei Vishinsky, V. M. Molotov, Joseph Stalin, I. M. Maisky, Andrei Gromyko, Fleet Admiral William D. Leahy, and Secretary Stettinius. Seated in back of the President is Harry Hopkins, and standing is H. Freeman Matthews. (Sovfoto)

low. There was general agreement with this statement, and Matthews added that the United States hoped that the necessary transfers of population would not be carried out in too precipitate a fashion.

With respect to Italian boundaries, Eden said that he wanted the Soviet Union, the United States, and Great Britain to tell Marshal Tito of Yugoslavia that the existing boundaries would remain for occupation purposes. Any change in the boundaries would be taken up later as part of the general peace settlement. I agreed with this proposal.

At my request Matthews explained our desire that the Balkan Control Commissions be insured freedom of movement and communication and that we wanted to be sure that our representatives were consulted before the Control Commissions acted. Eden replied that he was preparing a memorandum of the British desires on this problem for Molotov and would furnish us with a copy of the document.

We then discussed the question of Iran. Matthews made it plain that we felt the Russians should stop putting pressure on the Iranians for oil concessions at this time. Eden recommended that we go further and say that when the supply route to Russia across Iran was no longer needed, which he felt would occur by the following June, we should by agreement begin the removal of *all* troops.

He added that, since the southern Iranian oil fields were still vital to the prosecution of the war against Japan, he was not sure whether the British military would not insist that troops still be stationed there. I remarked that the latest information in possession of our government indicated that the rail and unloading facilities at Odessa and other Black Sea ports would not be sufficient—even though satisfactory arrangements were made with Turkey for passage through the Dardanelles—to permit the Persian Gulf ports to be closed. Eden observed that the British did not want spheres of influence for any nation in Iran and that withdrawal of troops was the best way to prevent this from occurring. I told him that this was the United States' position, as soon as troops were no longer needed there for the war.

We next discussed the traditional Russian interest in a warm-water port, and Eden said that he had urged the Prime Minister to put everything on the table—including that problem—at the forthcoming Conference.

We then raised the Chinese question and stressed the importance which the United States attached to British-Soviet-American support for an understanding between the Nationalist Government and the Chinese Communists in order to further the war effort and to prevent possible civil strife. Eden observed that Hopkins had told him a few days before in London that the President thought the British were opposed to an agreement between the two Chinese groups. The British Foreign Minister insisted that this was not accurate and that Great Britain not only wanted Chinese unity but wished to persuade the Russians to adopt the same position.

We next discussed the State Department's proposal for an Emergency High Commission for liberated Europe. I pointed out that the President had not made up his mind on this suggestion when he left Washington.

After a brief and inconclusive discussion of such questions, as supplies for liberated Europe, prisoners of war, and war criminals, we closed our conference with an analysis of the world organization. The Foreign Office, Eden said, approved of our voting formula in the Security Council, but he observed that the Foreign Office had to have further talks with the Prime Minister to make sure that he understood it. I remarked that we intended to have further talks with the President on the voting question when he reached Malta.

We mentioned that it was the State Department's belief that France should be added to Great Britain, the Soviet Union, China, and the United States as the fifth sponsoring power for the conference to draft the world charter. The British were in complete agreement that this step should be taken. As the meeting was breaking up some mention was made of dates for the conference. I expressed preference for an early meeting, shortly after April 15, but Cadogan felt that this would be too early.

After a hard, long day of conferences and discussions, Hopkins, Eden, Cadogan, and I joined the Prime Minister for dinner aboard the *Orion*. We stayed until almost midnight and had a most intimate conversation with the Prime Minister. We talked at great length about the need of economic and political aid for liberated peoples. The questions of feeding the people and furnishing them with transportation were recognized as matters of absolute necessity. The Prime Minister stated that they were as much wartime necessities as ammunition. He agreed, furthermore, that while the Foreign Office, the State Department, and the Russians had recognized this, as yet the military had not.

During the course of conversation Churchill expressed utter dismay at the outlook of the world. He said that there probably were more units of suffering among humanity as of this hour, while we were meeting, than ever before in history. As he looked out on the world, he added, it was one of sorrow and bloodshed. It was his opinion that future peace, stability, and progress depended on Great Britain and the United States remaining in close harmony at all times.

It seemed to me, immediately after this conversation, that the Prime Minister was very much depressed over the future of the world. The Prime Minister's mood of depression may have been caused by worry over relations with the Soviet Union or he may have been upset over the desperate condition of Greece. By the time he reached Yalta, however, most of this pessimism seemed to have left him.

The morning after the dinner with the Prime Minister, the President's heavy cruiser, the U.S.S. *Quincy,* sailed into the harbor. The President's arrival was a most dramatic moment. It was warm and sunny and the sky was cloudless. A half-dozen Spitfires darted back and forth above the harbor. A company of Marines was lined up on the *Sirius* and on the *Orion* across the way, and we could see Churchill walking back and forth smoking his usual long cigar.

Eden, Hopkins, Harriman, and other members of our group had been on deck about half an hour when the *Quincy* came in view around the bend. With glasses I had borrowed I quickly picked out the President, wearing a brown coat and a tweed cap, seated on the bridge. We all waved as the *Quincy* came abreast, and the President waved back. The Marines on the *Sirius* stood stiffly at attention and the band struck up "The Star-Spangled Banner." Then, as the *Quincy* passed the *Orion,* the Marines and the band on that ship repeated the performance.

On board the *Quincy* with the President were Admiral William D. Leahy, Admiral Ross T. McIntire, James F. Byrnes, director of the Office of War Mobilization, Stephen T. Early, secretary to the President, General Edwin M. Watson, military aide to the President, Edward J. Flynn, Democratic party leader, and the President's daughter, Mrs. Anna Roosevelt Boettiger.

After the *Quincy* had moored, Hopkins, Harriman, and I immediately went to call on the President. Admirals Leahy and Wilson Brown received us as we were piped aboard, and we were shown to the bridge where the President, somewhat rested from the ocean voyage, was sitting with his daughter.

I found the President in good spirits, and we chatted for a few minutes about our respective trips to Malta. The President said that he had a critical, urgent, and top-secret matter for the State Department. He had decided, at the last minute, to take Flynn on the trip to the Crimea, and Flynn had no passport. The President added that he did not want Flynn to spend the rest of his days in Siberia. Steps were taken immediately to secure the passport. Although Flynn took no part in the official business of the Conference, after it was over, at the President's request, he visited Moscow to discuss the improvement of relations between the Roman Catholic Church and Russia and then went to Rome, where he discussed the same subject with the Pope.

I reported to the President that we had had conversations with the Foreign Office the day before and were generally seeing eye to eye on most of the points that the President had asked us to discuss with the British. I also told him of my talks with Churchill and predicted that he and the Prime Minister—now that the Prime Minister had "beaten me up first" as Hopkins had put it—should have a harmonious time together.

The President seemed greatly relieved when I told him that General Marshall and Field Marshal Brooke had finally approved the plan for the German zones of occupation and that Eden and I had sent instructions to our representatives on the European Advisory Commission in London.

After visits from the governor of Malta, Admiral King, and General Marshall, the President had a luncheon aboard the *Quincy*. He was at the head of the table with the Prime Minister on his right, and Mrs. Boettiger was at the other end with Eden on her right. The others present at the lunch were Admiral Leahy, Sarah Oliver, James Byrnes, and I.

We had a typically fine Navy meal. There was a small candle, such as he had at 10 Downing Street, on the Prime Minister's tobacco tray to light his cigars, a friendly, delicate touch by the President. The Prime Minister accepted a regular-sized cigar furnished by his host, but before long he was contentedly puffing at one of his own eight-inch Churchillian cigars.

Both the President and the Prime Minister seemed in high spirits. By the time of this meeting in Malta the two men had established an easy intimacy and a high degree of frankness in their relationship. "It is fun to be in the same decade with you," the President had cabled the Prime Minister in 1942, while Hopkins later described Churchill's attitude en route for the Atlantic Charter meeting with the President: "You'd have thought Winston was being carried up into the heavens to meet God!"[3]

From my personal experience with both of them I know that they had deep respect and affection for each other. In all of their military and diplomatic discussions, on the other hand, their friendship and mutual respect never made either one of them forget his position or the nation he represented.

At this luncheon the President mentioned that the Atlantic Charter had never been a signed document and that he, as a result, had written the Prime Minister's name on the copy he had. In a jocular fashion Roosevelt expressed the hope

[3] Ibid., pp. 351, 494.

RENDEZVOUS AT MALTA

that perhaps on this trip the Prime Minister would countersign, so that the document would be bona fide.

Churchill remarked that he had recently read the Declaration of Independence and was delighted to find the Atlantic Charter incorporated in the same book. The Prime Minister declared that he still stood for what the Atlantic Charter said. At this point, in a quite serious vein, he observed that the four freedoms were all right, but that the most important of them was freedom from fear.

He remarked that the President had never made clear to the world his ideal of freedom from international fear. There were many countries on the face of the globe at the present moment, the Prime Minister pointed out, where the populations were in fear of their own governments. People must be freed of such fear, and he concluded his point dramatically by saying, "As long as blood flows from my veins, I will stand for this."

At one point during the luncheon the Prime Minister joked with the President about America's interest in China and Madame Chiang Kai-shek, and referred to China as the "Great American Illusion." The Prime Minister also treated in a light vein the President's refusal to change the location of the Yalta Conference after the warning that he had received from the intelligence services.

The President discussed his recent election and took great delight in pointing out that ninety per cent of the press had opposed him. Churchill stated that he liked the way people in a democracy could criticize their government. He then mentioned how he recently had insulted two members of Parliament in the hallway and thus guaranteed two votes against himself, as these two members of Parliament had originally intended not to vote at all. The Prime Minister stated that he was confident about winning the British elections four months hence. I remembered this prediction of Churchill's at the San Francisco Conference the following May, when Eden told me that there was a distinct possibility that the Conservative party might be defeated. He remarked to me at that time that I might be seeing Ernest Bevin at the next Foreign Ministers' Conference.

The President also remarked to Churchill that, although he expected the war in Europe to end that year, he thought the Japanese war might continue until 1947. There seemed to be unanimous agreement on this point.

Shortly after lunch the President privately told the Prime Minister, Eden, and me that he wanted to meet Ibn Saud of Saudi Arabia, King Farouk of Egypt, and Haile Selassie of Ethiopia on this trip. Churchill said that he thought it would be a splendid idea to invite them to visit aboard the *Quincy*.

Eden, following the luncheon, remarked to me that the President looked better, seemed much calmer and more relaxed than when he had last seen him. He thought that Mr. Roosevelt was in particularly fine shape. Cadogan, in contrast to Eden, told me that when he saw the President at Malta he was shocked at the change in the President's appearance since he had last seen him. I wrote in my notes that day:

> *The President seemed rested and calm and said he had gotten plenty of sleep on the way here. He said he had been resting ten hours every night since leaving Washington but still couldn't understand why he was not slept out.*

I had been concerned over the President ever since his inaugural address on the porch of the White House on January 20. That day he had seemed to tremble all over. It was not just his hands that shook, but his whole body as well. By the time he reached Malta he seemed, however, to be cheerful, calm, and quite rested.

It seemed to me that some kind of deterioration in the President's health had taken place between the middle of December and the inauguration on January 20. In spite of this development, however, I wish to emphasize that at all times from Malta through the Crimean Conference and the Alexandria meeting I always found him to be mentally alert and fully capable of dealing with each situation as it developed. The stories that his health took a turn for the worse either on the way to Yalta or at the Conference are, to the best of my knowledge, without foundation. The President's ability to participate on fully equal terms day after day in the grueling give-and-take at the conference table with such powerful associates as Churchill and Stalin is the best answer to these stories.

On the Yalta trip the President's daughter Anna was a great comfort to her father. Theirs was a beautiful relationship rarely found between a father and daughter. In addition to her kindness and devotion she had wisdom and tact and had learned how to guide difficult situations. She was most skillful, when a conversation at the dinner table seemed to be disturbing her father, in quietly suggesting another topic.

At Yalta the President was extremely steady and patient. At no time did he flare up. He was kind and sympathetic, but determined.

In midafternoon of February 2, General Bedell Smith came to the *Sirius* to discuss some urgent matters with me. I had met General Smith in 1940 when he was assistant secretary to the General Staff under General Marshall. My long friendship with Marshall had made it possible for Smith and me to build a warm friendship during the hectic days of the initial defense effort, when I first went to Washington. Eisenhower had taken Smith with him to London, and Smith had just flown in to Malta from Eisenhower's headquarters.

I talked at length with Smith. He described particularly the difficulties and troubles Eisenhower and he were having at SHAEF with Field Marshal Sir Bernard Montgomery. Montgomery was reporting directly to Churchill and these communications, Smith told me, were proving to be a great embarrassment to Eisenhower. Smith asked that I explain the situation to President Roosevelt. Although I subsequently told the President about this talk with Smith, the news was not particularly new or astounding to the President. He was quite familiar with the difficulties Eisenhower had had with Montgomery in the past.

In addition to the message about Montgomery, Smith told me of the Allied recovery from the German counterattack at the Battle of the Bulge and of the expectation of a successful Allied assault soon to be launched. He added that there was an outside chance that the Russian advance might be at an end. There was the possibility, he believed, that if the Germans lost Berlin they might retire to southwest Germany and conduct guerrilla fighting for months or even years.

That evening the President, the Prime Minister, Eden, and I dined together on the *Quincy,* and Eden and I, in an informal, conversational manner, reviewed for the two leaders the talk we had had the day before. At various times Eden or I mentioned our discussion of the international organization; the treatment of Germany; Poland; the Allied Control Commissions in Romania, Bulgaria, and Hungary; Iran; and China.

This meeting served again to clarify the American and British attitudes on these questions. Since the President and the Prime Minister expressed their ideas on these questions many times around the council table at Yalta, the details will be developed in the subsequent chapters of this book.

After dinner that evening we all flew to the Crimea. The President would have preferred to go by ship, since air travel made his sinus condition most painful. Although Dr. McIntire, too, preferred that the President travel by ship, it was finally ruled out as being too dangerous for the President to go on a battleship through the Dardanelles.

The airport at Malta that night was a busy place. We were taking a large number of military personnel, and the President jokingly remarked that, in view of the small Russian contingent to be at Yalta, our combined delegations would look to them like a minor invasion.

I invited Hopkins to join our State Department group for the flight and he was immediately put to bed. Our plane—flight number 5—left shortly after midnight on this blacked-out trip across the Mediterranean, the Aegean, and the Black Sea, fourteen hundred miles to the Crimean Conference or Argonaut, as it was called in the secret code.

PART TWO

At the Conference

CHAPTER 4

Argonaut

Seven hours after leaving Malta, at 7:30 A.M. on February 3, our C-54 landed at Saki airfield on the west coast of the Crimean Peninsula. The runways were made of concrete blocks resembling a tile floor. They were only just long enough, and a coating of ice made landings dangerous. The four-motored planes came in at approximately ten-minute intervals and each used the entire length of the runway.

All around the perimeter of the airfield the Russians had stationed guards with tommy guns at twenty-foot intervals. A spectacular band and a crack regiment, as well as many Soviet and United States Signal Corps photographers, were lined up on the field to welcome the British and American delegations.

As we alighted from the plane we were greeted by Foreign Commissar Molotov, Deputy Foreign Commissar A. Y. Vishinsky, Air Marshal Khudiakov, Admiral Kuznetsov, General Antonov, Ambassador Gromyko, and Ambassador Gusev.

The Russians had arranged three refreshment tents where buffets were set with eight-ounce glasses of hot tea with lemon and sugar. Bottles of vodka, brandy, and champagne, dishes of caviar, smoked sturgeon and salmon, white and black bread, fresh butter, cheese, and hard- and soft-boiled eggs filled the tables. Many criticisms have been levied at the Russians for their lack of technique, but the reception they gave us that early morning at Saki was a memorable performance.

Eden had arrived before us and, as we stood together, the planes bringing General Marshall, Admiral King, the British Chiefs of Staff, and the other members of our combined parties landed.

The President's plane, with an escort of six Lockheed Lightnings, came in about an hour later. Mrs. Boettiger, General Watson, and Admiral McIntire all alighted, but the President stayed aboard until Churchill's plane arrived approximately a half hour later.

After landing, Churchill went right over to the President's plane, the Sacred Cow. Roosevelt was let down to the ground in an elevator especially designed by the Douglas Aircraft Company, and was lifted by his bodyguard, Mike Reilly, into a Lend-Lease jeep, which the Russians had provided so that the President might review the guard of honor. Molotov joined the two leaders and introduced the Soviet representatives. Churchill, smoking a freshly lit eight-inch cigar, and Molotov stood by the President's jeep while the commander of the guard, standing rigidly at attention with his sword held straight up in front of him, made a short speech of welcome. Then the band played "The Star-Spangled Banner," "God Save the King," and the Soviet anthem. After the band had finished "The Star-Spangled Banner" the Pres-

Ambassador Gromyko, Mr. Stettinius, and Sir Alexander Cadogan awaiting the arrival of the President and the Prime Minister at Saki airfield. (Sovfoto)

The three foreign ministers sign the Protocol of the Yalta Conference on February 11, 1945. (Sovfoto)

President Roosevelt and Prime Minister Churchill reviewing a Russian guard of honor at Saki airfield. Beyond Mr. Churchill are Molotov, Stettinius, Vishinsky, and Harriman. (Sovfoto)

ident turned to Molotov, who was standing next to me, and told him that the band had played the American anthem beautifully.

As soon as the guard had marched by in review the President was lifted from the jeep into a sedan where Mrs. Boettiger was already waiting, and the motor caravan got under way for the long drive to Yalta.

As I rode through the countryside with Admiral Leahy and Averell Harriman, in a car just behind the President, I was struck with how the gently rolling and treeless country resembled our own great plains. We were all impressed, too, by the widespread war destruction. We saw burned-out freight trains, burned-out tanks, and other damaged matériel.

A few miles from the city of Simferopol the country changed and our road wound its way up over the mountain range lying between Simferopol and Yalta. As we descended to the east coast of the Crimea the weather was much milder than at Saki, and there were no traces of snow in the vicinity of Yalta.

Although the distance between Saki and Yalta was only about ninety miles, it took us six hours to make the journey over a road that was paved in just a few sections. Along the entire route, Red Army sentries, some of them sturdily built women, stood at attention every fifty to one hundred yards.

Our cars reached Livadia Palace, situated a mile and a half from the town of Yalta, at about six in the evening. The palace, built in 1911 as a summer residence for Tsar Nicholas II, looked out over a beautiful semicircular Black Sea harbor with Yalta, the most fashionable bathing resort in the Crimea, at its head. On both sides of the harbor mountains rose precipitously from the sea. It was a breath-taking sight and reminded me of parts of our Pacific coast.

The Germans, when they retreated from the Crimea, had looted Livadia Palace. It was our understanding that the Russians had had to draw upon three Moscow hotels for supplies to refurnish the palace for the Conference. The President was quartered in the Tsar's bedroom, and he used the billiard room as his private dining room. I was in a two-room suite overlooking the sea, and Byrnes, Hopkins, Leahy, Early, Harriman, Bohlen, and others of our party were provided with comfortable quarters on the ground floor of the three-story stone palace. The only acute shortage was bathrooms.

The State Department group was small enough to be comfortably housed at Livadia Palace, but this was not true of the military staff. General Marshall and Admiral King occupied respectively the imperial bedroom and the Tsarina's boudoir on the second floor. There was so large a United States military staff present, however, that five to seven generals were housed in one room and ten colonels in another. Throughout the Conference the overcrowded conditions for the military contingent were a source of much amusement. On the second floor of the palace the military organized a mess hall where American and Russian foods were served to the American delegation.

The British headquarters was in the hundred-year-old Vorontsov Villa, at Alupka, about half an hour away from Livadia Palace by car. The Russians were staying at Koreis Villa, an estate once belonging to Prince Yusupov, reputed assassin of Rasputin. One of the inconveniences of the location was that the three delegations were located in separate quarters a considerable distance away from each other by motor.

On the evening of our arrival, Ambassador Harriman, his daughter Kathleen, Mrs. Boettiger, Admiral Leahy, General Watson, and I had dinner with Mr. Roosevelt. The President, with his rich sense of humor, made much of the fact that he was the only Chief of State at the Conference. He smilingly observed that, since he was the senior officer present, people were going to come to see him.

This Saturday night dinner was the last leisurely social gathering at the Yalta Conference. The pressure of the next few days was most exhausting. My usual daily schedule, for instance, was to confer with Matthews, Bohlen, and Hiss just after I got up in the morning. I next discussed Conference problems with the President. Every morning, too, there were countless emergency problems to be dealt with, documents to be drafted, conferences with General Marshall, Hopkins, and members of the other delegations, and incoming cables from the Department in Washington to be studied.

After these meetings I attended the foreign ministers' conferences, which started at noon and continued on through rather lengthy luncheons. The chairmanship of these meetings was rotated and we met at the different headquarters in succession. After the foreign ministers' sessions broke up I usually saw the President again for a last-minute briefing before the plenary sessions. The plenary sessions all met at Livadia Palace and began at four o'clock and lasted until eight or later. Then often came tiring and lengthy dinners which, like the luncheons, called for both frequent toasts and constant alertness. After these dinners I usually conferred again with Matthews, Bohlen, Hiss, and Foote, read cables from Acting Secretary of State Grew in Washington, drafted cables to the Department, and then went to bed, often as late as two in the morning.

Following the dinner on February 3, Harriman, at the President's request, called on Molotov at Koreis to discuss plans for the next day's meeting. Harriman explained that the President was extremely satisfied with the arrangements at Livadia Palace and said that if it were agreeable to Marshal Stalin the President would be glad to receive him at Livadia the next afternoon at three or three-thirty for a purely personal talk. After this talk the President suggested a discussion of the military situation with the Prime Minister, the Marshal, himself, the military staff, and the foreign secretaries.

Molotov explained that the Marshal wanted to call on the President the next afternoon but preferred, if possible, to do it at 4 P.M. The formal meeting of the first plenary session could then convene an hour later. When Harriman agreed to this, Molotov suggested that, after they had discussed the military situation, they turn to German political questions. Stalin, Molotov reported, planned first to make a report on the military situation on the eastern front.

After these arrangements were settled, Harriman extended an invitation to the Marshal and the Foreign Minister to a dinner to be given the following evening by the President at Livadia Palace. Molotov replied that he was sure that Marshal Stalin would be delighted to be present, but he would have to confirm it the following morning.

The next morning at ten-thirty Harriman, Matthews, Hiss, Bohlen, and I met with the President on the sun porch overlooking the sea, to review our proposals for the Conference agenda. We arrived just before the President's meeting with the military chiefs broke up. Since the military chiefs were about to leave, I suggested that they remain in order that they might be fully informed of the diplomatic position of the State Department, and thus be in a position to correlate this with the secret military conferences that were to take place between the Chiefs of Staff of the three countries.

I then presented the following items (all of which have been explained earlier) to the President:

MEMORANDUM OF SUGGESTED ACTION ITEMS FOR THE PRESIDENT

1. International Organization. *We should seek adoption of United States proposal for voting formula and agreement to announce immediately calling of general United Nations Conference. (Copies of text of United States proposal and analysis thereof are available if you wish to hand them to Churchill and Stalin.)*

Argumentation: Our proposal safeguards unity of the great powers so far as is possible by any formula—enforcement action will require unanimous vote—only with respect to discussion will a party to a dispute not be able to vote. Latin American and other small powers will be disillusioned if discussion can be vetoed.

Note: If the voting issue is settled, additional points would have to be agreed to before a United Nations Conference could be called: International Trusteeships, France as fifth sponsoring power, list of nations to be invited, date of conference and its being held in United States on behalf of other four sponsoring powers, United States to consult China and France on behalf of Britain and Russia, form of announcement of agreement on International Organization matters (we have available the necessary papers on these points).

2. Adoption of Emergency European High Commission. *(Copies of draft text of declaration and of accompanying protocol are available if you wish to hand them to Stalin and Churchill.)*

Argumentation: Unity of great power policy with respect to liberated and Axis satellite countries is highly desirable, and France should be included as one of the great powers for this purpose.

3. Treatment of Germany.

(a) Final agreement should be reached with respect to control machinery and zones of occupation. Announcement should be made of such agreement and of the earlier agreement on surrender terms.

(b) Boundaries: It is not expected that definitive, detailed commitments will have to be made at this time. However, if it proves necessary, our detailed position has been prepared and is available.

(c) Minorities: We should oppose, so far as possible, indiscriminate mass transfer of minorities with neighboring states. Transfers should be carried out gradually under international supervision.

(d) Long range economic policies: We should favor abolition of German self-sufficiency and its position of economic domination of Europe, elimination of certain key industries, prohibition of manufacture of arms and of all types of aircraft, and continuing control to achieve these aims.[1]

4. Poland.

(a) Boundaries: We favor the Curzon line in the north and center and, in the south, the eastern line of Lwow Province, which would correspond generally with one of the frontiers proposed in 1919 to the Supreme Allied Council. Transfer of German territory to be limited to East Prussia (except Koenigsberg to Russia), a small coastal salient of Pomerania, and Upper Silesia.

(b) We should be prepared to assist in the formation of a new representative interim government pledged to free elections when conditions permit. We should urge inclusion in a provisional government of Mikolajczyk (Peasant Party is most important in Poland) and other moderate Poles abroad. We should not agree to recognize the Lublin "government" in its present form.

---

[1] By the "abolition of German self-sufficiency," the State Department meant the abolition of German autarchy for warmaking purposes.

5. Allied Control Commissions in Rumania, Bulgaria, and Hungary. *Our representatives must be assured of: (a) freedom of movement, and (b) consultation before decisions are made by the Control Commissions.*

6. Iran. *We should seek Soviet agreement not to press for oil concessions in Iran until termination of hostilities and withdrawal of Allied troops.*

7. China. *We should seek Soviet and British support for our efforts to bring about Kuomintang-Communist agreement.*
Argumentation: Cooperation between the two groups will expedite conclusion of the war in the Far East and prevent possible internal conflict and foreign intervention in China.

The President agreed to hand the State Department memorandum on voting in the Security Council to Stalin and Churchill. We of the State Department had been greatly concerned three days before at Malta when we had received a radio message from the President on the *Quincy* saying that he had a new idea on voting in the Security Council. It turned out that Justice Byrnes had been discussing the issue with the President. According to Roosevelt, Byrnes had suggested that, in order to avoid inability to act because of the unanimity principle, there ought to be provision for action to be taken by four of the Great Powers. The President, in spite of his wire, did continue, however, his support of the State Department formula.

On the Polish question, he examined a map and said that if the Russians would not agree to the Poles retaining Lwow, perhaps they might at least agree to the Poles retaining the oil fields as a matter of saving face. Bohlen commented that, while the oil fields were not too important from the Russian point of view, they were important to Poland. He added that

Poland would receive about one third less German territory than she would lose to the Soviet Union.

On the composition of the Polish Government, the President agreed with us that the Lublin Government should not be recognized. He was quite familiar with Mikolajczyk's proposal for a presidential council, composed of representatives of the various Polish groups, which would operate as an interim government until elections could be held. "They wouldn't have a king," the President observed, "and they needed a regency council." He asked us to prepare a short paper, expressing our views on Poland, for him to hand to Stalin and Churchill.

He did not think highly of the State Department proposals for a European High Commission to handle liberated areas. He made it clear that he felt the European Advisory Commission, established by the Moscow Pacts of 1943, had not been a success and, furthermore, he stated that he did not want "another organization." Meetings of the foreign ministers could adequately handle the question, he remarked. When it was pointed out to the President that the Secretary of State could not be absent from Washington too frequently, the President replied that a secretariat could furnish continuity. Although he decided not to introduce the proposal for the European High Commission at Yalta, he did introduce the "Declaration on Liberated Europe," which was an integral part of the State Department's recommendation.

Later that Sunday afternoon Byrnes, in a talk with our State Department delegation, supported the President's opposition to the European High Commission. The American people and Congress, he declared, would not like an American commissioner with independent authority. Although we pointed out that the commissioner would be subject to instructions, the justice felt that our ambassador in a given country could carry out the objectives of the proposed commission. Congress would not object to this, he felt, since ambassadors are approved by the Senate and are directly answerable to the Secretary of State.

Furthermore, he said, any agency tends to perpetuate itself after its usefulness has passed. American troops wanted to go home right away, and it would be unpopular if they had to remain in Europe because of the decisions of this commission. Most important of all, according to Byrnes, was that the United States would be loath to accept responsibility for internal matters in Europe. It was pointed out that we could hardly expect the British or the Russians or the French, who might be occupying a particular territory, to follow our advice if we refused to accept any responsibility for internal European matters.

In addition to the European High Commission proposal, we discussed at some length with the President the German zones of occupation. He brought up, at this point, the desire of the French to have a zone, and he felt that the final tripartite agreement should wait until the French zone was settled. Admiral Leahy suggested that we give the French our zone, saying that our troops wanted to return home promptly. Although the admiral was undoubtedly speaking in a light vein, he was also reflecting a general American attitude on postwar commitments in Europe.

The President then asked about the activities of UNRRA in Poland. He was told that the Lublin Government had recently authorized UNRRA supplies to come into Poland by overland shipments from the port of Constanza. He inquired about Red Cross activities in Poland and was told that the Russians had recently agreed to the shipment of some urgently needed supplies. He said that he did not think it was a good idea to have both the Red Cross and UNRRA operating in the same territory, and expressed the hope that the Red Cross activity would be completed promptly. It was most important, he added, to give new life to UNRRA in Poland.

Then he asked us whether we had given any consideration to making German land available for those Dutch farmers whose lands had been flooded by the Germans. Queen Wilhelmina had recently discussed this with the President, and he commented to us that we should permit these Dutch farmers to take any land they wanted in western Germany for a period of five years, or for whatever time might be required to restore productivity to the land flooded by sea water.

Although, as Secretary of State, I was with the President on this particular meeting with his military advisers, I was not present at the combined staff conferences of the military leaders of the Big Three at Yalta. As far as the decisions of our own Chiefs of Staff affected diplomacy, however, I was kept informed.

I knew at Yalta, for instance, of the immense pressure put on the President by our military leaders to bring Russia into the Far Eastern war. At this time the atomic bomb was still an unknown quantity, and our setback in the Battle of the Bulge was fresh in the minds of all. We had not as yet crossed the Rhine. No one knew how long the European war would last nor how great the casualties would be.

The Joint Chiefs of Staff of the United States, just before our departure for Yalta, had sent the State Department copies of documents relating to Russian participation in the war against Japan. These documents stated:

> ... We desire Russian entry at the earliest possible date consistent with her ability to engage in offensive operations and are prepared to offer the maximum support possible without prejudice to our main effort against Japan. ...

At the Quebec Conference in August 1943, Hopkins had with him a military document which read:

> Finally, the most important factor the United States has to consider in relation to Russia is the prosecution of the war in the Pacific. *With Russia as an ally in the war against Japan, the war can be terminated in less time and at less expense in life and resources than if the reverse were the case. Should the war in the Pacific have to be carried on with an unfriendly or a negative attitude on the part of Russia, the difficulties will be immeasurably increased and operations might become abortive.*[2]

When Cordell Hull was at Moscow in October 1943, Marshal Stalin had declared that Russia would join the war against Japan, and at Teheran, a few weeks later, he made the same statement to the President and to the Prime Minister.

Up to this point Stalin had said nothing about the exact timing or the conditions for Russian entry into the war against Japan. Then, in October 1944, while Churchill was in Moscow discussing European matters with Stalin, Harriman and General John R. Deane, our military attaché in Moscow at that time who was representing the United States Joint Chiefs of Staff, discussed the Far East with Stalin. Stalin said that the Soviet Union would enter the Japanese war three months after the termination of the German war, but that there would first have to be an agreement with China. On this occasion Harriman and Deane did not explore what Marshal Stalin had in mind.

[2] Sherwood, op. cit., pp. 748–49.

Soon after the President arrived at Yalta he had top-level conferences with the Marshal over the question of Russia's entrance into the Japanese war. Most of the American delegates present knew nothing about these discussions, nor was the question raised at the plenary sessions of the Big Three or at the foreign ministers' meetings. Approximately halfway through the Yalta Conference, Harriman and Hopkins told me that the President had asked them to advise me that discussions were taking place between the President and the Marshal on this question.

I was told, among other things, that Stalin had said that it was clear that certain concessions desired in the Far East by the Russians were essential for Russian entry into the war against Japan. Without these conditions, Stalin had contended, the Supreme Soviet and the Russian people would wonder why they had entered the war in the Far East. They understood the German war because of the German attack on their country, but, since there had been no overt move by the Japanese in the Far East, concessions would be necessary to justify Soviet entry into the war.

After Harriman and Hopkins had mentioned the Far Eastern discussions to me I asked the President, in one of my private conversations with him, whether or not there was anything in connection with this matter that he wished the State Department delegation to pursue. The President stated that, since it was primarily a military matter and since Mr. Harriman had had many private discussions about it with him and with representatives of the Soviet Union over a period of time, he thought it had best remain on a purely military level.

After my talk with the President, he, Harriman, and Hopkins continued discussing the Far Eastern question with

Stalin and Molotov. On February 11 the following agreement was signed by Marshal Stalin, Prime Minister Churchill, and President Roosevelt:

> The leaders of the three Great Powers—the Soviet Union, the United States of America and Great Britain—have agreed that in two or three months after Germany has surrendered and the war in Europe has terminated, the Soviet Union shall enter into the war against Japan on the side of the Allies on condition that:
>
> 1. The status quo in Outer-Mongolia (the Mongolian People's Republic) shall be preserved;
>
> 2. The former rights of Russia violated by the treacherous attack of Japan in 1904 shall be restored, viz.:
> (a) the southern part of Sakhalin as well as all the islands adjacent to it shall be returned to the Soviet Union,
> (b) the commercial port of Dairen shall be internationalized, the preeminent interests of the Soviet Union in this port being safeguarded, and the lease of Port Arthur as a naval base of the U.S.S.R. restored,
> (c) the Chinese-Eastern Railroad and the South-Manchurian Railroad, which provides an outlet to Dairen, shall be jointly operated by the establishment of a joint Soviet-Chinese Company, it being understood that the preeminent interests of the Soviet Union shall be safeguarded and that China shall retain full sovereignty in Manchuria.
>
> 3. The Kurile Islands shall be handed over to the Soviet Union.[3]
>
> It is understood that the agreement concerning Outer-Mongolia and the ports and railroads referred to above will require concurrence of Generalissimo Chiang Kai-shek. The

[3] The Kurile Islands, of course, were Japanese territory before the Russo-Japanese War of 1904. During the nineteenth century both Russia and Japan had had claims to the Kuriles, and Japanese ownership was recognized near the close of the century.

> *President will take measures in order to obtain this concurrence on advice from Marshal Stalin.*
>
> *The Heads of the three Great Powers have agreed that these claims of the Soviet Union shall be unquestionably fulfilled after Japan has been defeated.*
>
> *For its part the Soviet Union expresses its readiness to conclude with the National Government of China a pact of friendship and alliance between the U.S.S.R. and China in order to render assistance to China with its armed forces for the purpose of liberating China from the Japanese yoke.*

This "Agreement Regarding Japan"—a top-secret document—did not appear in the protocol of the Yalta Conference. It was taken to Washington and deposited in the President's personal safe. Few of the President's closest advisers knew of its existence. It was feared that, if too many people knew about it, the information would leak out and reach Japan. With this information, Japan then might upset the Allied plans by launching an early attack on the Soviet Union before Soviet troops could be shifted from Europe to the Far East.

The Chinese were not notified immediately of this agreement at Yalta for fear the secret would not be kept in Chungking. Marshal Stalin told President Roosevelt at Yalta that the Russians would start sending divisions across Siberia but insisted that this must be done in complete secrecy. The President agreed, therefore, that only after the troop movements were completed would he explain the decision to the Chinese. The President, of course, did not live long enough to do this.

I was advised by one of my friends in the British Government that Eden had tried to keep the Prime Minister from signing the agreement since he had not been present at the principal discussions and because it was such a complex matter. Churchill, however, had declared that the whole position of the British Empire in the Far East might be at stake. He was going to sign, I was told the Prime Minister said, in order that Great Britain might stay in the Far East. The Prime Minister, I understand, added that he had great faith in President Roosevelt and felt that he could rely completely on the President's judgment in this matter.

The State Department was not a factor in the Far Eastern agreement. Although Ambassador Harriman had conducted conversations with Stalin on the question, he had a unique assignment at Moscow. There was nothing, during the war, quite like it. His task was totally different from that of a mere ambassador. He was the over-all co-ordinator of both civilian and military matters in Moscow. The military representatives, General Deane, and the civilian agencies, like the Office of War Information, the War Production Board, the Lend-Lease Administration, the War Shipping Administration, and even the Office of Strategic Services, reported to Harriman.

President Roosevelt and the War Department had assigned Harriman the task of discovering what was necessary to bring Russia into the Far Eastern war. By the time Harriman reached Yalta, I have understood, he already had some idea of what was necessary to bring the Russians into the Japanese conflict. I was told by Harry Hopkins in the days just before we reached Yalta that good headway had already been made on the question. The Far Eastern agreement was carefully worked out and was not a snap decision made at Yalta because, as some have alleged, President Roosevelt was tired and wanted to avoid further arguments.[4]

Much of the criticism which has been directed against

[4] Sherwood, op. cit., p. 867.

the Far Eastern agreement concerns the secrecy which surrounded both its negotiation and the final document. Two points should be remembered in appraising this criticism. The first is the nature of political power inside Russia, where authority and responsibility are tightly held, and exercised with extreme secrecy. This forced the President to handle the problem almost alone, since Stalin would have refused, I am certain, to make any commitments to enter the war in the Pacific before a larger negotiating group. The second is that this Russian predilection for secret and even personal diplomacy was reinforced, in this instance, by clear military considerations. The war was approaching a climax both in Europe and in the Pacific, and any risk of possible disclosure of such far-reaching military plans was a dangerous risk. As I have said, I was informed about the negotiations, although other important members of the United States delegation were not. The document was in the White House safe when President Roosevelt died. I had not actually seen it nor, to the best of my belief, had President Truman when he moved into the White House. I have already written that faulty liaison between the White House and the Department of State was one of the major problems with which I had to deal. But in this instance it is certainly hard to fix any blame for a situation which arose out of such compelling wartime circumstances and which was made worse by the President's sudden and tragic death.

Military considerations of the highest order dictated the President's signing of the Far Eastern agreement. The military insisted that the Soviet Union had to be brought into the Japanese war. Stimson has described the Army's attitude on the Japanese war even as late as July 1945:

> *As we understood it in July, there was a very strong possibility that the Japanese Government might determine upon*

resistance to the end, in all the areas of the Far East under its control. In such an event the Allies would be faced with the enormous task of destroying an armed force of five million men and five thousand suicide aircraft, belonging to a race which had already amply demonstrated its ability to fight literally to the death.

The strategic plans of our armed forces for the defeat of Japan, as they stood in July, had been prepared without reliance upon the atomic bomb, which had not yet been tested in New Mexico. We were planning an intensified sea and air blockade, and greatly intensified strategic air bombing, through the summer and early fall, to be followed on November 1 by an invasion of the southern island of Kyushu. This would be followed in turn by an invasion of the main island of Honshu in the spring of 1946. The total U. S. military and naval force involved in this grand design was of the order of 5,000,000 men; if all those indirectly concerned are included, it was larger still. . . . We estimated that if we should be forced to carry this plan to its conclusion, the major fighting would not end until the latter part of 1946, at the earliest. I was informed that such operations might be expected to cost over a million casualties, to American forces alone. Additional large losses might be expected among our allies and, of course, if our campaign were successful and if we could judge by previous experience, enemy casualties would be much larger than our own. . . .[5]

At a top-level policy meeting in the White House, just before the San Francisco Conference opened on April 25, President Truman, the military leaders, and I discussed the failure of the Soviet Union to abide by the Yalta agreement on the Balkans. At this meeting the United States military representatives pleaded for patience with the Soviet Union because they feared that a crack-down would endanger Russian entry into the Far Eastern war.

---

[5]Henry L. Stimson and McGeorge Bundy, *On Active Service in Peace and War* (New York: Harper & Brothers, 1948), pp. 618, 619.

Even as late as the Potsdam Conference, after the first atomic bomb had exploded at Los Alamos on July 16, the military insisted that the Soviet Union had to be brought into the Far Eastern war. At both Yalta and Potsdam the military staffs were particularly concerned with the Japanese troops in Manchuria. Described as the cream of the Japanese Army, this self-contained force, with its own autonomous command and industrial base, was believed capable of prolonging the war even after the islands of Japan had been subdued, unless Russia should enter the war and engage this army.

With this belief, the President's military advisers urgently desired Russian entry into the war. Our casualties would be far smaller if the Japanese had to divert forces to meet the Russians in the north.[6] Although Russian troops were to engage the Japanese Army in Manchuria, the Far Eastern agreement signed at Yalta specifically pledged Russian recognition of Chinese sovereignty over Manchuria. It is not true, therefore, that the President agreed to permanent Russian control of Manchuria. It has also been charged that President Roosevelt at Yalta agreed to Russian entry into northern Korea. Actually Russian entrance into northern Korea was agreed to, after Yalta, by American military authorities as part of the taking of the surrender of Japanese troops.

[6] I have had the opportunity of private discussions on this matter with General Deane.

CHAPTER 5

The Big Three Meet

February 4

Marshal Stalin and Foreign Commissar Molotov arrived at Livadia Palace at 4 P.M. on Sunday afternoon, February 4, in a large black Packard limousine for a short meeting with the President. Although short in stature, the Marshal, with his powerful head and shoulders set on a stocky body, radiated an impression of great strength.

The President and Stalin, after exchanging greetings, discussed the offensives of the British, American, and Russian armies. The President said that he hoped the armies were getting close enough now for General Eisenhower to communicate directly with the Soviet commanders in the field rather than through the Chiefs of Staff in London and Washington as in the past. Stalin agreed with the suggestion and also promised that the Russian military staff would start immediate consultation with the other two military staffs present at Yalta.

Roosevelt told the Marshal that he was struck by the

extent of German destruction in the Crimea. All of this made him, the President said, more bloodthirsty toward the Germans than he had been a year ago.

Stalin replied that everyone was more bloodthirsty than he had been a year ago. The destruction in the Crimea, he pointed out, was nothing, however, compared to what had occurred in the Ukraine. The Germans were savages, he added, and they seemed to have a sadistic hatred for the creative work of human beings.

The President then asked the Marshal how he had found General de Gaulle during the French leader's recent visit to Moscow. The Marshal replied that he had not found De Gaulle to be a very "complicated person." Ambassador Harriman had cabled the State Department on January 4 that Stalin had told him, after the meeting with the Free French leader, that De Gaulle was an "awkward and stubborn man." De Gaulle, on the other hand, had told Harriman that his experience in Moscow had left him with a poor impression of the crudeness of Soviet foreign policy. He had then predicted that the Western countries would henceforth have serious difficulties with the Soviet Union.

It was unrealistic, Stalin told the President, for De Gaulle to insist upon full rights with the Big Three, in view of the fact that France had not done much fighting in the war. The President recalled his conversation with De Gaulle two years before at Casablanca, when De Gaulle had compared himself with Joan of Arc as the spiritual leader of France and with Georges Clemenceau as its political leader.

Relations between the President and General de Gaulle, as was well known, had been tense and most unsatisfactory. It was not until after the landing in Normandy on June 6, 1944, that the United States was willing to recognize De

Gaulle and the French Committee of National Liberation as the *de facto* authority in the civil administration of France. The President had been unwilling to recognize De Gaulle until it could be demonstrated that he really was supported by the French people. The President had no desire to try to force an unwanted government on France. In spite of this lack of political support for De Gaulle on our part, we had extended Lend-Lease aid to the Free French as early as November 11, 1941. After the Allies had reconquered part of France, and popular support for De Gaulle's government was apparent, we had announced on October 23, 1944, after consultation with Great Britain and the Soviet Union, that we recognized the De Gaulle *de facto* authority, which had been broadened by the addition of resistance elements, as the provisional government of the French Republic.

The President told Marshal Stalin at Yalta on February 4 that he had recently been informed that the French were willing to give up outright annexation of German territory, provided this territory was placed under international control. Stalin replied that this had not been De Gaulle's attitude at Moscow. The Rhine, De Gaulle had stated, was the natural boundary of France, and he wished to have French troops there permanently.

As to the zones of occupation in Germany, Marshal Stalin seemed to concur with the President on the agreement that had been reached by the European Advisory Commission on tripartite zones. The outstanding question, the President said, was a zone for the French. He explained that he had discussed with Churchill the question of the French having a zone, and that he thought "it was not a bad idea." When Marshal Stalin asked the President why he favored a zone for France, Roosevelt replied that he favored it only out of kindness. Both the Marshal and Molotov, in vigorous tones, said that this was certainly the only reason to give the French a zone. The Marshal made it clear that he did not believe the French deserved a zone, and he added that this question had to be considered further at Yalta.

The President and the Marshal then closed their discussion and adjourned to the conference room at Livadia Palace, formerly used by the tsars as a banquet hall and ballroom, for the first plenary session of the Yalta Conference.

There were present at this first formal conference:

The President	The Prime Minister	Marshal Stalin
Mr. Stettinius	Mr. Eden	Mr. Molotov
Admiral Leahy	Field Marshal Sir Alan Brooke	General Antonov
General Marshall	Admiral Cunningham	Admiral Kuznetsov
Admiral King	Field Marshal Sir H. Alexander	Air Marshal Khudiakov
General Kuter	Major General Sir Hastings Ismay	Mr. Vishinsky
General Deane	Sir Charles Portal	Mr. Gromyko
General McFarland	Major Birse	Mr. Gusev
Mr. Harriman		Mr. Maisky
Mr. Bohlen		Mr. Pavlov

The members of the Conference sat around a great circular table. Although this first meeting on February 4 included military figures because of the nature of the discussion, the military leaders, with the exception of Admiral Leahy, did not attend any other plenary sessions. They had their own sessions, separate from the diplomatic conferences.

The customary seating arrangement, after this first meeting, was—working clockwise and starting with the President: Bohlen, Harriman, Cadogan, Eden, the Prime Minister, Sir

Edward Bridges, Gromyko, Vishinsky, Molotov, the Marshal, Maisky, Gusev, Leahy, and I, on the President's right. In addition, other members of the three delegations usually sat behind their respective representatives. The Americans, sitting behind the President, varied somewhat from session to session but usually included Hopkins, Matthews, and Hiss, and sometimes Foote. Whenever Byrnes attended the plenary sessions he sat at the conference table.

Each delegation had its own interpreter. Bohlen acted as the American interpreter, Birse the British, and Pavlov the Russian. Bohlen, however, was more than a professional interpreter. He was an expert, as well, on substantive matters. It was the general practice for each speaker to utter only one sentence or a paragraph and then allow it to be interpreted by his own interpreter.

Eden frequently commented to me that it was extremely cumbersome to have either the American or British interpreter do the interpreting of English into Russian. It would have been much better, he felt, to allow the Russian interpreter to do this, and to have the British or American interpreter translate the Russian into English. Better still, I thought, would have been to have an expert official interpreter to act for all the delegations, as had been done in the League of Nations.

It would also have been better at Yalta to have had a stenographic record made of the discussions. The record then could have been distributed to and approved by each delegation and become the official record of the proceedings. There was, however, no single official record of the meetings, nor was there any stenotypist recording every word. Instead, each delegation kept its own minutes. Bridges, for instance, took notes in shorthand for the British, while

Bohlen had the double task of interpreting and note taking for the United States. In addition, some members of the American delegation, at least, kept their own personal notes. Every noon at the foreign ministers' meetings to discuss problems assigned by the three leaders, Edward Page of the American Embassy in Moscow served both as interpreter and as note taker for the American delegation. All of these mechanical arrangements for the Crimea Conference had been worked out beforehand by the British and American embassies in Moscow in consultation with the Soviet Foreign Office.

The military followed a different practice in keeping a record of their discussions. Although each of the three nations had its own representative taking notes, these three individuals cleared their versions with each other and with all the participants. In the case of the diplomatic discussions, this practice was unfortunately not followed. As a result, the British, Russian, and American records may well vary in their descriptions of just what word or phrase was used by any given speaker. On the other hand, of course, the official documents introduced by the three countries should appear the same in all the minutes, and the final agreements reached were identical, since Eden, Molotov, and I, with our respective staffs, prepared the official protocol with great care.

At the plenary sessions as well as during the formal dinners President Roosevelt, in addition to explaining the American position, usually proved to be the arbiter and conciliator between Marshal Stalin and Prime Minister Churchill. Churchill's eloquence and skillful maneuvering were generally answered by the Marshal in blunt and direct remarks. Sometimes when tension was acute between the two men the President would introduce seemingly irrelevant comments in order to relieve the atmosphere. It was by no means planned that the President should be cast in the role of conciliator. In fact throughout this period the British were rather sensitive about the President finding himself in this position.

At this first session at Livadia Palace, Marshal Stalin started the meeting by expressing the hope that the President would open the Conference just as he had the Teheran Conference. The Marshal stated in a direct and friendly manner that, since the President was both Chief of State and head of government (he and Mr. Churchill were only heads of government and President Kalinin and King George VI were not present), he felt that the President should preside at the Conference. The President answered that he was honored to open this great Conference, and that he wished to express on behalf of the American guests their deep appreciation for the hospitality and splendid arrangements of the hosts.

He said that he knew the people he represented wished peace above all and wanted the war to come to a successful conclusion at the earliest possible date. We all understood each other now much better than in the past, he said, and this understanding was increasing month by month. He felt safe, therefore, he added, in proposing that the talks be conducted in an informal manner so that each could speak his mind frankly and freely. He said he had discovered through experience that the best way to conduct business expeditiously was through frank and free discussion.

Although he knew that they would cover the map of the world at the Conference, he suggested that the military situation on the eastern front should be discussed first. The advance of the Russian armies into Germany, he declared, had electrified the peoples of the United States and of Great Britain.

Marshal Stalin then called upon Colonel General Antonov, Deputy Chief of the Soviet General Staff, who read a prepared paper giving in great detail the background of the Soviet winter offensive. He described how Soviet forces from January 12 to 15 had gone into an attack on a front of seven hundred kilometers stretching from the Niemen River to the Carpathians. Forces under General Cherniakhovsky had advanced toward Königsberg; forces under Marshal Rokossovsky had moved along the north bank of the Vistula, cutting East Prussia off from central Germany; forces under Marshal Zhukov had moved south of the Vistula against Poznan; forces under Marshal Konev had moved against Chenstokhov-Breslau; and forces under General Petrov, in the area of the Carpathians, had moved against Novo Targ.

During an eighteen-day advance, according to General Antonov, the Soviet troops had averaged twenty-five to thirty kilometers of forward movement each day. As a result of the offensive, Red armies had reached the Oder River north of Frankfurt, seized the industrial area of Silesia, cut off enemy forces in East Prussia from central Germany, broken through German positions in East Prussia in the directions of Königsberg and Latvia, and destroyed in all forty-five German divisions.

General Antonov concluded by urging Great Britain and the United States to speed up the advance of Allied troops on the western front. He also recommended that Allied air action be taken to hinder the Germans from shifting troops from Italy, Norway, and the western front to the eastern front.

The President asked General Antonov whether in their advance into Germany the Russians had changed the gauge on the railroads to the wider Russian gauge. The general replied that they had found the vast majority of German rolling stock so badly damaged that it was useless to them. As a result, it had been necessary for them to widen the gauge "on a few important lines."

When the President suggested that the combined military staffs should decide where the different railroad gauges would meet in Germany, Marshal Stalin replied that most of the German railroads would remain at the standard gauge. The Soviet Union, he added, lacked the equipment to convert more than a few strategic lines. He spoke in forceful language, and at one point he rose from his chair and emphasized his points with dramatic gestures.

During the discussion Stalin placed great emphasis on what he called widespread statements that he was having the Russian military situation presented because of demands from the President and from the Prime Minister. He was proud, he added, that he was taking the initiative and making this explanation voluntarily without pressure from the President or the Prime Minister. I had the feeling, as the Marshal made this statement, that he was answering, for the record, criticism within the Politburo that he was giving in too frequently to Roosevelt and Churchill.

After Stalin and Antonov had answered detailed questions from both the Prime Minister and the President, Churchill suggested that General Marshall, with the President's approval, present the situation on the western front. Marshall thereupon presented extemporaneously one of the clearest and most concise summaries I have heard in my life of operations on the western front and of the immediate plans for the future. It was obvious that his report made a profound impression on the representatives of the Soviet Union.

He explained that the German bulge in the Ardennes had

now been eliminated, and that Allied forces in certain areas had advanced beyond the line held when the Germans launched their counterattack in December. He then described how Eisenhower and Montgomery hoped to cross the Rhine shortly after March 1. He also explained that British and American fighter planes and light bombers had destroyed great amounts of German transport. Heavy bombers, he added, were being used primarily against German oil supplies. These operations were so successful that German oil production had been reduced to twenty per cent of its former capacity. Heavy bombers, too, were disrupting rail communications and assembly yards, and destroying tank factories.

Marshall then declared that there were indications that the Germans, as the result of technological developments, were about to resume large-scale submarine warfare. At the time of the North African landings in 1942, he said, there were approximately a hundred enemy submarines operating in the Atlantic. At the present time there were thirty to thirty-five in operation. Heavy bombers, he added, were striking at German submarine assembly yards.

When he had concluded, the Prime Minister pointed out that Danzig was a great submarine assembly point, and the fact, therefore, that the Russian front lines were approaching that city was a great satisfaction to him.

When Stalin asked whether the Allied reserves were sufficient for their planned offensive, Marshall explained that on March 1 General Eisenhower would have eighty-nine divisions, covering the front from the Mediterranean to Holland, at his disposal. Approximately one out of every three divisions would be a tank division. Stalin was also told that there were nearly ten thousand Allied tanks and four thousand heavy bombers in the European theater. The Prime Minister, in reply to an observation by Stalin that they had one hundred and eighty Soviet divisions against eighty German divisions on the front in Poland, remarked that the Anglo-American armies had never had superiority in manpower. Their superiority rested, the Prime Minister stated, in air power and armor. Marshall then pointed out that ten days before there had been seventy-nine German divisions opposing seventy-eight Anglo-American divisions on the western front.

Stalin then asked what were the wishes of the British and Americans in regard to the Red Army.

The Prime Minister remarked that first of all he wished to express the gratitude of Britain, and, he was sure, of America, for the massive power and success of the Soviet offensive. All he could ask for was that the Russians continue their attack.

Stalin in his reply seemed somewhat irritated. He declared that the present offensive was not the result of any wish of the Allies. The Soviet Union, he added, was not bound by any agreement made at Teheran to conduct a winter offensive. Furthermore, in spite of what some people had thought, no demand or request had been received from either the President or the Prime Minister in regard to such an offensive.

The President had asked him, Stalin said, to receive a representative, Air Marshal Tedder, from General Eisenhower's staff to discuss the Red Army's winter offensive, and he had immediately agreed. Tedder had asked that the Soviets continue their offensive until the end of March, and Stalin had observed that, weather and road conditions permitting, they would do so. He mentioned this, he remarked, only to emphasize the spirit of the Soviet leaders, who not only fulfilled formal obligations but who went further and acted upon what they considered to be their moral duties to their Allies.

The President observed that he concurred with Marshal Stalin's statement about Teheran. It had been agreed there, he pointed out, merely that each partner would move as quickly as possible against the common enemy. He personally at that time, he noted, had been facing an election and that had made it impossible for him to plan too far into the future. At that time, too, our armies had been separated by many miles. Now, however, with our armies approaching each other, he thought it should be possible to co-ordinate our plans more closely.

The Prime Minister observed that the reason no request had been made to Marshal Stalin was the complete confidence which the President and he felt in the Marshal, the Russian people, and the efficiency of the Russian Army. It was, therefore, unnecessary to strike any bargain. It was now, however, of the highest importance, Churchill said, for the three military staffs, assembled for the first time, to work out detailed plans for the co-ordination of the joint blows against Germany. If the Soviet offensive came to a halt because of bad weather or road conditions, the Allied armies should be free to move. The best situation of all, he added, was for both armies to attack simultaneously from the east and the west.

Stalin replied that he felt it would be most useful for the staffs to discuss the coming offensive, and also one for the summer. He added that he was not at all sure that Germany would have surrendered by summer. The Chiefs of Staff of the three countries were then instructed to meet the following morning to co-ordinate the military plans of the Big

Three. This was the first time such a step had ocurred in the war. Although the three nations had been fighting for their very existence for years, it was not until Yalta that there was enough mutual confidence to bring them together for specific co-ordination of the military situation.

The whole spirit of the meeting, I recorded in my notes, "was most co-operative. . . ." Stalin impressed me as a man with a fine sense of humor. At the same time one received an impression of power and ruthlessness along with his humor. During the various conferences at Yalta, I noticed that the other members of the Soviet delegation would change their minds perfectly unashamedly whenever Marshal Stalin changed his.

An amusing episode occurred at the end of the meeting when two NKVD men, assigned to guard the Marshal, somehow lost him when he hurried to the washroom. There was a great scurrying and immense furore in the corridors until the Marshal reappeared.

At eight-thirty that evening the President gave a dinner at Livadia Palace for Churchill and Stalin. The only Americans present besides the President were Harriman, Bohlen, Byrnes, and myself. The leaders of the Big Three were in good humor throughout the meal. There were dozens of toasts. I was highly amused to notice that Stalin would drink half of his glass of vodka and, when he thought no one was watching, surreptitiously pour water into the glass. I also noticed that he seemed to prefer American to Russian cigarettes.

In one of Churchill's toasts he observed that the whole world had its eyes on this Conference, and, if we were successful, we could have peace for a hundred years. In firm tones he expressed his belief that the three powers who had shed the blood and fought the war would have to maintain the peace.

Stalin made it quite plain in his toasts that he agreed with the Prime Minister that the three Great Powers which had borne the brunt of the war should be the ones to preserve the peace. He said that it was ridiculous to believe that a small country like Albania should have an equal voice with the Big Three. He was prepared, he declared, to join with the United States and Great Britain to protect the rights of the small powers, but he would never agree to having any action of any of the Great Powers submitted to the judgment of the small powers.

The President and the Prime Minister replied that they were agreed that the Big Three would necessarily have to bear the major responsibility for the peace, but they pointed out that it was essential to exercise this power with moderation and with respect for the rights of the smaller nations. "Yugoslavia, Albania, and such small countries do not deserve to be at this table," the Marshal declared. "Do you want Albania to have the same status as the United States?" he asked. "What has Albania done in this war to merit such a standing? We three have to decide how to keep the peace of the world, and it will not be kept unless we three decide to do it."

The Prime Minister replied to this statement: "The eagle should permit the small birds to sing, and care not wherefor they sang."

At one point in the dinner conversation Vishinsky, in a side remark to Bohlen, warned that Russia would never agree to the right of the small powers to judge an act of the Great Powers. When Bohlen observed that the United States delegation at Yalta had to keep in mind the concern of the American people that the rights of the smaller nations be protected, Vishinsky replied, "The American people should learn to obey their leaders." Bohlen then said that if Vishinsky would visit the United States he would like to see him undertake to tell that to the American people. Vishinsky replied that he would be delighted to come to America and tell this to the American people.

Argentina's failure to co-operate with the Allies was discussed, and Stalin said that Argentina should be punished. If she were in this section of the world, he observed, he would see that she was punished. The President replied that the Argentine people were good but that there were some bad men in power at the moment.

The whole problem of dealing with the smaller powers was not too simple, observed Roosevelt. "We have, for instance, lots of Poles in America who are vitally interested in the future of Poland," he declared. Stalin immediately replied: "But of your seven million Poles, only seven thousand vote." He added with emphasis that he had looked it up and he knew that he was right. Although Stalin may have looked into the Polish-American question, actually, of course, voters of Polish descent are numbered in the hundreds of thousands. The inaccurate information that the Russians had about the United States was a source of continual amazement to us. They had their embassy and consular staffs to report to them, as well as, presumably, the American Communist party. Possibly, of course, their representatives in the United States sent home only what they thought the Kremlin wanted to hear.

After a toast by Churchill to the proletarian masses of the world, there was considerable discussion about the right of people to govern themselves. The Prime Minister noted that, although he was constantly being attacked as a reactinary, he was the only leader present who could be thrown out at any time by the votes of his own people. Personally, he added, he gloried in this danger.

When Stalin ironically remarked that Mr. Churchill seemed to fear the coming elections, the Prime Minister stated that he not only did not fear the elections but he was proud that the British people could change their government at any time they saw fit.

During the course of the dinner Molotov and I drank toasts to each other and to a continued friendship. In his toast Molotov expressed the hope that I would soon be able to visit Moscow. The President immediately interjected, "Ah-ha, he wants him to go to Moscow." The President then asked, "Do you think Ed will behave in Moscow as Molotov did in New York?" President Roosevelt, with his joshing humor, was suggesting that Molotov had had a gay time when White House Secret Service men, some time before, had taken Molotov around New York City to see the sights. Stalin replied: "He could come to Moscow incognito."

Our dinner that night at Yalta was a typically American one. Although caviar and sturgeon were added, as always at every meal, we had chicken salad, meat pie, fried chicken Southern style, and vegetables. There was Russian champagne, and there was much good-humored jesting with the President over the question of whether he had wired Moscow for five hundred bottles of champagne, but Stalin said that anyway he would give it to the President on a long-term credit of thirty years.

"There is one thing I want to tell you," the President said at this point. "The Prime Minister and I have been cabling back and forth for two years now, and we have a term of endearment by which we call you and that is 'Uncle Joe.'"

Stalin then asked just what this meant. The President told him it was a term of endearment, as though he were a member of the family. When Stalin appeared to be offended, Molotov told us not to be deceived. "He is just pulling your leg," Molotov told us. "We have known this for two years. All of Russia knows that you call him 'Uncle Joe.'" I had heard the story earlier that on some occasion before Yalta the Prime Minister was supposed to have asked the Marshal whether he minded being called "Uncle Joe." Stalin was supposed to have replied that he would like to wait on this until Mr. Churchill knew him a little better.

After this exchange on the "Uncle Joe" nickname the President, glancing around the table and noticing that the glasses were empty, called for more champagne. Stalin then asked if it were time to go home. The President said no, but Stalin replied that he was late for his military duties. He finally said that he would leave at ten-thirty. Actually he did not leave until eleven-ten. He and his generals and all of his staff followed the custom of working all night until 5 A.M., sleeping for five hours, and then starting to work again at 10 A.M. They maintained this schedule for seven days a week. A number of times during the Conference Molotov in particular spoke in an apologetic manner about the Marshal's having to depart from a meeting, explaining that he had to direct the military campaign as well as attend to the business of the Conference.

After the dinner had adjourned and Stalin and the President had left, I discussed the voting question in the Security Council with Churchill and Eden. The Prime Minister insisted that he was inclined to accept the Russian suggestion of unanimity at all times, because he felt that everything depended on maintaining the unity of the three powers. Without that, he added, the world would be doomed to inevitable catastrophe, and therefore anything that preserved that unity would have his vote.

Eden took vigorous exception to the Prime Minister's statement, and declared that there would be no reason for the small powers to join a world organization based on the principle of complete unanimity. The United States formula, he insisted, was the minimum essential to attract the support of the small nations. Furthermore, he made it clear that he did not believe the British people would accept the principle of unqualified unanimity.

The Prime Minister said he did not agree in the slightest with Eden. He said that he was thinking of the realities of the international situation. Eden, however, warned the Prime Minister that if he accepted the Russian position on voting we would never even have a United Nations conference. I then entered the discussion and explained to the Prime Minister the reasons for the American proposal, and I think I made some progress with him. At least, Eden said to me later that he believed this was the first time the Prime Minister grasped the basic issue.

When the Prime Minister left Livadia Palace, Eden, Harriman, Bohlen, and I remained to discuss the evening's conversation. We were in agreement that the trend at the moment seemed to be more toward a three-power alliance than anything else. No progress, we felt, had yet been made at Yalta toward building a world organization based on recognition of the sovereign rights of all nations.

CHAPTER 6

The German Question

February 5

On the second day of the Conference, I went to the President's room after breakfast for a talk. I was able, while his mind was fresh and he was unhurried by outside pressure, to determine his innermost feelings about some of the critical matters that were coming up over the horizon. We discussed extra votes for the U.S.S.R., the location of the forthcoming conference on world organization, the make-up of the American delegation that was to be selected, and finally, how to deal with the atomic bomb question if it arose at the Conference.

The President informed me that he and Harriman planned to discuss with Stalin the question of Soviet entrance into the Japanese war and that with the heavy burden I was carrying in other matters there was no need for me to become involved in this subject. The President reaffirmed his unalterable opposition to sixteen votes for the Soviet Union. We had a general exchange on the possibility of a number of cities as the site for the world organization conference, but none seemed to satisfy the President, and he asked that I continue my studies and present a concrete proposal to him later. It was obvious, he stated, that we should have a bipartisan delegation at the conference; he favored two representatives of each party from the Senate and the House and two or three others, making perhaps a delegation of seven. He asked me to give the matter thought and to make specific recommendations to him as soon as possible. I also mentioned my talk with General Marshall in the Azores about the atomic bomb, and he agreed with the general's position that we should handle any Russian questions if and as they arose.

After my talk with the President, I took a short stroll around the palace grounds and out the main gate. During this walk I noticed a completely burned-out villa about a hundred yards down the road from the palace. I was told that the retreating Germans had either burned or left in ruins most of the villas in this vicinity. They had been retreating so fast, however, that they had not had time to destroy Livadia Palace, which they had been using.

That morning, among other things in a hectic schedule, I talked with Hopkins, Byrnes, and Harriman about the political questions which would be raised at the afternoon meeting of the President, the Prime Minister, and the Marshal. Then I had a series of appointments with other people and attended to incoming dispatches from Washington.

At noon Anthony Eden and I were luncheon guests of Molotov at Koreis Villa. Justice Byrnes, Ambassador Harriman, and Edward Page accompanied us to this luncheon meeting. When Harriman informed Molotov of the thrilling news that Manila had just been captured, Molotov immediately proposed a toast to this victory of the Allied armies.

THE GERMAN QUESTION

During the course of the luncheon Molotov suggested, after serious discussion, that the Conference be formally named the "Crimean Conference." Although the Big Three agreed to this name and the communiqué officially contained it, the name never won popular acceptance.

When Eden asked Molotov just what the Russians proposed discussing that afternoon at the plenary session, Molotov replied that they were prepared to discuss any question the United States or the United Kingdom desired. This was a stock answer I was to hear many times later at the San Francisco Conference. On the question of the partitioning of Germany as well as German economic and political matters, Molotov expressed the feeling that the Americans and the British were considerably ahead of the Russians in their studies on the German problem.

Eden replied that the British had studied the German matter on a technical level, but that the War Cabinet had not discussed it. He recommended, and Molotov agreed, that the three foreign ministers should study the question further and bring definite proposals to the three leaders in two or three days.

In a side remark to Molotov, I stated that the United States Government attached great importance to reaching an agreement on certain German economic questions. He promptly replied that the Soviet Government expected to receive reparations in kind from Germany. He also expressed the hope that the Soviet Union would receive long-term credits from the United States.

I immediately stated that my government had studied the question of Soviet credits and that I personally was ready to discuss the matter either here or later in Moscow or Washington. Molotov expressed the opinion that, now that the end of the war was in sight, it was most important for agreement to be reached on these economic questions.

The State Department had actually been devoting considerable study to the question of a loan to the Soviet Union. On January 3, 1945, Ambassador Harriman had discussed the matter with Molotov. Harriman had pointed out that Congress had given the Executive power to deal only with credits during the life of the Lend-Lease Act. At the end of hostilities, Harriman had explained, new authority would be necessary under a new act by Congress. Molotov understood this situation and asked if the present moment were appropriate for raising the question of postwar credits. Our ambassador had cabled to us in Washington that he had answered that the moment was entirely favorable for arriving at final agreement about Lend-Lease orders for the war period and for opening preliminary discussions on credits after the war. He had pointed out that since it would take some time to work out an agreement and to receive the required authority from Congress discussions should be begun before the war was over.

Secretary of the Treasury Morgenthau had sent a letter to the President on January 1, 1945, stating that he had discussed Soviet credits several times with Harriman. "We are not thinking of more Lend-Lease or any form of relief but rather of an arrangement that will have definite and long-range benefits for the United States as well as for Russia," he wrote. "I am convinced that if we were to come forward now and present to the Russians a concrete plan to aid them in the reconstruction period it would contribute a great deal towards ironing out many of the difficulties we have been having with respect to their problems and policies."

General William J. Donovan and his staff in the Office of

THE GERMAN QUESTION

Strategic Services had drafted an estimate for us just before the Yalta Conference of the war damages suffered by the Soviet Union. It was the opinion of this agency that Russia had lost approximately sixteen billion dollars of fixed capital in terms of 1937 prices, or twenty-five per cent of the fixed capital within her pre-1939 borders. In addition, Russia had lost probably another four billion dollars' worth of manufacturing inventories and personal property. The Soviet Union, as we know, did not receive a loan at the close of the war. Whether such a loan would have made the Soviet Union a more reasonable and co-operative nation in the postwar world will be one of the great "if" questions of history.

The first foreign ministers' meeting on that second day at Yalta was not particularly fruitful from the standpoint of policy matters. We could deal only with the problems assigned to us by the plenary sessions. Since the first plenary session, the day before, had discussed only military matters, the foreign ministers had to wait until the second plenary session for assignments. From February 6 to the end of the Conference, however, the foreign ministers were to have a rigorous schedule of problems for discussion.

The President opened the second plenary session that afternoon by remarking that one of the first questions for discussion was that of occupying Germany. The French desired a zone of occupation, he observed, and occupation involved control machinery.

Marshal Stalin said that he desired to discuss the following questions:

(1) *The partition of Germany.* There had been an exchange of views at Teheran, he pointed out, and also when Churchill visited him at Moscow, but they had reached no

decisions. If we definitely agreed on dismemberment, he declared, he wanted to know what form the dismemberment would take.

(2) Would the Big Three establish a government in Germany? If Germany was divided, he added, would each part have its own government?

(3) Was there not need to work out the definite terms of unconditional surrender?[1]

(4) The types of reparations and their amount.

All of these questions, the President said, and Eden spoke up and agreed, were long-range ones and grew out of the question of the zones of occupation.

Marshal Stalin, however, continued his explanation of the partitioning of Germany by stating that the President had suggested partition into five parts at Teheran. Roosevelt had discussed the possibility at Teheran of five autonomous states: (1) Prussia (reduced), (2) Hanover and the northwest, (3) Saxony and the Leipzig area, (4) Hesse-Darmstadt, Hesse-Kassel, and the area south of the Rhine, (5) Bavaria, Baden, and Württemberg. The Kiel Canal and Hamburg, the Ruhr and the Saar were to be under United Nations control. Stalin now remarked that he had associated himself with the President's suggestions at Teheran but that this, of course, had been only an exchange of views. The Prime Minister, Stalin added, had talked at Moscow of dividing Germany into two parts, Prussia and Bavaria, and placing the Ruhr and Westphalia under international control. No agreement, however, had been reached, since Roose-

[1] It appeared from this remark that Stalin was not familiar with the protocol, which the Russian, British, and American representatives on the European Advisory Commission had already signed.

velt was not present. The time had come for a decision, Stalin thought.

The Prime Minister observed that, although they were all agreed on dismemberment, the tracing of boundaries was a much too complicated matter of geography, history, and economics to settle in five or six days at Yalta. It deserved prolonged discussion by a special committee. He himself was not ready to answer the question of how to divide Germany. His personal view, although he would feel free to change it, was that a second German state might be possible with its capital at Vienna. There were other questions, he thought, although already decided in principle, which now presented themselves for consideration:

(1) We are agreed that Germany should lose certain territories largely conquered by Russian troops or needed in the Polish settlement.

(2) There was the question of whether the Ruhr and the Saar should be under France, made independent, or be controlled by a world organization for an extended period.

(3) Finally, there was the question as to whether Prussia should be divided internally.

The Prime Minister emphasized that he had no fixed opinions on these matters. On all these questions, however, he urged that the French be consulted. He also suggested that at Yalta they should establish the machinery for a thorough investigation of these questions. As to the immediate surrender of Germany, he felt that all details had already been worked out by the three governments and were well known to them. There remained, he felt, only formal agreement on the zones of occupation and the control machinery.

Stalin asked if it would not be wise to include a mention of the intention to dismember in the terms of unconditional surrender to be imposed on the Germans. The Prime Minister declared that it was not necessary to discuss this with the Germans. All we had to do, he added, was to inform them that they had to await our joint decision as to their future.

At this point the President remarked that the Conference had not reached a decision on Marshal Stalin's question as to whether it favored dismemberment. The Marshal wanted the matter settled in principle but not as to details. The President added that it was clear that the Prime Minister was not yet ready to specify boundaries. It seemed to him, the President said, that both the Prime Minister and the Marshal were actually talking about the same thing. Therefore the President suggested that we all agree that Germany was to be dismembered and simply inform the Germans as to the principle and not as to the details. He warned that, if they were not careful, there would be a hundred plans for dismemberment. He therefore urged that the three foreign secretaries be instructed to bring in a plan as soon as possible for the study of the dismemberment question. The Prime Minister then announced that His Majesty's Government was now prepared to agree to the principle of dismemberment and to have a body study the question of dismemberment.

Stalin remarked that he thought the President's suggestion should be accepted. As he understood it, they agreed (1) to dismember Germany and empower the foreign ministers to develop concrete plans; (2) to add to the surrender terms the statement that Germany would be dismembered without giving any details. The Prime Minister's idea of not telling the Germans about dismemberment, the Marshal said, was

While the President was discussing whether the Conference agreed on the dismemberment of Germany, I passed this note:

Mr. President:
    We can readily agree to referring this—the 1st meeting of Foreign Ministers.   Ed

risky. The advantage of adding dismemberment to the surrender terms, he declared, was that the German group in power should bear the responsibility for it when they signed a surrender document.

The President remarked that the Marshal's idea of this was something like his own. It would be better all around to have it in the terms of surrender.

When Churchill warned that including this point in the surrender terms would make the Germans more determined to resist, Roosevelt said that the German people had suffered so much already that he doubted that questions of psychological warfare would affect them any longer. After a further brief discussion the three leaders agreed to refer to the foreign ministers the inclusion of the word "dismemberment" in the surrender terms prepared by the European Advisory Commission.

On the matter of granting the French a zone of occupation, Churchill spoke in favor of granting France a part of the British and American zones. He asked Stalin if he approved of the British and Americans jointly working out a zone to allot to the French out of their zones.

Stalin replied that it might establish a precedent for other states to ask for zones. He also pointed out that the Prime Minister's proposal would mean that France would become part of the control machinery for Germany. Instead the Marshal suggested that the British might secure the help of France or Holland or Belgium in the occupation but not give them any rights in the control machinery. The Soviet Union, too, might invite states to help occupy its zone, but these states would not be allowed to have representation in the control machinery.

Churchill replied, however, that the French had had long

experience in occupying Germany and they would not be lenient. France must become strong again to help check a revived Germany, he declared. Great Britain did not know how long the United States would be willing to remain in the occupation of Germany, he added. Therefore the French Army should grow in strength and help share the burden. If Russia wanted to share her zone with some other power, we should not object, he concluded.

At this point Stalin asked the President to express an opinion as to how long the United States would be willing to keep occupation forces in Germany. The President replied: "I can get the people and Congress to co-operate fully for peace but not to keep an army in Europe for a long time. Two years would be the limit."

Although this may now sound astonishing, it must be remembered that there was already a ground swell of public opinion demanding that our forces be returned home as soon as the war was over. Furthermore, it is reasonable to assume that, had Russian-American relations remained at the high-water mark reached at Yalta, public opinion would not have favored American troops being stationed in Europe for too long a time after the close of the war. It was the deterioration in Soviet-American relations after Yalta that rapidly changed American opinion on this question.

After the President's statement Stalin said he agreed with Mr. Churchill that the French should again become strong, but he added that in this war France had "opened the gates to the enemy." Russia and Great Britain would not have had so many losses and so much destruction in this war if the French had put up a determined fight. The control and administration of Germany must be only for those powers which had stood against the enemy from the beginning, he added, and therefore France did not belong to this group.

Although the Prime Minister agreed that France had not been much help in the war, he countered by saying that France was the most important neighbor of Germany. Furthermore, British public opinion would not understand it if decisions vital to France were made without regard to that country. We should not, he added, decide upon an indefinite exclusion of France for all time. He pointed out that he had opposed inviting De Gaulle to the Crimean Conference, but the fact remained that France had to take her place again in world affairs.

When France was thus suggested as a future addition to the Big Three, Stalin smilingly said that this was an extremely exclusive club, restricted to a membership of nations with five million soldiers. Churchill quickly corrected him and said three million.

The Prime Minister declared that Great Britain would need the help of France in its future defense against Germany. "We have suffered badly from German robot bombs," declared Churchill, "and should Germany once more get near to the channel coast we would suffer again. After the Americans have gone home, we have to think seriously of the future." The Prime Minister then proposed that France be offered a part of the present British and American zones and that technical studies be conducted as to the French relation to the control machinery.

Stalin interjected that he still was against France having a place in the control machinery. The President then suggested that the French have a zone of occupation but that discussion of their participation in the control machinery be postponed.

He indicated that although he favored the French having

Livadia Palace, the official headquarters of the Yalta Conference and the American residence. (U.S. Army Signal Corps photos)

The courtyard at Livadia Palace.

President Roosevelt's study in Livadia Palace.

(U.S. Army Signal Corps photos)

Russian maids making President Roosevelt's bed.

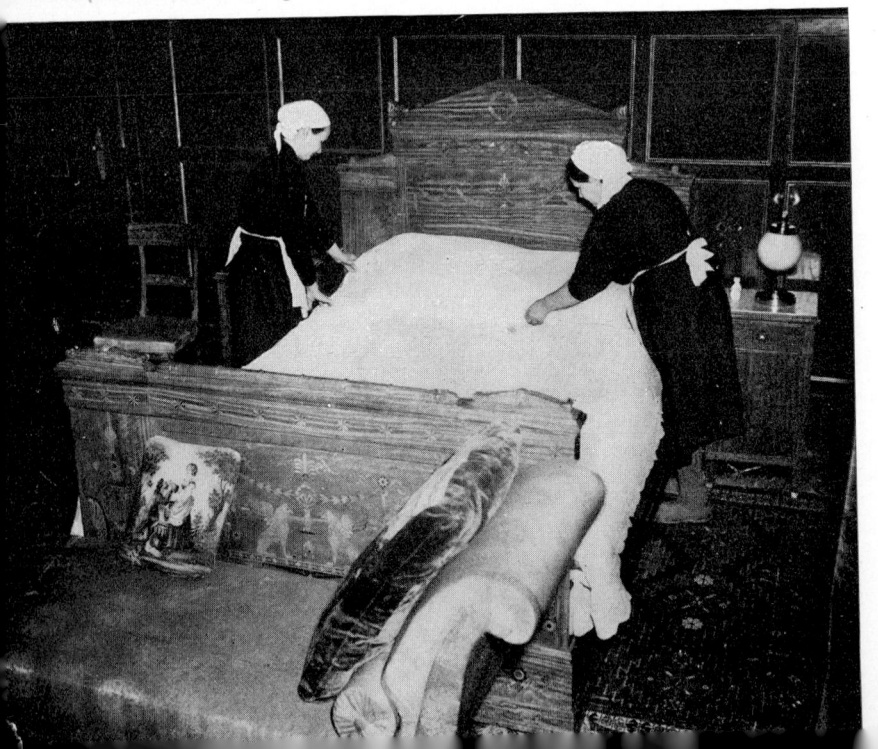

a zone of occupation, at this point he agreed with Stalin that France should not take part in the control machinery. He then added that other nations might want to come into the control machinery. Holland, for instance, had suffered the loss of great areas of land by flooding. We must set aside German land to make up for this, the President declared, and the Netherlands might therefore ask for a seat on the Control Commission.

Eden then asked how, if the French were to have a zone, they could be excluded from the control machinery. If they were excluded, he added, how could the operation of their zone be controlled?

When Stalin replied that they could be controlled by the power from which they obtained the zone, both Churchill and Eden declared that Great Britain could not undertake to do this and that the French would never submit to it. The French, Eden explained, had pressed the British on the question of a place on the Control Commission, and he asked Stalin if they had not raised the question in Moscow. Stalin replied that they had, but they had been told it could only be discussed by all three powers.

The Prime Minister again asked if it were agreed that the British and Americans should set aside a zone for France. The foreign ministers, he added, should discuss further the control question. Stalin answered that it was agreed that France should have a zone and that the foreign ministers should study the question of the relationship of the French zone to the Control Commission.

All through this discussion, as well as during most of the Conference, Stalin showed an obvious desire to reach an agreement with Roosevelt. This was not so true, however, of Stalin's attitude toward Churchill.

The President next raised the question of German reparations. He pointed out that the United States did not desire reparations in the form of labor, and he was sure that Great Britain held the same view.

Stalin replied that they had a proposal for reparations "in kind," but were not prepared to talk about the use of manpower. He then called upon his associate, Maisky, to explain the Russian proposal. Maisky, with his clipped, pointed beard and scholarly manner, was an attractive and able person. He had formerly been the Soviet Ambassador to the Court of St. James and spoke fluent English, though with a distinct accent. He delivered his report in a forceful manner and seemed to have the full support of Stalin and Molotov. I have always wondered why Maisky was removed not only from reparations matters but also from power and influence not long after the Crimean Conference.

The Soviet Union, Maisky said, had two ideas in mind. Within two years after the end of the war, factories, heavy machinery, machine tools, rolling stock, and investments abroad should be withdrawn from the national economy of Germany. In addition, there should be yearly payments in articles of production or in kind for a period of ten years.

For the security of Europe and to restore the Soviet economy, he insisted that it was necessary to reduce German heavy industry by eighty per cent. All munitions production, as well as synthetic petroleum production, for example, should be prohibited. The twenty per cent of heavy industry left to Germany would be sufficient, he declared, for the needs of the German peacetime economy. The list of reparations in kind, to be paid over a ten-year period, could be settled later on. In order to make Germany pay, he added, there had to be strict tripartite control over Germany. The

THE GERMAN QUESTION

details of the control could be settled later, but it must be established that all industries of value for war purposes were to be internationalized. Representatives of the three great Allies should serve on the boards of directors for the ten-year period.

It had to be realized, Maisky said, that war damages to state and private property were so astronomical that reparations would not be able to cover the total bill. Priorities among countries should therefore be established. He recommended that the priority of a country be based on (1) the proportional contribution of the country to the winning of the war, and (2) its losses of material in the war. The Soviet Union, he added, desired not less than ten billion dollars of total reparation in kind through withdrawals and yearly payments over this ten-year period. He then proposed that the Big Three establish a reparations commission in Moscow to work out the details of the reparations program.

When Maisky had completed his presentation the Prime Minister recalled the sad experience with reparations following the last war. He pointed out that Germany had been able to pay in part only because of large loans from the United States. On the other hand, in view of Russia's high losses, he would favor the removal of some plants and equipment to the U.S.S.R. He added that he was sure that we would never get out of Germany anything like two hundred and fifty million pounds a year. Great Britain, too, had suffered. Houses had been destroyed and the nation was faced with an acute export problem. England had to export in order to buy food to live, one half of which had had to be imported even before the war. Britain, too, had incurred extremely heavy debts apart from Lend-Lease. No victorious country would come out of the war so burdened financially as Great

Britain, the Prime Minister declared. As a result, if there were any benefits in reparations, he would be glad to have them, but he was doubtful if any important benefits would flow from reparations. Other countries also had suffered great devastation—France, Belgium, Holland, and Norway. In addition, he declared, we also had to consider the phantom of a starving Germany and who would pay for that. If you wished a horse to pull a wagon, he concluded, you would at least have to give it fodder.

Stalin interjected that there would be food for the Germans, but care should be taken to see that the horse did not turn around and kick you when you were not looking.

The Prime Minister continued, however, that he favored the proposal that a commission be set up in Moscow to study reparations as the Soviet Union had recommended.

The President commented that after the last war the United States had loaned far more money to Germany than was ever received back from that country. Such a situation could not occur again, he said. The United States, he declared, wanted no German manpower, machines, or factories. The only thing, therefore, the United States could obtain was German property in America. He explained that he hoped to secure legislation to have this property taken over and placed under a public trust.

The President then pointed out that the United States had been traditionally generous to other nations, but that it could not guarantee to finance the future of Germany. He envisioned, he said, a Germany that was self-sustaining and not starving. There would be no lending of money to Germany after this war. Our objective was to see that Germany should not starve, while helping the Soviet Union to get reparations for rebuilding and helping the British to get rep-rations in exports to former German markets. Therefore the time had come to set up a reparations commission. In rebuilding we must get all the reparations we could from Germany, but we could not get all the cost of rebuilding from German reparations. Leave Germany enough industry and work to keep her from starving, the President concluded.

Maisky asserted that, while he appreciated the Prime Minister's remarks about reparations after the last war, the mistake was not that they were too high but that they were in monetary form. He must add, he said, that the financial policies of both Great Britain and the United States had contributed to the German refusal to pay. Ten billion dollars was not very much for Russia to expect from Germany, he observed. It was only ten per cent of the United States' budget that year, he declared, and six months of Great Britain's war expenditures. He agreed that Germany should not have a higher standard of living than middle Europe. He disagreed with Churchill that Germany might starve. Germany, he declared, could live a modest, decent life based on light industries and agriculture.

Stalin then insisted that the three Great Powers should have first claim on German reparations. France, he said, had not exerted enough effort in the war to receive a first claim to reparations. Churchill, however, recalled the saying of "each according to his needs," and declared that he did not think exertion in the war should be taken into consideration in determining the distribution of reparations.

The President remarked that in his opinion the proposed reparations commission should be limited to the representatives of the Soviet Union, Great Britain, and the United States. Stalin agreed with this, and the Prime Minister expressed his agreement that in the first instance the representatives of the three major powers should consider the question.

The meeting adjourned at 8 P.M., after the three leaders had agreed to the establishment of a reparations commission in Moscow and had instructed the foreign ministers to prepare directives for the commission. The directives, however, were to be referred back to the three leaders before being sent to the commission.

After the meeting the President asked a small group to dine with him. There were present General Marshall, Admiral Leahy, Admiral King, Admiral Wilson Brown, Admiral McIntire, Justice Byrnes, Mr. Early, Ambassador Harriman, Miss Kathleen Harriman, Mrs. Boettiger, the President, and I. It was purely a family dinner, at the end of a hard day.

CHAPTER 7

The Big Three Veto Power

February 6

On the third day of the Conference, Eden and Molotov joined me at Livadia Palace for a discussion of the dismemberment of Germany, which had been referred to us by the plenary session the previous evening. Before we examined this question, however, we agreed on a press release announcing the Crimean Conference. The German radio had been circulating all kinds of rumors, and we felt that it was advisable to issue a general statement. That afternoon the three leaders signed the communiqué we presented:

> The President of the United States of America, the Premier of the Soviet Union and the Prime Minister of Great Britain, accompanied by their chiefs of staff, the three foreign secretaries and other advisers, are now meeting in the Black Sea area.
>
> Their purpose is to concert plans for completing the defeat of the common enemy and for building, with their Allies, firm foundations for a lasting peace. Meetings are proceeding continuously.

The conference began with military discussions. The present situation on all the European fronts has been reviewed and the fullest information interchanged. There is complete agreement for joint military operations in the final phase of the war against Nazi Germany. The military staffs of the three Governments are now engaged in working out jointly the detailed plans.

Discussions of problems involved in establishing a secure peace have also begun. These discussions will cover joint plans for the occupation and control of Germany, the political and economic problems of liberated Europe and proposals for the earliest possible establishment of a permanent international organization to maintain peace.

A communiqué will be issued at the conclusion of the Conference.

At my meeting with Eden and Molotov, I pointed out that much research and study would be necessary before agreement could be reached on the dismemberment of Germany. I did, however, hope that we could agree on the general principles involved. I suggested that the surrender terms agreed upon in the European Advisory Commission be amended by adding the word "dismemberment." I also urged that consideration be given to assigning this topic to the European Advisory Commission in London.

Molotov immediately agreed to the addition of the word "dismemberment." He suggested that the paragraph begin: "In order to secure peace and security of Europe, they will take measures for the dismemberment of Germany."

Eden objected that this wording would too fully commit the three powers before the question had been thoroughly studied. When Molotov continued to press for the Russian draft, Eden declared that the British would go no further than the addition of the words "and the dismemberment."

I proposed as a possible alternative, although I still preferred my first suggestion, a phrase to the effect that "including dismemberment to the degree necessary to safeguard the peace and security . . ."

Molotov was inclined to prefer my second proposal, but Eden strongly objected to going further than my first suggestion. It was finally decided to sum up the discussion by stating that all three foreign secretaries agreed to the addition of the word "dismemberment" and that Mr. Eden would consult with Mr. Churchill to determine whether he would accept my second proposal.

It was agreed, in view of the approaching luncheon hour, to postpone discussion of referring the dismemberment question to the European Advisory Commission. Molotov did suggest, however, that since it was a specific matter it might be better to establish a special commission.

The sunroom of Livadia Palace, where I gave a luncheon for the foreign ministers, was a large, pleasant room. It had a bay window looking out over the Black Sea far below. The luncheon was informal and friendly in character. Molotov had to leave at two-thirty for an urgent meeting with Stalin and as a result we adjourned to meet again at the plenary session at four o'clock.

After the luncheon I met immediately with Hiss and Foote to go over my notes for the afternoon meeting of the three leaders. The President that morning had restudied with me our voting formula for the Security Council. He again told me that it was a satisfactory plan and asked me to present it at the plenary session that afternoon.

It was to be a most important moment for me. I had devoted many days and nights to the problem of building a world organization, ever since I left the Lend-Lease Administration for the State Department. If we could now persuade the Russians to accept our voting proposal, a United Nations conference could be called and our plans for a world organization for peace and security would be nearer realization.

The Big Three meeting took place at 4 P.M. in the great hall of the palace with its white Corinthian columns and a log fire blazing in the great fireplace at the far end of the room. I sat at the President's right. Behind the President sat Hopkins, Matthews, and Hiss.

Stalin wore his plain khaki uniform with its high collar and a single decoration. I noticed that today he was smoking Russian cigarettes, and that he doodled on a piece of paper more than usual.

Churchill wore the uniform of a colonel. He was, as usual, rosy-cheeked. As he talked, his horn-rimmed glasses repeatedly slid down toward the end of his nose. Every once in a while he would cast an awesome look over the top of these spectacles.

The President opened the meeting by asking me to report first on that morning's meeting of the foreign ministers. I explained our agreement to add the word "dismemberment" to the unconditional surrender terms for Germany, but I pointed out that Mr. Molotov had some additional phrases he wanted to add. Molotov, however, interjected that he now was withdrawing his suggested amendment. This was obviously a result of the after-luncheon conference that he had had with Stalin.

The Prime Minister declared that he had not had time to obtain the consent of the War Cabinet to the insertion of the word "dismemberment," but that he personally was glad to accept the decision on this point on behalf of the British Government.[1]

[1] The wording of the final agreement that was later worked out by the

I then stated that the foreign ministers desired to have more time before reporting to the three leaders on reparations and on the relationship of the French to the Control Commission.

As regarded the French zone, the Prime Minister observed that he felt the future importance of France had been greatly enhanced by the limitation the President had placed the previous day on the length of time during which American forces might remain in Europe. Great Britain alone, he added, would not be strong enough to guard the western approaches to the Channel.

The President immediately pointed out that he had spoken purely on the basis of present conditions. American public opinion, he felt, would be willing to support an international organization along the lines proposed at Dumbarton Oaks. This, of course, might change their attitude in regard to the question of maintaining troops in Europe.

The President then proposed that they proceed to a consideration of the United States formula on voting in the Security Council. All the peoples of the world, he said, shared a common desire to see the elimination of war for at least fifty years. He was not so optimistic, he added, as to believe that eternal peace was as yet attainable, but he did believe, provided a world organization were formed, that fifty years was possible. He then turned to me and asked me to present on his behalf the United States position on voting in the Security Council.

---

foreign ministers read: "The United Kingdom, the United States of America and the Union of Soviet Socialist Republics shall possess supreme authority with respect to Germany. In the exercise of such authority they will take such steps, including the complete disarmament, demilitarisation and the dismemberment of Germany as they deem requisite for future peace and security."

I made the following statement:

REVIEW OF STATUS OF THIS QUESTION.

It was agreed at Dumbarton Oaks that certain matters would remain under consideration for future settlement. Of these, the principal one was that of voting procedure to be followed in the Security Council.

At Dumbarton Oaks, the three Delegations thoroughly explored the whole question. Since that time the matter has received continuing intensive study by each of the three Governments.

On December 5, 1944, the President sent to Marshal Stalin and to Prime Minister Churchill a proposal that this matter be settled by making Section C, Chapter VI of the Dumbarton Oaks proposals read substantially as follows:

"C. VOTING

"1. Each member of the Security Council should have one vote.

"2. Decisions of the Security Council on procedural matters should be made by an affirmative vote of seven members.

"3. Decisions of the Security Council on all other matters should be made by an affirmative vote of seven members including the concurring votes of the permanent members; provided that, in decisions under Chapter VIII, Section A and under the second sentence of paragraph 1 of Chapter VIII, Section C, a party to a dispute should abstain from voting."[2]

Stalin inquired whether there was anything new in the proposal that had not been included in the President's message of December 5. I replied that there had been only a minor drafting change.

[2] Note: This became Article 27 of the Charter of the United Nations with a slight change of verb tense; what had been Chapter VIII of the Dumbarton Oaks proposals became Chapter VI in the Charter; and Chapter VIII, Section C, became Article 52 of Chapter VIII.

The interpreters became quite confused trying to explain what this change was, and there was an unpleasant moment when the Russians thought we were trying to slip something over on them. At this point Gromyko helped us straighten out the matter with Stalin and Molotov. Pasvolsky, on my instructions, had held several consultations with Gromyko in Washington before the Yalta Conference, explaining to him the reasons for the American voting formula. I had written to the President on January 20: "The Ambassador asked many questions on the voting issue and seemed to be trying to get into his mind our arguments in favor of the formula which you proposed to Mr. Stalin. . . . it is most interesting to know that at least the Ambassador, personally, seems to have a very great interest in the subject. . . ." As a result of the Washington meetings Gromyko at Yalta was quite helpful in explaining the American position to Stalin and Molotov.

After the misunderstanding over the drafting change had been clarified with Stalin and Molotov, I proceeded to make the following analysis of the American proposal:

(a) We believe that our proposal is entirely consistent with the special responsibilities of the great powers for the preservation of the peace of the world. In this respect our proposal calls for unqualified unanimity of the permanent members of the Council on all major decisions relating to the preservation of peace, including all economic and military enforcement measures.

(b) At the same time our proposal recognizes the desirability of the permanent members frankly stating that the peaceful adjustment of any controversy which may arise is a matter of general world interest in which any sovereign member state involved should have a right to present its case.

We believe that unless this freedom of discussion in the

> *Council is permitted, the establishment of the World Organization which we all so earnestly desire in order to save the world from the tragedy of another war would be seriously jeopardized. Without full and free discussion in the Council, the Organization, even if it could be established, would be vastly different from the one we have contemplated.*[3]
>
> *The paper which we have placed before the other two delegations sets forth the text of the provisions which I have read and lists specifically those decisions of the Council which, under our proposals, would require unqualified unanimity, and, separately, those matters in the area of discussion and peaceful settlement in which any party to a dispute would abstain from casting a vote.*

While I was making this presentation I stopped after each sentence or paragraph to allow my remarks to be interpreted. As a result it took an extremely long time for me to complete the report. After presenting the formula and analyzing its significance, I then proceeded to explain the reasons for the American position:

> *From the point of view of the United States Government there are two important elements in the matter of voting procedure.*
>
> *First, there is the necessity for unanimity among the permanent members for the preservation of the peace of the world.*
>
> *Second, it is of particular importance to the people of the United States, that there be provision for a fair hearing for all members of the organization, large and small.*
>
> *We believe that the proposals submitted by the President to Marshal Stalin and Prime Minister Churchill on December 5*

---

[3] At the San Francisco Conference the Russians for a long time insisted that a question could not even be discussed by the Security Council without the unanimous vote of all five permanent members, unless one of them was involved in the dispute. Editorial writers and some columnists accused the State Department of failing to raise the general issue of freedom of discussion in the Council when the voting problem was discussed at Yalta. As the record shows, we not only raised this issue, but the principle was accepted at Yalta by the Russians.

of last year provide a reasonable and just solution and satisfactorily combine these two main considerations.

I then expressed the hope that our two great allies would find it possible to accept this proposal of the President. Before the Prime Minister and the Marshal began a general discussion of the American formula the President asked me to explain the effect of the proposal on the decisions of the Security Council. I thereupon made the following statement:

> Under the above formula the following decisions would require the affirmative votes of seven members of the Security Council including the votes of all the permanent members:
>
> I. Recommendations to the General Assembly on
>   1. Admission of new members;
>   2. Suspension of a member;
>   3. Expulsion of a member;
>   4. Election of the Secretary General.
>
> II. Restoration of the rights and privileges of a suspended member.
>
> III. Removal of threats to the peace and suppression of breaches of the peace, including the following questions:
>   1. Whether failure on the part of the parties to a dispute to settle it by means of their own choice or in accordance with the recommendations of the Security Council in fact constitutes a threat to the peace;
>   2. Whether any other actions on the part of any country constitute a threat to the peace or a breach of the peace;
>   3. What measures should be taken by the Council to maintain or restore the peace and the manner in which such measures should be carried out;
>   4. Whether a regional agency should be authorized to take measures of enforcement.
>
> IV. Approval of special agreement or agreements for the provision of armed forces and facilities.

V. Formulation of plans for a general system of regulation of armaments and submission of such plans to the member states.

VI. Determination of whether the nature and the activities of a regional agency or arrangement for the maintenance of peace and security are consistent with the purposes and principles of the general organization.

After this exposition I concluded with the following statement:

The following decisions relating to peaceful settlement of disputes would also require the affirmative votes of seven members of the Security Council including the votes of all the permanent members, except that a member of the Council would not cast its vote in any such decisions that concern disputes to which it is a party:

I. Whether a dispute or a situation brought to the Council's attention is of such a nature that its continuation is likely to threaten the peace;

II. Whether the Council should call on the parties to settle or adjust the dispute or situation by means of their own choice;

III. Whether the Council should make a recommendation to the parties as to methods and procedures of settlement;

IV. Whether the legal aspects of the matter before it should be referred by the Council for advice to the international court of justice;

V. Whether, if there exists a regional agency for peaceful settlement of local disputes, such an agency should be asked to concern itself with the controversy.

When I had finished my lengthy presentation, Stalin and Molotov made it clear that the Soviet Government attached

Secretary of State Hull congratulating Edward R. Stettinius, Jr., on becoming Under Secretary of State (October 1943). In the rear is Assistant Secretary of State Dean Acheson. (Acme)

Mr. Stettinius with Alger Hiss of the State Department delegation at the Conference. (U.S. Army Signal Corps)

great importance to the question of voting in the Security Council, and therefore wished to study the United States proposal and would be ready to discuss the question at the next plenary session.

The Prime Minister declared that his reason for not having agreed with the original proposal made at Dumbarton Oaks was his concern that full consideration be given to the realities of the situation, as far as the three Great Powers were concerned. Now, after having heard the full explanation, his anxieties were removed, and on behalf of the British Commonwealth of Nations, the Empire, and, he believed, the self-governing dominions, he could state that the American proposal was entirely satisfactory.

In the last resort, he added, peace depended on the friendship and the co-operation of the three Great Powers, but the British Government would consider that the leaders of the three powers were committing an injustice if provision were not made for small countries to state their grievances in a frank fashion. If this were not done, he warned, it would look as though the three powers were trying to rule the world, while their real desire was to save the world from repetition of the horrors of war. He felt that the three major powers should make what he termed "a proud submission" to the rights of the smaller powers.

He had looked at the whole matter from the point of view of British interests, he continued, and he did not think the American proposal would harm British interests. For instance, he said, if China should raise the question of the return of Hong Kong, both China and Britain would be precluded from voting in regard to the method of settling the controversy, but in the last analysis Great Britain would be protected against any decision adverse to her interests through the exercise of the veto right under paragraph III (Removal of threats to the peace and suppression of breaches of the peace) of the Secretary of State's analysis.

Stalin interrupted to ask what would happen if Egypt raised the issue of the return of the Suez Canal. The Prime Minister asked the Marshal to let him finish his illustration. Under paragraph III, Great Britain would have the right by its veto to stop all action against Great Britain by the Security Council. Great Britain thus would not be required to return Hong Kong unless she herself agreed to do so. China would and should, however, have the right to speak, and the same would apply to Egypt in regard to the Suez Canal. The same considerations, he felt, would apply in the event, for instance, that Argentina made a complaint against the United States.

At this point the President recalled that they had stated in the Teheran Declaration: "We recognize fully the supreme responsibility resting upon us and all the United Nations to make a peace which will command the good will of the overwhelming mass of the peoples of the world. . . ." The President added that he thought this statement was most pertinent to their present discussion and helped to explain the American position.

The Prime Minister emphasized, since he saw no reason to fear the American proposal, that he was glad to associate the British Government with it. He added that because of the great power of the three countries, which was still protected by the veto, we should allow the other nations the right to be heard.

Stalin stated that he would like to study the document, since it was impossible to catch all the implications from an oral presentation. He felt that the Dumbarton Oaks proposals had already provided the right of discussion for any nation in the Assembly, and he could not believe that any nation would be satisfied simply with expressing its opinion. If Mr. Churchill thought, for instance, that China would be satisfied with merely expressing its opinion on Hong Kong, Mr. Churchill was mistaken. China would want a favorable decision, and the same was true of Egypt on the Suez Canal.

It was not a question of one power or three powers desiring to be masters of the world, the Marshal insisted, because the Dumbarton Oaks proposal placed a brake on that. The Marshal then asked the Prime Minister for further clarification as to what powers Mr. Churchill had in mind when he referred to a desire to rule the world. Stalin said that he was sure Great Britain had no such desire nor had the United States and that, commented the Russian leader, left only the U.S.S.R.

Churchill explained that he had been speaking of the three Great Powers collectively, who could place themselves so high over the others that the rest of the world would say that these three desired to rule.

In an ironic tone Stalin then replied that it looked as though two Great Powers had already accepted a document which would avoid any such accusation, but that the third had not yet given its assent. The Marshal continued by saying that there was a more serious question than voting procedure or the domination of the world. They all knew, he said, that as long as the three of them lived none of them would involve their countries in aggressive action. But, after all, ten years from now none of them might be present. A new generation, not knowing the horrors of war, would come into being. It was, therefore, their obligation to create for this future generation the kind of organization which would truly secure peace for at least fifty years.

The main task, the Marshal added, was to prevent quarrels among the three Great Powers and guarantee their unity for the future. The charter of the new world organization should have this as its primary objective. The greatest danger, he believed, was conflict among the three Great Powers represented around the table. If unity could be preserved, however, there was little danger of the renewal of German aggression. A covenant must therefore be worked out which would prevent conflict among the three Great Powers.

Stalin continued by apologizing for not having had an opportunity to study the Dumbarton Oaks proposals in detail. As he understood my explanation, there were two categories of disputes:

(1) *Conflicts which would require the application of sanctions, economic, political, or military.*

(2) *Conflicts which could be settled by peaceful means.*

In regard to the first, the permanent members of the Security Council had a right to vote even if they were parties to the dispute. Under the second category, however, the parties in the dispute would not be allowed to vote. It seemed to me apparent from this concise analysis of our proposals that he had given rather careful study to the question. It should not be assumed, as has been written, that he and his subordinates were uninterested in a world organization.[4] The many conversations that I had with Gromyko and the other members of the Russian delegation at Dumbarton Oaks had con-

[4] James F. Byrnes, *Speaking Frankly* (New York: Harper & Brothers, 1947), p. 37.

vinced me that the leaders of the Soviet Union were greatly interested in a world organization at that time. We knew, of course, that at the same time the Soviet Union was using all the power at its command to build its own sphere of influence.

The Russians were accused, Stalin added at this plenary session, of spending much time on the question of voting, which he admitted was true. They attached great importance to this matter, since all decisions of the Security Council were made by votes, and Russia was interested in the decisions, not in the discussions. He also warned that, if China or Egypt raised complaints against Britain, these nations would not be without friends or protectors in the Assembly who would advocate their cause.

Both the Prime Minister and I insisted at this point that under the American proposal the power of the world organization could not be directed against any of the permanent members. Stalin, however, seemed uncertain of this, and said that he feared any conflicts or dispute in the world organization which might break the unity of the three powers.

The Prime Minister admitted the importance of this argument, but replied that he did not believe the world organization would eliminate disputes among the three powers. The settlement of these disputes, he believed, would still remain the function of diplomacy.

Stalin declared that his colleagues in Moscow could not forget that, during the Finnish War in 1939, Great Britain and France had instigated the expulsion of the Soviet Union from the League of Nations and that they had also mobilized world opinion against her, even going so far as to speak of it as a crusade.

The Prime Minister replied that at the time the British

and the French were *"very, very angry"* with the Soviet Union. But in any event such action would be impossible under the Dumbarton Oaks proposals.

The Marshal replied that he was not now thinking of expulsion but of one country's mobilizing opinion against another. This might happen to any country, replied Churchill, but he doubted very much that either the President or Marshal Stalin would lead a savage attack against Great Britain, and he felt that this also applied to the President and to him in their relations with the Soviet Union.

The President then closed this entire discussion by saying that he felt that the unity of the three Great Powers was one of the paramount aims and that our proposals would promote rather than impair the achievement of this aim. No matter what voting procedure was adopted, he said, the world would know about any differences among the Great Powers. In any event there was no method of preventing the discussion of differences in the Assembly. Furthermore, full and free discussions in the Security Council would in no sense promote disunity, in his opinion, but would serve, on the contrary, to demonstrate the confidence which the Great Powers had in each other and in the justice of their own policies.

After this statement the Russians asked for a short intermission, and I took Churchill and Eden into my quarters. Churchill declared that, as a result of my presentation of the voting formula, now he—and he thought Stalin—really understood it for the first time. Eden and Churchill both agreed that we had made progress, and now they had high hopes that we would have a world organization after all.

CHAPTER 8

"Captain of Her Soul"

February 6

President Roosevelt, in his capacity as chairman of the Conference, announced when the third plenary session reconvened that the next item for discussion was the Polish situation. The United States was further away from Poland than the other two powers, the President remarked, and there were times when a long-distance point of view was useful on a given problem.

He had stated at Teheran, he recalled, that he believed the American people were inclined to accept the Curzon Line as the eastern frontier of Poland, but if the Soviet Union would consider leaving Lwow and the oil fields in the province of Lwow to Poland, that would have a salutary effect on American public opinion. He pointed out, however, that he was merely suggesting this for consideration rather than insisting on it.

In regard to the Polish Government, he wished to see the creation of a representative government which could have the support of all the Great Powers. One possibility which had been suggested, he pointed out, was the creation of a presidential council composed of Polish leaders, which in turn would form a government from the chiefs of the five political parties. One thing that must be made certain, the President emphasized, was that Poland should maintain the most friendly and co-operative relations with the Soviet Union.

Stalin interjected that Poland should maintain friendly relations not only with the Soviet Union but with the other Allies as well. (The italics are mine.)

The President added that if the three powers could find a solution to the perplexing Polish issue it would be a great help to everyone. He did not know personally any of the present members of either the London Government or the Lublin Government, he said, but Mr. Mikolajczyk had spent much time in Washington the previous summer and he had been impressed with him as a sincere and honest man.

The Prime Minister declared that he had consistently stated in Parliament and elsewhere that the British Government would support the Curzon Line, including leaving even Lwow to the Soviet Union. Both he and Mr. Eden had been criticized for this, but he felt that in view of the burdens which Russia had borne in the war the Curzon Line was not a decision of force but one of right. Of course, he noted, if the mighty Soviet Union could make a gesture like the relinquishment of Lwow to a much weaker country, this act of magnanimity would be acclamied by the whole world.

He was far more interested, he added, in the sovereignty and independence of Poland than in the question of frontiers. He desired to see the Poles have a home of their own where they could organize their lives as they saw fit. He had, he observed, heard Marshal Stalin firmly proclaim this objective, and he placed his trust in this declaration. The Prime Minister reiterated that he did not consider the question of the frontier as being as vital as the independence of Poland.

It must not be forgotten, he went on, that Great Britain had gone to war in 1939 to protect Poland against German aggression, and this act had almost cost Great Britain its freedom in the world. Therefore, although Great Britain had no material interest in Poland, it was a question of honor and his government would never be content with a solution which failed to establish Poland as a free and independent state.

The freedom of Poland, however, he insisted, did not mean any hostile designs or intrigue against the Soviet Union, and he was sure that none of those present would permit this to occur. It was the earnest desire of His Majesty's Government, he observed, that Poland be mistress in her own house and "captain of her soul."

The British Government, he continued, had recognized the present Polish Government in London but did not have an intimate relationship with it. Mr. Mikolajczyk, Mr. Grabski, and Mr. Romer he had found to be reliable and honest men. He inquired if at Yalta the three leaders could not agree on a Polish Government which would have places for these men. If this could be accomplished, the three Great Powers could then recognize it as an interim government until such time as the Polish people could themselves select their own government by a free vote. Churchill closed by saying that he was most interested in the President's suggestion on this point.

After a ten-minute intermission, suggested by Stalin, the Marshal presented his views on the Polish question. He commenced by saying that he could understand Mr. Churchill's statement that Poland was a question of honor for Great Britain, but for the Russians it was a question of both honor and security. It was a question of honor for Russia, he pointed out, because Russia had many grievances against Poland and wanted to eliminate these grievances. It was a question of strategic security not only because Poland was a neighbor but also because Poland throughout history had been the corridor for attacks on Russia. Twice during the last thirty years, Stalin observed, with great emphasis in his voice and with a determined gesture of his hand, Germany had passed through this corridor as it marched onto Russian soil.

The U.S.S.R. desired a strong, independent, and democratic Poland, Stalin declared, to help protect the Soviet Union, since the Soviet armies alone could not close this corridor from the outside. It was not only a question of honor for the Soviets, he again stated, but one of absolute necessity, to have Poland independent, strong, and democratic. It was for this reason, he added, that the Soviet Government had made a great change from the tsarist nineteenth-century policy of suppressing and assimilating Poland.

In regard to the Curzon Line and Mr. Churchill's reference to a magnanimous act in the case of Lwow, it was necessary to remind the Conference, the Marshal said, that not the Russians but Lord Curzon and Clemenceau had fixed this line at the close of the First World War. The Russians had not been invited to these discussions after the First World War, and the line had been established against their will. Lenin had opposed, for instance, giving Bialystok Province to the Poles, but the Curzon Line did give it to Poland. "We have, therefore," the Marshal declared, "retreated from Lenin's position." Furthermore, he added, the Conference could hardly expect him to be less Russian than Curzon and Clemenceau on the Polish frontier question. "We could not then return to Moscow," I noted that he observed, "and face the people who would say, 'Stalin and Molotov have been less determined defenders of our interests than Curzon and Clemenceau.'"

It was, therefore, impossible for the Soviets to agree with the proposed modification of the Curzon Line, declared Stalin. He added that he would prefer to have the war continue, in spite of the blood it would cost Russia, in order to secure land from Germany to compensate Poland. When Mr. Mikolajczyk had been in Moscow, Stalin added, he had been delighted to hear that Poland's western frontier would extend to the western Neisse River. The Soviet Union favored the Polish frontier on the western Neisse, the Marshal declared, and he therefore requested that the President and the Prime Minister support this proposal.

As to the question of the Polish Government, Mr. Churchill's suggestion that it be created at Yalta, Stalin observed, must have been a slip of the tongue, since it was impossible to create a Polish Government without the participation of the Poles. Although he was called a dictator and not a democrat, Stalin commented, he had enough democratic feeling to refuse to create a Polish Government without consulting the Poles.

The previous autumn in Moscow, when Mikolajczyk and Grabski met with the Lublin Poles, various agreements had been reached, Stalin pointed out. But when Mikolajczyk returned to London, he was expelled from office by the London Poles because he was willing to reach an agreement. It would be difficult to bring the two groups together, the Marshal predicted, because Arciszewski of the London group had characterized the Lublin Poles as bandits and criminals and they naturally regarded him in the same light. Bierut and Osubka-Morawski of the Warsaw Poles were opposed even to discussing a fusion with the London Poles and, the Marshal added with emphasis, these two leaders had told him that they refused to listen to a proposal that would result in Mikolajczyk's becoming Prime Minister.

The Marshal declared that he was prepared to support any attempt to reach a solution that would offer some chance of success. He suggested that some of the Warsaw Poles be asked to come to Yalta or perhaps to Moscow. The Warsaw Government, he observed, had a democratic base equal at least to that of De Gaulle's.

The Marshal then added that, as a military man, he demanded from a country liberated by the Red Army that there should be no civil war in the rear. "We demand order and we do not want to be shot in the back," he remarked. The Warsaw, or Lublin, Government had fulfilled this requirement, but, Stalin charged, agents of the London Government had been killing Red Army soldiers and attacking Soviet supply bases. When he compared what the representatives of the Lublin Government had done with the activities of the London Government, he could only see that the Lublin Government was good and the London Government was bad. "We require tranquillity behind our lines," he repeated. As a military man, he could follow no other course than to support the government which assured the Red Army of this requirement.

The Prime Minister immediately declared that the British and Soviet governments had different sources of information on Poland, and so they received different views of the situation. Although some of their information might be incorrect,

Churchill could not believe that the Lublin Government represented more than one third of the people. The British earnestly sought a solution of the Polish question, he said, in order to prevent the Polish underground from colliding with the Lublin Government. He added that he agreed with Mr. Stalin that anyone who attacked the Red Army should be punished, but he repeated categorically that the British Government could not agree to recognize the Lublin group as the government of Poland.

After this statement by the Prime Minister, the Conference adjourned that night at an extremely late hour. The President sent the following letter, prepared by the Department and Hopkins, to Stalin before going to bed that evening:

My dear Marshal Stalin:
I have been giving a great deal of thought to our meeting this afternoon, and I want to tell you in all frankness what is on my mind.

In so far as the Polish Government is concerned, I am greatly disturbed that the three great powers do not have a meeting of minds about the political setup in Poland. It seems to me that it puts all of us in a bad light throughout the world to have you recognizing one government while we and the British are recognizing another in London. I am sure this state of affairs should not continue and that if it does it can only lead our people to think there is a breach between us, which is not the case. I am determined that there shall be no breach between ourselves and the Soviet Union. Surely there is a way to reconcile our differences.

I was very much impressed with some of the things you said today, particularly your determination that your rear must be safeguarded as your army moves into Berlin. You cannot, and we must not, tolerate any temporary government which will give your armed forces any trouble of this sort. I want you to know that I am fully mindful of this.

You must believe me when I tell you that our people at home look with a critical eye on what they consider a disagreement between us at this vital state of the war. They, in effect, say that if we cannot get a meeting of minds now when our armies are converging on the common enemy, how can we get an understanding on even more vital things in the future.

I have had to make it clear to you that we cannot recognize the Lublin Government as now composed, and the world would regard it as a lamentable outcome of our work here if we parted with an open and obvious divergence between us on this issue.

You said today that you would be prepared to support any suggestions for the solution of this problem which offered a fair chance of success, and you also mentioned the possibility of bringing some members of the Lublin government here.

Realizing that we all have the same anxiety in getting this matter settled, I would like to develop your proposal a little and suggest that we invite here to Yalta at once Mr. Bierut and Mr. Osubka-Morawski from the Lublin government and also two or three from the following list of Poles, which according to our information would be desirable as representatives of the other elements of the Polish people in the development of a new temporary government which all three of us could recognize and support: Archbishop Sapieha of Cracow, Vincente Witos, Mr. Zurlowski, Professor Buyak, and Professor Kutzeba. If, as a result of the presence of these Polish leaders here, we could jointly agree with them on a provisional government in Poland which should no doubt include some Polish leaders from abroad such as Mr. Mikolajczyk, Mr. Grabski and Mr. Romer, the United States Government, and I feel sure the British Government as well, would then be prepared to examine with you conditions in which they would disassociate themselves from the London government and transfer their recognition to the new provisional government.

I hope I do not have to assure you that the United States will never lend its support in any way to any provisional government in Poland that would be inimical to your interests.

It goes without saying that any interim government which could be formed as a result of our conference with the Poles here would be pledged to the holding of free elections in Poland at the earliest possible date. I know this is completely consistent with your desire to see a new free and democratic Poland emerge from the welter of this war.

Most sincerely yours,
Franklin D. Roosevelt

CHAPTER 9

"A Step Forward"

February 7

At breakfast on February 7, I received a radio message from the State Department in Washington informing us of a plane crash which had killed Constantine A. Oumansky, Soviet Ambassador to Mexico. We immediately prepared a warm note to Marshal Stalin for the President's signature, expressing sympathy over the death and offering an American Army plane to bring Oumansky's ashes back to the Soviet Union. This offer was quickly accepted and it was a gesture that the Russians seemed to appreciate deeply.

Just after breakfast Harry Hopkins and James Byrnes met with the State Department staff and remarked that they thought the voting problem in the Security Council was of greater importance than anything else at that moment. They urged me to subordinate all other questions in the meeting with Eden and Molotov that was to be held at noon until the two other foreign ministers thoroughly understood our proposal.

The foreign ministers met that day at the Soviet headquarters. It was a villa with beautiful formal gardens, large pools, and statuary. The mountain above the villa was covered with pine, fir, oak, and trees similar to California redwoods. Many of the plants and trees in the area had been brought in years ago from all over the world.

I told the other two foreign ministers that I would be happy to answer any questions on the voting procedure which I had discussed at yesterday's meeting of the three leaders. Molotov remarked that matters affecting the world security organization had not yet been referred by the plenary session to the foreign secretaries. Although he did have several questions to raise, he was not prepared, therefore, to discuss the subject at this meeting.

We turned to the question of the dismemberment of Germany. We agreed to appoint a subcommittee consisting of Vishinsky, Cadogan, and Matthews to redraft the surrender terms in order to include the word "dismemberment." Molotov suggested that a commission consisting of Eden, Winant, and Gusev be established in London to study the procedure for the dismemberment of Germany.

I stated that the creation of this commission was a most important matter, but that the prestige of the European Advisory Commission, functioning since the Moscow Conference, would be greatly diminished if the question were not referred to it. In view of the fact that the EAC was created to deal with just such questions, I pointed out that a separate commission would seriously threaten the prestige and effectiveness of the EAC.

Eden remarked that if this matter were referred to the European Advisory Commission the French would then participate in the work, although the Conference had not yet decided on French participation in the control of Germany.

Molotov observed that the subject under discussion was the study of the procedure for the dismembering of Germany, not the actual dismemberment. It therefore could be assigned to a special committee and later, perhaps, it might be handed over to the European Advisory Commission.

Eden then raised the question of the terms of reference for the body created to study this problem. The body, he suggested, should examine when the partitioning should take place and what the boundaries of the newly created states should be. An examination also should be made to guarantee the proper functioning and survival of these states. Furthermore, he observed, the relation of these states to foreign powers should be explored. Eden expressed his concern over the absence of France if he and Winant and Gusev alone were to handle the problem.

When Molotov suggested that the question of French participation in the dismemberment discussions be subsequently decided in London by Eden, Winant, and Gusev, both Eden and I expressed approval of that recommendation.

We then turned to the question of integrating France into the German Control Commission. Molotov no longer maintained Soviet opposition to a French zone of occupation but recommended that France be allowed to exercise control only in its zone under the general guidance of the Control Commission.

Eden, however, felt that France should participate in the Control Commission itself. He declared that he foresaw all kinds of difficulties if the French were not in the Control Commission. General de Gaulle, he believed, might refuse to accept a zone if he did not have the same powers in the control machinery as the other three occupying powers. He could not see, Eden argued, why it was any more of a departure to have France on the Control Commission than on the European Advisory Commission. The Prime Minister had made it clear, Eden declared, that French participation in the Control Commission did not mean that France would be included in conferences of the three Great Powers.

I suggested that the question of French participation be turned over to the EAC for study.

It was finally decided that we three should submit the following report on this matter to the plenary session that afternoon:

> (*a*) *It had been agreed upon to give France a zone of occupation.*
>
> (*b*) *With respect to the question concerning the participation of France in the Control Commission, Messrs. Molotov and Stettinius considered it appropriate to submit this question to the consideration of the EAC, while Mr. Eden considered it appropriate to study the question at the present time and to assign to France a place on the Control Commission.*

Eden observed that he believed that, if France were admitted to the Control Commission, the three foreign ministers should agree that no other power should be granted a zone of occupation. Molotov remarked, however, that there was not sufficient time at the present meeting to discuss this suggestion.

We then turned to the question of German reparations, and Molotov submitted a statement suggesting that the three powers establish a reparations commission in Moscow to work out a detailed plan for exacting reparations according to the principles to be adopted by the three powers at the Crimean Conference. The activities of the reparations commission would be conducted in strict secrecy, and the three powers would decide when, and to what extent, other Allied powers would be invited to join in the work of the commission.

Molotov then submitted the following document on "Basic Principles of Exaction of Reparations from Germany":

1. Reparations are to be received in the first instance by those countries which have borne the main burden of the war and have organized victory over the enemy.
All other countries are to receive repartions secondly.

2. Setting aside for the moment the use of German labor by way of reparations, this question to be considered at a later day, reparations in kind are to be exacted from Germany in the two following forms:
   (a) Removal in a single payment at the end of the war from the national wealth of Germany located on the territory of Germany herself as well as outside her territory (equipment, machine-tools, ships, rolling stock, German investment abroad, shares of industrial, transport, shipping and other enterprises in Germany, etc.) these removals to be carried out chiefly for the purpose of military and economic disarmament of Germany.
   These removals are to be completed within two years of the end of the war.
   (b) Annual deliveries of commodities during 10 years after the end of the war.

3. The total of German reparations in the form of removal from her national wealth as well as in the form of annual deliveries of commodities after the end of the war is fixed at 20 billion dollars.
   This amount shall be distributed as follows:
   (a) U.S.S.R.—10 billion dollars.
   (b) United Kingdom and U.S.A.—8 billion dollars.
   (c) All other countries—2 billion dollars.

At Molotov's request, Maisky, who was present for this discussion as the Soviet expert on reparations, stated that the Soviet authorities had reached a figure of twenty billion dollars for the total of reparations. Ten billion dollars' worth of property were to be removed at once and the other ten billions were to be paid in kind over the next ten years. The national wealth of Germany at the beginning of the war, Maisky declared, amounted to a hundred and twenty-five billion dollars. During the course of the war, the Soviet Union estimated, this national wealth would be reduced forty per cent, thus leaving Germany with a national wealth of seventy-five billion dollars. Their analysis of the national wealths of the more highly industrialized countries had revealed, Maisky observed, that the mobile wealth which could be transferred abroad amounted to approximately thirty per cent or, in the case of Germany, to twenty-two to twenty-three billion dollars.

The Soviet Union, therefore, Maisky said, proposed at the close of the war the removal of ten billion dollars of this mobile wealth. The remainder left to Germany would mean a standard of living comparable to what prevailed in central Europe. Although the standard of living of central Europe was lower than in Germany, it still was a decent standard, he remarked.

As to the reparations to be exacted each year for a ten-year period, the Soviet Union had estimated, Maisky declared, that the national income of Germany before the war amounted to thirty billion dollars annually. The war would lower this income to approximately eighteen or twenty billion. The Soviet Union, therefore, proposed that one billion dollars annually, for the ten-year period, be extracted. It was not a large sum, he remarked, and could be supported by Germany.

Eden stated that he would like to see in Item 1 of the Soviet document on "Basic Principles of Exaction of Reparations from Germany" some reference to the sacrifices undergone by the Allies. It had been said at the plenary session, Eden recalled, that the test for reparations should be not only the exertion of a country in the war, but also the sufferings a nation had endured at the hands of the enemy. On either basis, commented Eden, the Soviet Union would come out well. He added that he agreed in principle with Item 2 in the Soviet document, but wished to give a thorough study to the document before continuing any discussion of it.

Molotov replied that there would be no objection to adding to Item 1 the words suggested by the British Foreign Secretary.

I said that I, like Mr. Eden, wanted to give a thorough study to the Soviet document. Mr. Roosevelt had instructed me to make clear that the United States did not desire reparations except with respect to German foreign investments and perhaps raw materials. I suggested we report to that afternoon's plenary session that we had agreed on a reparations commission to be established in Moscow to give preliminary study to the whole question.

Molotov stated that whenever the British and American representatives were ready he would be prepared to continue the discussions. The amount of reparations desired by the United States and Great Britain was, of course, he said, entirely the concern of those countries. In view of their losses, however, the Soviet Government felt it only just to make mention in the reparations statement of compensation going to the United States and Great Britain. He said that he agreed with my suggestion that the foreign ministers report to the plenary session that they had agreed on a reparations commission to be established in Moscow and that the commission would start to work immediately.

In view of the fact that the United States had great misgivings on reparations in the form of labor, I asked whether the Soviet Union intended to raise the question of the use of German manpower at the Crimean Conference. Molotov replied that they needed to study the matter further and were not prepared to discuss it at the Conference. He agreed that it should be discussed by the reparations commission in Moscow.

Eden asked whether the reparations commission in Moscow should not also be authorized to study German industry in connection with the future security and control. Molotov maintained, however, that the commission should deal with German industry only in connection with reparations. The commission should keep security in mind, but this was not the basic task of the commission.

I recommended that the German Control Commission should have the responsibility for the control of German industry for security purposes. The reparations commission, however, should co-ordinate its work with the policy of the Control Commission. Molotov expressed agreement with my suggestion, and we then adjourned the foreign ministers' meeting just before the plenary session.

President Roosevelt opened the afternoon session that day by remarking that he wanted to emphasize again that he was less interested in tracing Polish frontier lines than he was in the problem of the Polish Government. He said that he did not attach importance to the continuity or legality of any Polish Government, since he felt that for some years there had been in reality no Polish Government. Before proceeding on the Polish question, however, he suggested that they hear the report on the meeting of the foreign ministers.

Since, as has already been stated, we followed the practice of rotating the chairmanship of the foreign ministers' meetings, Molotov, as chairman that day, submitted the following report:

DECISIONS ADOPTED AT THE MEETING OF THE THREE MINISTERS OF FOREIGN AFFAIRS, V. M. MOLOTOV, MR. STETTINIUS AND MR. EDEN.

February 7, 1945

1. Regarding the Dismemberment of Germany.

(a) A. Y. Vishinsky, Mr. Cadogan and Mr. Matthews were entrusted with the preparation of the final draft of Article 12 of the instrument "unconditional surrender of Germany" having in view the insertion in the text of Article 12 of the word "dismemberment."

(b) The study of the question of the procedure of the dismemberment of Germany was referred to a committee consisting of Mr. Eden, Mr. Winant and F. T. Gusev.

2. Regarding the Zone of Occupation in Germany for France.

(a) The allotment to France of a zone in Germany to be occupied by French occupational forces has been agreed upon.

(b) As regards the question of the participation of France in the Control Commission, V. M. Molotov and Mr. Stettinius feel [it] desirable to refer the question to the EAC. Mr. Eden considers it necessary to discuss this question now and give France a place on the Control Commission.

3. Regarding the Reparations to be Exacted from Germany.

(a) It was agreed that in the paragraph one of the Soviet proposals mention should be made of sacrifices borne.

(b) It was decided that the residence of the Reparations Committee should be in the City of Moscow. It was agreed

that the Committee should begin its work immediately upon the approval of the principles of the exacting of the reparations.

(c) It was decided that the discussion of the two documents relating to the matter of the reparations which have been submitted by V. M. Molotov, first, regarding the basic principles of exacting the reparations from Germany, and, second, regarding the organization of an Allied Reparations Committee, should be continued at the Crimean Conference.

Roosevelt and Churchill expressed their gratitude for our productive work. Churchill, however, said that he wished to study the English translation of Mr. Molotov's report although, except for one point, he thought that he would be in agreement.

The Prime Minister stated that the British Government was unconvinced by the argument that it would be possible to grant France a zone without participation in the Control Commission. The French would cause endless trouble if such a procedure were followed, he warned, and added that French participation in the Control Commission would be necessary to secure uniformity in the zones. He repeated his statement that French participation in the Control Commission would not give them any right to attend a conference such as the present one. It was obvious, he added, and he thought they would be right, that the French would accept no zone unless they were on the Control Commission.

It was useless to refer the question to the European Advisory Commission, the Prime Minister declared, since the EAC would reach a deadlock with the British and the French on one side and the Soviet Union and the United States on the other. The matter should be settled at Yalta although it still required further study.

"A STEP FORWARD"

When the President asked if it would not be better to postpone the problem for two or three weeks, Churchill answered that it would be difficult to settle the question after they all had left the Crimea.

Stalin observed that the three governments had been able to settle many things by correspondence. Furthermore, if the question were left to the European Advisory Commission, the French as a member of the EAC could express the attitude of France.

The Prime Minister replied that he believed he could anticipate what the French attitude would be. He repeated that he did not, at least for a while, want France to be included in the present "exclusive club." On the other hand, he felt that permitting France to join the Control Commission would satisfy the French for a while.

The President declared that he agreed that France should not join the Big Three at present, but he said that he was doubtful whether membership on the Control Commission would satisfy them. The President then suggested that they return to the Polish question.

Stalin said that he had received the President's letter, suggesting that they invite Poles to Yalta, and then had attempted to telephone the Lublin Poles to ascertain their views on the subject, but as yet had not reached them. Mr. Molotov was having the reply to the President's letter typed, added the Marshal, and until that was finished, he recommended they turn to the voting question in the Security Council.

Stalin stated that the Soviet delegation had carefully considered the voting formula and as a result of the clear explanation given the previous day, the Soviet Union was now happy to accept the entire American proposal, since they

Although the President suggested that the three leaders leave the problem of French participation in the German Control Commission to discuss the Polish question, he wrote the following note to make sure that he did not fail to raise the Control Commission question later at the Conference:

> Refer again to the French participation
> in the Allied Control Commission.

were now convinced that it fully guaranteed the unity of the Great Powers.[1] The Soviet announcement did not come to us as a complete surprise. Just before the plenary session convened that afternoon, the Prime Minister had come over and sat on the edge of a chair between the President and me and said to the President: "Uncle Joe will take Dumbarton Oaks."

---

[1] Other members of the American delegation recorded that Molotov made this statement, but my notes distinctly refer to the Marshal's having made it. This variation furnishes an excellent example of differences that may appear in the records of different people since we did not have official minutes approved by all delegations.

Molotov then raised the issue of the participation of the Soviet Republics as initial members in the Assembly of the world organization. The Soviet Government, Molotov declared, would not press for membership of all sixteen of the republics as it had requested at Dumbarton Oaks. This was the first announcement that the Soviet Union would not continue its demand for sixteen votes in the Assembly. We had made it abundantly clear that the United States would never participate in a world organization that had such a provision.

The Soviet Union, Molotov announced also for the first time, would be satisfied with the admission of three or at least two of the Soviet Republics as original members. The three were the Ukraine, White Russia, and Lithuania. The Soviet attitude, Molotov explained, was based on constitutional changes of February 1944, whereby, he said, the Soviet Republics had achieved control of their own foreign policy. Furthermore, not only were these three republics heavily populated, but, he said, they had borne the greatest sacrifices of the war, particularly the Ukraine. He hoped that Mr. Churchill and Mr. Roosevelt would accept the Soviet proposal.

When the President asked whether Mr. Molotov meant membership for these republics in the Assembly, Mr. Molotov replied, "Yes." He declared that the British dominions had gradually achieved important positions in international affairs, and he felt that it was only right that three, or at least two, of the Soviet Republics should be allowed to find a worthy place among the members of the Assembly.

The President expressed his pleasure at the Soviet agreement on the voting procedure, and said that he thought the people of the world would welcome this as "a step forward."

> *This is not so good.*

When Molotov asked that three or two of the Soviet Republics be admitted to membership in the Assembly, the President wrote and passed to me:

> This is not so good.

The next step, he thought, was to plan to call a conference to organize the world organization, and he suggested late March or sooner as the time for the conference.

As to the Soviet Union's request regarding the Soviet Republics, each of the Big Three was different in structure and tradition. The British system included large countries like Canada and Australia. The United States, on the other hand, had one language and one Foreign Minister, while the Soviet Union was still different in national structure. Molotov's proposal, he observed, had to be studied in the light of the possibility that if the larger nations were given more than one vote it might prejudice the theory of one vote for each member.

"A STEP FORWARD"

Roosevelt suggested, therefore, that the foreign ministers study the Soviet proposal and, at the same time, recommend a date and place for the conference to establish the world organization. The three ministers should also, he said, decide what nations should be invited.

Churchill then expressed his heartfelt thanks to Marshal Stalin and Mr. Molotov for the great step which would bring satisfaction and relief to the peoples of the world. The question of membership for the Soviet Republics, in this form, he pointed out, was before the Big Three for the first time. He agreed with the President that the United States and Great Britain were quite different in organization. The self-governing dominions had now taken their own place in world affairs and had worked for peace and for the furtherance of democratic processes. They had come into the war in 1939 on their own accord, although they knew full well Britain's vulnerability at that time.

Great Britain, of course, could not agree to any organization which would reduce the status of the dominions or exclude them from full participation. The Prime Minister added that he had great sympathy with the Soviet request. His heart, he declared, went out to mighty Russia, which, though bleeding, was beating down the tyrants in her path. He could clearly understand the Soviet point of view. After all, Russia was represented by only one vote in comparison with the British Commonwealth, which, with the exception of India, had a smaller population. He was happy that the President had been willing to consider the Soviet proposal for extra votes. He himself, however, could not exceed his authority and would like to discuss the proposal with the Foreign Secretary and possibly communicate with the War Cabinet before giving a precise answer.

The President remarked that all he had proposed was that the foreign ministers study the question as well as the time and place of the conference and the countries which should be invited.

The Prime Minister said he did not disagree with this suggestion, but that he felt that the foreign ministers had already had a great deal of work thrust upon them. He added that he foresaw great difficulties if the President pushed for the conference to be held in March. The war would be at its height, British domestic problems would be pressing, and as far as England was concerned, the War Cabinet, including Mr. Eden, would be fully occupied in Parliament. The turmoil of Europe and the world, too, might make it difficult to enlist the undivided attention of the foreign ministers of many countries for an early conference.

The President observed that he only had in mind a conference to arrive at the principles for a charter of an organization. The world organization itself would probably not be able to come into actual being for some three to six months afterward.

The Prime Minister replied that in the spring some nations would still be under the German yoke and would be represented, as a result, by governments in exile, whose authority was questionable. Other countries, like Holland, would be starving and in misery. Still other countries would be present which had not suffered at all in the war. He wondered how such a gathering could effectively undertake the immense task of creating the future organization to protect the peace and security of the world.

The President bluntly repeated his suggestion that the foreign ministers consider the Soviet membership proposal, the date and place of the conference, and the nations that

Stimson takes this same view.

√7/05

While the Prime Minister was objecting to an early date for the Conference to draft a charter of the world organization, I passed the following note to the President, advising him that Secretary of War Henry L. Stimson agreed with Churchill.

should be invited to attend. It was clear during this discussion at Yalta, as well as earlier, that it was the President's determination for the early establishment of the world organization that brought about a conference before the close of the war. Had the three countries waited until the close of the war to draft the Charter, it is doubtful, because of the rapid deterioration of Russian-American and Russian British relations, that the United Nations could have been formed.

Churchill finally said that he had no objection to the foreign ministers' discussing this matter, but he emphasized that this was not a technical question but a great political decision.

Stalin remarked that the foreign ministers would not make decisions but would merely report their suggestions back to the leaders.

After a short intermission the Prime Minister suggested that the foreign ministers should also consider the question of Iran and other matters of perhaps secondary importance. Both the President and the Marshal agreed.

At this point Harry Hopkins passed the following handwritten note to Roosevelt:

> Mr. President:
> When are you going to spring your T.V.A. for Europe?
> Harry

The President then said, in a joking fashion, that he had hoped that forestry would be one of the points considered, since he had not seen a tree in his visit last year to Teheran. He added that Iran was a good example of the type of economic problem that might confront the world if we were to bring about an expansion of world trade and the greater ex-

Mr President
    When are you going to spring your T. V. A. for Europe?

        Harry

2/7/45

change of goods. Persia, he said, did not have the purchasing power to buy foreign goods, and if expansion of world trade were to occur, measures must be considered for helping countries such as Persia. Before the advent of the Turks, he remarked, Persia had had plenty of timber and water, and her people had been reasonably prosperous. At the present time, however, he had never seen a poorer country than Persia. He hoped very much, therefore, that the new world organization would conduct a world-wide survey with a view to extending help to countries and areas that did not have sufficient purchasing power.

It was this kind of vision on the President's part that made it such a privilege for those of us who had a deep interest in improving the lot of the less fortunate to work with him. The President's conviction that less developed countries must be aided was in line with the thinking of some of us in the State Department which prompted our insistence over the months of planning that provision should be made in the United Nations Organization for an Economic and Social Council. On January 12, 1944, the President had sent Hull the following memorandum:

> Iran is definitely a very, very backward nation. It consists really of a series of tribes, and 99 per cent of the population is, in effect, in bondage to the other 1 per cent. The 99 per cent do not own their land and cannot keep their own production or convert it into money or property.
>
> I was rather thrilled with the idea of using Iran as an example of what we could do by an unselfish American policy. We could not take on a more difficult nation than Iran. I should like, however, to have a try at it. The real difficulty is to get the right kind of American experts who would be loyal to their ideals, not fight among themselves and be absolutely honest financially.

If we could get this policy started, it would become permanent if it succeeded as we hope during the first five or ten years. And incidentally, the whole experiment need cost the taxpayers of the United States very little money.[2]

The President then told the plenary session that there was a parallel in Europe where certain countries had adequate and cheap supplies of electric power from both water and coal, while countries fifty miles away had neither. This situation, he felt, was wrong. He observed that in the Soviet Union and its various republics, as well as in the United States, with the TVA, consideration had been given to the problems of a region as a whole. This statement was a good example of the President's technique of introducing an apparently irrelevant topic to ease tension. The subject was, of course, of vast importance to the President, but he invited no further discussion of it at that moment.

The plenary session then returned to the Polish question, and Molotov made the following proposal on behalf of the Soviet Union, which, in the Soviet delegation's own English translation, read:

1. It was agreed that the line of Curzon should be the Eastern frontier of Poland with a digression from it in some regions of 5–8 kilometers in favor of Poland.

2. It was decided that the Western frontier of Poland should be traced from the town of Stettin (Polish) and farther to the South along the River Oder and still farther along the River Neisse (Western).

3. It was deemed desirable to add to the Provisional Polish Government some democratic leaders from Polish émigré circles.

[2]*Hull, op. cit.*, Vol. II, p. 1507.

4. *It was regarded desirable that the enlarged Provisional Polish Government should be recognized by the Allied Governments.*

5. *It was deemed desirable that the Provisional Polish Government, enlarged as was mentioned above in paragraph 3, should as soon as possible call the population of Poland to the polls for organization by general voting of permanent organs of the Polish Government.*

6. *V. M. Molotov, Mr. Harriman and Sir Archibald Clark Kerr were entrusted with the discussion of the question of enlarging the Provisional Polish Government and submitting their proposals to the consideration of the three Governments.*

When Molotov had finished presenting these proposals he said that they had still been unable to secure a telephone connection with the Poles in Poland. As a result, it was apparent that time would not permit the summoning of Poles to the Crimea as the President had suggested. He added that he felt that his proposals went far toward meeting the President's wishes.

While Molotov was describing the Soviet proposal, Harry Hopkins scribbled and passed this note to the President: "Why not refer to foreign ministers for detailed discussion and report tomorrow or next day?"

The President, in replying to Molotov, said that progress was certainly being made. He did not like, however, the word "émigré." In any event, he would like to have an opportunity to study these proposals with Mr. Stettinius. Stalin expressed agreement with this request.

While this discussion was taking place I scribbled the following note to the President as a warning, since I thought things were moving too fast and too far: "Have we the au-

Have we the authority to deal with a boundary question of this kind [giving a guarantee]

I raised this question with the President, since under the Constitution he alone could not commit the United States to a boundary agreement. On February 10, at the plenary session, the President explained the problem involved and the wording on the boundary agreement was changed from "The three powers" to "The three heads of Government."

thority to deal with a boundary question of this kind, giving a guarantee?"

When the Prime Minister began to speak, the President scribbled back: "Now we are in for ½ hour of it."

The Prime Minister said that he shared the President's dislike of the word "émigré." The word had originated during the French Revolution and meant in England a person who had been driven out of a country by his own people. This was not true in the case of the Poles, he declared, who had left their country as a result of the brutal German attack. He therefore preferred in place of the word "émigré" to refer to them as "Poles temporarily abroad."

As to Item 2 in Mr. Molotov's proposal, the Prime Minister continued, he would always support the movement of Poland's frontier westward, since they should receive compensation. But they should not take more territory than they could handle, he insisted. "It would be a pity to stuff the Polish goose so full of German food that it gets indigestion," he declared.

Although he personally would not be shocked, he knew that many people in Great Britain would be if it were proposed to move large numbers of Germans. He felt that if removals were confined to East Prussia the problem could be handled, but the addition of the area west to the western Neisse would create a tremendous problem.

Stalin remarked that most Germans in those areas had already run away in the face of the advance of the Red Army. The Prime Minister replied that this, of course, simplified the problem. The fact that Germany had had six to seven million casualties and would probably have a million more before surrender would provide space in Germany for deported people.

Harry Hopkins' note to the President suggesting that the foreign ministers study the Soviet proposal on Poland. On the same sheet of paper Roosevelt, when Churchill began to speak on the Polish issue, wrote the second message to me.

He was not afraid, the Prime Minister repeated, of the problem of transferring populations provided that it was proportioned to the capacity of the Poles to handle it and to the capability of the Germans to receive the numbers. The whole question needed study, he added, not only in principle but as a practical matter. He also thought that some reference should be made in the Soviet proposal to other democratic leaders from within Poland itself. Stalin agreed to concede this point to the Prime Minister, and the words "and from inside Poland" were added to the end of Point 3 of the Soviet statement.

The Prime Minister concluded that he agreed with the President that it would be well to sleep on this problem and take it up tomorrow. He did feel, however, that some progress had been made. At the President's suggestion, this exhausting five-hour session was then adjourned until the following afternoon.

After the plenary session I dined with the President. It had been a most fruitful day, and we were all thoroughly gratified that we were now a step further along the difficult path to a world organization of nations. During that evening I had an opportunity of discussing privately with him the Russian request for two or three extra seats in the Assembly, the location of the world security conference, and the American delegation. I suggested that Senators Connally and Vandenberg and Representatives Bloom and Eaton should be on the American delegation. I also proposed the names of Dean Virginia C. Gildersleeve and Harold E. Stassen. I felt that we should have a woman member and also a liberal Republican from the Midwest.

The President's first reaction was that there should be a place on the delegation for Senator Warren Austin, who had been a staunch supporter of the Administration's foreign policy from the beginning. I, of course, agreed, but pointed out the importance of having the senior members of the Senate Foreign Relations Committee from both parties. Furthermore it was of the utmost importance, from the point of view of ultimate ratification by the Senate of the Charter of the world organization, to have Senator Vandenberg's full understanding and support from the beginning.

In reviewing the entire matter of additional seats for the Soviet Union, the President told me that evening at Yalta that Stalin felt his position in the Ukraine was difficult and insecure. A vote for the Ukraine was essential, the Marshal had declared, for Soviet unity. No one has been able to determine the extent of the Ukranian difficulty, but we in Washington, of course, had heard talk during the German advance that the Ukraine might leave the Soviet Union. The Marshal also felt that he would need the three votes to secure the acquiescence of his associates to Soviet participation in the world organization. The President had been indignant at the Soviet request at Dumbarton Oaks for votes for each of the sixteen republics. He had told me it would be just as logical for us to ask for forty-eight votes. However, he now told me that from the standpoint of geography and population he did not believe there was anything preposterous about the Russian proposal for two extra votes for the Ukraine and White Russia. Stalin during the plenary sessions had already declared that the Soviet Union did not consider it to be reasonable that a small country like Albania should speak with the same voice in the Assembly as one of the Great Powers.

Furthermore, the President knew that the British, although they had opposed sixteen votes, would not object to two extra votes for the Soviet Union. The British were in too embarrassing a situation from the standpoint of the make-up of the British Empire to oppose the Russian request. India was not self-governing—and Churchill had made it clear earlier that he did not favor Indian independence—and yet India was to have a vote.

As the President analyzed the question in my presence, he said that the most important thing was to maintain the unity of the three Great Powers, to defeat Germany, and then to get them all around a table to work out a world organization. There would be approximately fifty seats in the Assembly anyway, and after all, what practical difference would it make to the success or failure of the Assembly for the Soviet Union to have two additional seats to represent its vast population and territory? The actual power, said Roosevelt, would rest in the Security Council and each country in this body, large or small, would have only one vote.

CHAPTER 10

Planning the World Security Conference

February 8

The next morning I went to Dr. McIntire's room at Livadia Palace and said it was my desire, if Cordell Hull's health would permit it, that he be the head of the American delegation and chairman of the conference. "Mr. Hull is coming along nicely," Admiral McIntire said, "but if you put a burden of this kind on him, on which he would make a supreme effort, the task might break him." McIntire then told me that six weeks before Hull had expressed a desire to be present at the conference simply in the role of an adviser to the American delegation.

Shortly after this talk with McIntire, Harry Hopkins and I had a discussion in which he suggested that we should start to work immediately on the preparation of a communiqué about the coming world security conference. If we did not, he warned, the Prime Minister would sit up in bed some morning and dash it off himself. From past experience, Hopkins added, he knew it would be difficult to change it once it was on paper. I agreed and at Steve Early's suggestion instructed my staff to start work on a preliminary draft.

Later in the morning I drove to the British headquarters. The road was well paved, with many hairpin turns. It skirted the mountainsides on the edge of an awesome drop, down to the shore far below. There were many summer homes and villas, built for the tsarist aristocracy, along the way. The villas, many of which the retreating Germans had burned, had been built in a wide variety of architectural styles.

The British headquarters at Vorontsov Villa was a strange combination of Moorish, Gothic, and Scottish baronial architecture. It had a beautiful conservatory, formal gardens with boxwood hedges, fountains, and a large stone lion with one eye half open and the other shut.

The Germans had not stripped Vorontsov Villa the way they had Livadia Palace. Hitler had given it to one of his generals, and the general had left all the furnishings in order to occupy it himself after the war. The Germans had then retreated from the villa so fast that they had been unable to destroy it or even to loot it of its belongings.

Today it was Eden's turn to preside at the foreign ministers' meeting. After he opened the meeting I extended an official invitation of the United States Government to our great allies to hold the conference on world organization in the United States. I said that I hoped they were not shocked by the President's mention of March as the time for the conference. Although I was most anxious for a date no later than the latter part of April, I felt sure that the time could be arranged to fit the convenience of Mr. Eden and Mr. Molotov.

I recalled that at Dumbarton Oaks there had been considerable discussion of inviting the associated nations, that is, those who had broken relations with the Axis powers but had not declared war, as well as the United Nations, those that had declared war. I said I had now reached the conclusion that it would be most satisfactory to the United States to limit the invitations to those who had declared war on the common enemy and had signed the United Nations Declaration.

With respect to Molotov's proposal to admit two or three of the Soviet Republics, I stated that I was puzzled as to just how this membership could be arranged, since the Dumbarton Oaks proposals had specified that each sovereign state should have one vote. I stated that it was necessary for me to review the entire matter with the President again. In the light of my conversation with the President the night before, I did add, however, that the President had declared that the subject deserved sympathetic consideration.

Molotov replied that he had expressed his views the day before, and would like to hear Mr. Eden's reaction. Eden declared that he would be delighted to accept the invitation to hold the conference in the United States. He only wished to enter one suggestion. Mr. Winant, Mr. Gusev, and he were a little jealous at never having any large conferences in London. He hoped, therefore, there would be an early meeting of the foreign secretaries in London. Both Molotov and I readily assented to this request.

Eden said he preferred to postpone the opening of the conference until the second half of April. After some discussion I suggested, and it was agreed, that the conference should open on Wednesday, April 25, in the United States.

Eden then said that he was sympathetically inclined toward the Soviet proposal to include two or three of the Soviet Republics and would be ready to say so at whatever was considered the appropriate moment.

Molotov interjected the remark: the sooner the better. He

commented that, although the Dumbarton Oaks proposals provided only one vote for each government, Canada and Australia had individual votes. The fact that they were component parts of the British Empire did not prevent them from having individual memberships.

The Soviet Constitution, he added, had been amended to give the Soviet Republics the right to conduct foreign relations and in other ways to increase the rights of the constituent republics.

He then said that if only those nations which had declared war on Germany and had signed the United Nations Declaration were to be invited to the conference, certain questions naturally arose. Which Polish Government, for example, would be invited? Also certain countries which did not maintain diplomatic relations with the Soviet Union, as a result of our formula, would be invited. He added that he would like the opportunity to check the exact list of states which would be invited to attend the conference.

I then handed him a list of the countries which had signed the United Nations Declaration and I said I thought these nations should meet to prepare the charter, and that new members could be elected after the conference had convened.[1]

[1] The nations that adhered to the Declaration signed on January 1, 1942, were:

The United States of America
The United Kingdom of Great Britain and Northern Ireland
The Union of Soviet Socialist Republics

China	El Salvador	New Zealand
Australia	Greece	Nicaragua
Belgium	Guatemala	Norway
Canada	Haiti	Panama
Costa Rica	Honduras	Poland
Cuba	India	South Africa
Czechoslovakia	Luxembourg	Yugoslavia
Dominican Republic	Netherlands	

Eden suggested that a possible procedure would be for the United Nations to meet and draw up an agenda which would include the question of admitting the two Soviet Republics as original members. Molotov recommended an amendment to Eden's proposal to the effect that the three foreign secretaries agreed that it would be advisable to grant admission to the Assembly to two or three Soviet Republics.

I replied that I was favorably impressed with Mr. Eden's proposal and I desired to take the matter up with the President. Until I did, however, I wanted to make it clear that I could not make any firm commitment. I expected, however, I added, that the United States would be able to give a favorable reply before the end of the day. Although the President, the night before, had stated that he thought the Soviet request "was all right," I desired to reserve the United States' position at the foreign ministers' meeting until I had an opportunity to check again with the President in order to be certain that he had reached a definite conclusion on the matter. After we had decided to appoint a subcommittee to draft a report on this and other questions relative to the world security conference, we turned to the subject of Iran.

Eden recalled the Big Three pledge in the "Declaration of

The nations that adhered later to the Declaration, with the date of their notification of their adherence, were:

Mexico, June 5, 1942
Commonwealth of the Philippines, June 10, 1942
Ethiopia, July 28, 1942
Iraq, January 16, 1943
Brazil, February 8, 1943
Bolivia, April 27, 1943
Iran, September 10, 1943
Colombia, December 22, 1943
Liberia, February 26, 1944
France, December 26, 1944
Ecuador, February 7, 1945
Peru, February 11, 1945
Chile, February 12, 1945
Paraguay, February 12, 1945
Venezuela, February 16, 1945
Uruguay, February 23, 1945
Turkey, February 24, 1945
Egypt, February 27, 1945
Saudi Arabia, March 1, 1945

Iran" and he stated that, except for the privileges which Iran had granted to the Allies for the duration of the war, Iran should be master of its own house and free to make its own decisions. He urged that the Allies refrain from interfering in Iranian internal matters. It was no part of British policy, he declared, to prevent the Soviet Union from obtaining oil in northern Iran. The Soviet Union, he added, was a natural consumer for Iranian oil. He felt, however, that the Allies should not press for oil concessions until their troops had been withdrawn. He recommended therefore that they agree to an earlier withdrawal of troops than was provided for in the "Declaration of Iran." If such an agreement were reached, Eden observed, it would prove that the Allies were now prepared to carry out the Teheran Declaration.

Molotov declared that the question of oil concessions and the withdrawal of troops were two different matters. The question of the withdrawal of troops had never been placed before the Soviet Government until that moment, Molotov observed, and it would take some time to study the question.

In regard to oil concessions, he added, the Soviet Union had asked the Iranian Ambassador what the Iranian attitude would be to a request for concessions. When a favorable reply had been received, the Soviet Union had opened negotiations. Soon after that the Iranians had adopted the attitude that during the war there would be no concessions. Molotov observed, however, that he could see no reason why negotiations could not be reopened. No negotiations were being conducted at the moment, and, therefore, since the situation was not acute, he recommended that it be left alone to take its own course.

(When we arrived in London in January 1946 for the first

United Nations Assembly meeting, we were faced with the Iranian issue, and my mind went back to this discussion of the foreign ministers, in which Molotov had said that the situation was not acute.)

I pointed out that American oil companies had been carrying on negotiations for oil concessions but had now ceased their efforts. The United States, I declared, was content to leave the question of oil concessions until the end of the war.

The American troops stationed in Iran, I observed, were there to transport and guard Lend-Lease supplies from the Persian Gulf to the Soviet Union and for no other reason. We supported the British, I continued, in regard to an early withdrawal of all troops of all nations.

Both Eden and I agreed that our governments had no objection to Iran's granting oil concessions to the Soviet Union. Although the Allied treaty with Iran called for the withdrawal of troops no later than six months after the end of hostilities, Eden urged that the troops be withdrawn just as soon as the supply route was no longer necessary.

Molotov replied that he believed it might be advisable to limit the Iranian question to an exchange of views. He then offered to summon the Russian specialist on Iran to the Yalta Conference to make a report on the Iranian situation. Eden remarked that he would like to think this over, and added that he might have some new suggestions to make at another meeting. We adjourned at this point to prepare for the fifth plenary session that afternoon.

I had just a few minutes to talk to the President before Marshal Stalin arrived at Livadia Palace for a private discussion of military matters. I pointed out to the President that I had reserved the American position on extra votes for the Soviet Union at the foreign ministers' meeting until I could talk to him again and that, as a result, a subcommittee, consisting of Gladwyn Jebb, Gromyko, and Hiss, representing the three nations, was now at work preparing a report. I also stated that Eden had told Molotov that the British would support the Soviet request. The President thereupon commented to me that somehow we would now have to accept the proposal.

At this point the door to the President's study opened and Bohlen brought Stalin and Pavlov into the room. After the President had greeted the Marshal, I stated—before withdrawing from this conference and in order to bring my dicussion with the President to a close—that the foreign ministers had had a successful meeting and had reached agreements on . . . Before I could finish the sentence, however, the President interrupted me and said to the Marshal, "The foreign ministers have met and have reached agreement on today's agenda." The Marshal asked if they had agreed to the extra votes for the Soviet Union, and the President replied, "Yes."

The plenary session convened shortly after this statement. Hiss, our representative on the subcommittee, told me as the meeting was coming to order that he had just asked Eden for a copy of the report drafted by the subcommittee, which the British representative had agreed to have typed.[2] When Eden had somewhat reluctantly handed him a copy, Hiss noticed that it expressed American support for the extra votes, which had not been in the draft which he as American representative on the subcommittee had approved. He protested to Eden that the United States had not approved the extra votes, but Eden replied, "You don't know what has taken

[2] It was in the subcommittee that the British and Russian representatives had agreed to two rather than three extra votes for the Soviet Union.

place." It was obvious from Eden's remark that the President had had a private talk with the British after the subcommittee had adjourned and before the plenary session had convened.

In the military discussion between Stalin and Roosevelt that afternoon the President had requested that the United States Air Force be allowed to use certain airfields near Budapest for bombing operations against the Germans. At the present time, he pointed out, American planes based in Italy had to make a long and hazardous flight over the Alps to reach Germany. The President also asked that a group of American experts be permitted to make surveys of the effects of bombing, similar to one that had been made at Ploesti, in the areas recently liberated by the Red Army. Stalin immediately acceded to both these requests and said that he would give the necessary orders at once.

At the plenary session Eden was called upon to report on the foreign ministers' conference. He reported our agreement to recommend that the conference on world organization be convened on Wednesday, April 25, in the United States, and that the United Nations as they existed at the close of the Crimean Conference be the only states invited to the conference.

The world organization conference, he pointed out, would itself determine who should be the original members of the world organization. At this point the British and American delegates would support the request of the Soviet Union to admit as original members two of the Soviet Republics. It was later a great surprise to me, since we had merely agreed that we would support the Soviet request, to have Ambassador Gromyko back in Washington after Yalta make a great issue of having the two additional Soviet Republics invited for the opening meeting of the conference. I had serious trouble with Gromyko over this matter. The American and British position remained, however, as agreed at Yalta, that we would support the Russian request, but the entire question of the admittance of the two Soviet Republics as original members was to be decided by the conference itself.

The British delegation, Eden said as he concluded his report, did not think that it was right for other countries now to join the United Nations merely in order to participate in the conference, but he understood from consultation with the Secretary of State that the American delegation had other views. A subcommittee, he added, was considering this question.

Stalin remarked that there would be ten nations at the conference—in the list that had signed the United Nations Declaration—which had no diplomatic relations with the Soviet Union. He observed that it was somewhat strange for the Soviet Government to attempt to build future world security with nations which did not desire to maintain diplomatic relations with his country, and he asked what could be done about this situation.

The President replied that he knew most of these countries would like to establish diplomatic relations with the Soviet Union but just had not got around to it. There were a few nations where the influence of the Catholic Church was strong, and for this reason they had not established diplomatic relations. The President pointed out, on the other hand, that the Soviet Union had already sat down with these nations at conferences such as the Bretton Woods Conference to establish the World Bank and the International Monetary Fund, and the United Nations Relief and Rehabilitation Conference.

Stalin replied that this was correct, but the coming conference was to consider the very vital question of the establishment of world security.

The President then recalled that three years before, the State Department had advised some of the other American republics that it was not necessary to declare war on Germany but only necessary to break diplomatic relations. These countries, since they had followed the advice of the United States, felt that they were in good standing. Some of these republics, the President observed, had rendered great assistance in the war effort.

Speaking frankly, he added, our advice to the Latin American nations had been a mistake. Just a month ago, Mr. Stettinius had raised with him the entire question, and, as a result, the President said, he had sent letters to the presidents of six Latin-American countries urging them to declare war. Ecuador had done so just the day before, February 7, and he had reason to believe that others would do so promptly.

Stalin then asked Roosevelt about the status of Argentina. The President replied that we were talking about a conference of United and Associated Nations which had helped in the war effort.

Argentina, of course, was neither a United Nation nor an Associated Nation. All through the war we had been concerned over Axis activities in the Argentine. In July 1944 the State Department had informed the other American republics that we were determined not to recognize the Farrell regime, which had recently come to power through a revolution, until there were conclusive acts and demonstrations that there had been fundamental changes in Argentine policy toward the United Nations. Secretary Hull had hurled some of his strongest language at Argentina for having persisted in open and notorious aid to the Axis. Great Britain, however, because of its reliance on meat from the Argentine and its heavy investments there, had been reluctant to join the United States in strong action against Argentina.

Stalin told the President that he had no love for Argentina. He added that he felt there was a contradiction of logic in the whole matter of admitting nations. He wondered just what the criteria were for admission and raised the question of Turkey. There were some nations who had really waged war and had suffered, he said, and there were others who had wavered and speculated about being on the winning side.

The President replied that it was his idea that only those Associated Nations who declared war should be invited to the conference. He suggested that the time limit for this declaration be March 1, 1945. This was a decisive moment. President Roosevelt's frank appeal to the Prime Minister and the Marshal to help him out of the difficult situation caused by the Department's advice to the Latin-American Associated Nations persuaded the two men to accept March 1 as the deadline for a declaration of war by them. That night I sent a cable to Grew, asking him to have Assistant Secretary of State Nelson Rockefeller suggest to these countries that they take the necessary steps to declare war immediately. Peru, Chile, Paraguay, Venezuela, and Uruguay all declared war by February 23.

After Churchill and Stalin had agreed to the March 1 date, the Prime Minister observed that he sympathized with Marshal Stalin's statement that many countries had played a poor part in the war. He felt, however, that there would be some advantage to having a whole new group of nations declare war for the psychological effect of this on German morale.

The President observed that in addition to the South American countries there was Iceland, which was also an Associated Nation.

The Prime Minister said that in the case of Egypt that country had wished to declare war on two occasions but had been advised against it by the British Government. The British had felt, the Prime Minister continued, that it would be more useful to keep Egypt as a non-belligerent in order to save Cairo from systematic bombing. Egypt, however, had rendered a valuable service in such things as maintaining order and guarding bridges, and if Egypt now wished to declare war, it should have the opportunity. Iceland, too, he pointed out, had rendered a valuable service by permitting the entry of British and American forces, and this country should have the opportunity to declare war.

Stalin remarked that the opportunity to participate in the conference should not apply to former enemy states (I assume he meant countries like Italy) which had recently declared war on Germany. The Prime Minister and the President heartily agreed with this remark.

The Prime Minister said he certainly did not include Eire among the possible candidates for the conference, since that country still had German and Japanese missions there. Turkey, too, he knew, would not receive universal approbation. Turkey, however, had made an alliance with Great Britain at a difficult moment, and its attitude had been generally friendly and helpful.

When Stalin stated that he would agree to Turkey's being invited provided the Turks declared war before the end of February, Churchill expressed his pleasure with the Soviet attitude. Turkey and Egypt as it turned out signed the United Nations Declaration by March 1, and thus were invited to send delegations to the conference.[3]

The President then referred to Denmark, whose king had been a virtual prisoner ever since the German invasion. When Stalin observed that Denmark should wait, both Roosevelt and Churchill agreed, but they stated that once Denmark was liberated the Danes should be invited to join the organization.

Molotov asked if it would not facilitate the admission of the Ukrainian and the Byelorussian (White Russian) republics as members of the Assembly if they signed the United Nations Declaration before the first of March. Churchill observed that it did not seem quite right to him to allow small countries, which had done so little, to attend the conference by the expedient of their declaring war, and to exclude the two Soviet Republics.

Marshal Stalin agreed that it was illogical, and questioned whether, although the three powers had agreed to recommend the Ukraine and White Russia as members of the Assembly, the fact that they had not signed the United Nations Declaration by March 1 might not furnish an excuse for excluding them from the conference. Both the President and the Prime Minister again assured Stalin that they would support the request of the Soviet delegation at the conference.

The Prime Minister again emphasized that he had preferred confining the conference to the present United Nations but, if others were to be added, he thought the two Soviet Republics also should be added. Stalin declared that

[3]Saudi Arabia did not sign until April 12, but was at war with Germany effective March 1 and therefore was also invited to attend the conference.

he did not want to embarrass the President on this point. If the President would explain his difficulties, the Marshal added, he would see what could be done.

The President replied that it was a technical question but an important one. Up to that moment they had been discussing invitations to separate countries, but now it was not a question of a country but of granting one of the Great Powers three votes instead of one in the Assembly. This was a matter, he said, which should be put before the conference. "We have already agreed," he added, "to support this request at the conference." There had been no briefing of the President by the State Department on this particular question. Throughout this give-and-take, his mind functioned with clarity and conciseness, furnishing excellent proof that he was alert and in full command of his faculties.

Stalin then inquired again whether Ukrainian and Byelorussian signatures to the United Nations Declaration would not be advisable. The President replied that it would not be advisable and the Marshal withdrew his suggestion.

After this discussion the question of the world security organization and the approaching conference required very little of the time of the Crimean Conference. It is, however, of interest to describe how San Francisco was selected at Yalta as the location of the conference.

For months the State Department had surveyed possible locations and had discussed the advantages and disadvantages of many cities. The requirement was a city that could accommodate four to five thousand delegates, advisers, secretariat, and correspondents, with ample auditoriums and conference rooms, and with radio, cable, rail, and airfield facilities. We discussed the possibility of Atlantic City, New York, Philadelphia, Chicago, Cincinnati, Miami, French

Lick, Hot Springs (Virginia), Pinehurst, and other centers.

For various reasons, either because of the time of year or the lack of hotel facilities and auditoriums, or war congestion, or for questions of security, none of these places quite satisfied Roosevelt. In a final conversation that I had with him on the subject that day, as he lay in bed at the Livadia Palace, he said, "Go back to work, Ed, and come up with a better suggestion, as we haven't hit it yet." I went to bed that night perplexed.

I suddenly wakened at about three o'clock in the morning with a clear picture in my mind of San Francisco playing host to the United Nations. My mind raced with enthusiasm and freshness. I saw Nob Hill, the Opera House, the Veterans Building, the Pacific Union Club, the Mark Hopkins, the Fairmont and the St. Francis Hotel, each filling its purpose. I saw the golden sunshine, and as I lay there on the shores of the Black Sea in the Crimea, I could almost feel the fresh and invigorating air from the Pacific.

I went back to sleep and arose in the morning feeling that a solution to a great dilemma had been found. My mind was clear that the Pacific coast of the United States was the place to convene this historic conference and that San Francisco was the city; that it was directly accessible by air and water to the Latin-American countries and to the Philippines, China, New Zealand, Australia, and other countries across the Pacific; that the Nazis were soon to fall and it would be a striking reminder to the world that Japan was still to be conquered; that emphasis would be placed on the fact that aggression had been only half stamped out by the crushing of Nazi Germany.

I also thought it would be helpful from the standpoint of the whole concept of the United Nations to have the repre-

PLANNING WORLD SECURITY CONFERENCE

sentatives of various countries of the world travel through the United States and see for themselves its magnificence, greatness, and power. I recall now, for instance, Molotov's remark after he had been across San Francisco Bay to visit shipyards that he was at last beginning to understand the greatness of America.

I knew, as I thought of the wisdom of holding the conference in California, that Roosevelt always believed that the Assembly should meet in a different country from time to time so that during the course of fifteen years, for instance, all the delegates would have seen most of the world.

Early that morning I went to see General Marshall to tell him that I would like to propose San Francisco as the site of the meeting. Before doing so I wished to obtain his reaction because of the importance of Army and Navy operations in the San Francisco area at that particular time. Marshall discussed the matter and said he felt that, while San Francisco was terribly congested, there was no place in the United States that was not, and that from the standpoint of facilities this would be a splendid choice. I had a similar conversation with Admiral King, who pledged full co-operation on the part of the Navy.

I tried to find in my mind the reason why San Francisco had come to me so clearly in the middle of the night. I thought back to one of the meetings that Molotov, Eden, and I had had a day or so before when various locations were being discussed and of my analysis of the various sections of the United States where we could hold the meeting. Eden had privately whispered to me that he had never seen California, and my mind had been thus directed toward the West Coast.

After obtaining the assurances of Marshall and King, I

waited my opportunity to talk privately with the President. I soon saw him in his bedroom in Livadia Palace. I outlined briefly the requirements from the standpoint of hotels, auditoriums, and transportation. I advised him that I had discussed it with Marshall and King and he said, "It sounds most interesting, Ed, but we have called off all unnecessary movements of people, conventions, and so forth. What about transporting these people two or three thousand miles unnecessarily?"

He asked me to discuss this question with Jimmy Byrnes, who as director of the Office of War Mobilization issued all transportation orders. Byrnes advised me that this historic conference was one of world importance at the moment and that, no matter where it was held, it would involve movements of people, and he felt it would be understood and would not cause criticism if the conference were in San Francisco. I reported this to Roosevelt, who immediately said, "Well, that's encouraging. I am beginning to see your picture clearly."

The following night, February 10, Stalin, Molotov, Roosevelt, and I were dining with Churchill at the British headquarters. For some reason or other Molotov had the location of the conference very much on his mind.

As we were having vodka and caviar before going to dinner, Molotov edged up to me and asked, "We have agreed upon the date. Can you not tell us where the conference is to be held?" I crossed the room and leaned down to Roosevelt, who was still in his little portable wheel chair that we carried in the automobile for him, and said, "Molotov is pressing me on a decision as to a place for the conference. Are you ready to say San Francisco?" The President said, "Go ahead, Ed; San Francisco it is."

I went back to Molotov and told him that Mr. Roosevelt had just approved the selection of San Francisco. Molotov beckoned to Eden, and as we stood in front of an open fire in the presence of Roosevelt, Churchill, and Stalin, we drank vodka in the Crimea to the success of the San Francisco Conference, to open on April 25, just eleven weeks later.

When I reached Moscow on February 12, for a two-day visit immediately after the Yalta Conference, I cabled my old friend, Mayor Roger Lapham of San Francisco: "California, Here We Come."

CHAPTER 11

"The Glories of Future Possibilities Stretching Before Us"

February 8

After the plenary session of February 8 had completed its discussion of various aspects of the approaching world security conference, the three leaders turned their attention once more to the difficult problem of Poland. That morning Roosevelt had sent the following proposal to both Stalin and Churchill:

> . . . Counter proposals circulated by the United States Delegation to the Soviet and British Delegations of February 8, 1945.
>
> The proposals submitted by Mr. Molotov in regard to the Polish question in reply to the President's letter to Marshal Stalin dated February 6, 1945, have been given careful study.
> In regard to the frontier question, no objection is perceived to point One of the Soviet proposals, namely, that the Eastern boundary of Poland should be the Curzon line with modifications in favor of Poland in some areas of from five to eight kilometers.

In regard to point Two, while agreeing that compensation should be given to Poland at the expense of Germany, including that portion of East Prussia south of the Koenigsberg line, Upper Silesia, and up to the line of the Oder, there would appear to be little justification to the extension of the western boundary of Poland up to the Western Neisse River.

In regard to the proposals of the Soviet Government concerning the future Government of Poland, it is proposed that Mr. Molotov, Mr. Harriman and Sir Archibald Clark Kerr be authorized on behalf of the three Governments to invite to Moscow Mr. Bierut, Mr. Osubka-Morawski, Archbishop Sapieha, Mr. Vincente Witos, Mr. Mikolajczyk and Mr. Grabski to form a Polish Government of National Unity along the following lines:

1. There will be formed a Presidential Committee of three, possibly consisting of Mr. Bierut, Mr. Grabski and Archbishop Sapieha, to represent the Presidential office of the Polish Republic.

2. This Presidential Committee will undertake the formation of a government consisting of representative leaders from the present Polish provisional government in Warsaw, from other democratic elements inside Poland, and from Polish democratic leaders abroad.

3. This interim government, when formed, will pledge itself to the holding of free elections in Poland as soon as conditions permit for a constituent assembly to establish a new Polish constitution under which a permanent Government would be elected.

4. When a Polish Government of National Unity is formed, the three Governments will then proceed to accord it recognition as the Provisional Government of Poland.

Molotov asked whether the last point of the President's proposal meant that, after recognition of a Government of National Unity, the London Government would disappear.

"THE GLORIES OF FUTURE POSSIBILITIES"

Churchill replied that when the British recognized the new government recognition would be withdrawn from the London Government.

When Stalin asked what would happen to the property and resources of the London Government, after the new government had been recognized, the President replied that he believed the property would go to the new government.

After a brief recess the Prime Minister submitted a British proposal for Poland. It included the following items:

(1) *The Curzon Line, with some slight adjustments, would be the eastern frontier of Poland.*

(2) *Poland in the west would include Danzig, the regions of East Prussia west and south of Königsberg, the district of Oppeln in Silesia and the lands desired by Poland to the east of the Oder. All Germans in these regions were to be repatriated to Germany and all Poles in Germany, if they wished, would be repatriated to Poland.*

(3) *A fully representative provisional Polish Government should be established based upon all the democratic and anti-Fascist forces in Poland and including democratic leaders from abroad.*

(4) *Representative Polish leaders should consult together on the composition of this provisional government and V. M. Molotov, Mr. Harriman, and Sir Archibald Clark Kerr (later Lord Inverchapel, British Ambassador to Washington) should talk with these leaders and submit their proposals to the consideration of the three governments.*

(5) *As soon as possible, the provisional Polish Government, thus established, would hold free and unfettered elections on the basis of universal suffrage and a secret ballot.*

All democratic parties should have the right to participate and run candidates.

The Prime Minister added that with some slight amendments, however, he was willing to accept the President's proposals.

Molotov insisted that it was impossible to ignore, as these two proposals did, the existence of the present government in Poland. The Soviets therefore felt that they should discuss enlarging that government by the addition of other democratic elements from within Poland and abroad.

The Lublin Government, he asserted, enjoyed immense prestige and popularity in Poland. The Poles themselves would never agree to anything that would greatly change the provisional government. The leaders of the Lublin Government had been closely connected with the liberation of Poland, whereas Mr. Mikolajczyk, Mr. Grabski, and Mr. Witos had not. If we wished to achieve a practical result, he insisted, the only step was to enlarge the present government. All three countries agreed, Molotov pointed out, on the holding of free elections. In regard to the Polish frontiers, Molotov expressed his pleasure with the complete agreement on the eastern boundary. He stated, however, that he knew the Polish Provisional Government wanted the western frontier as outlined in the Soviet proposal.

Molotov agreed that it would be desirable for the Poles to meet with Harriman, Kerr, and himself in Moscow. Instead of creating a presidential council, he said he thought it would be a good idea to invite three members of the Lublin Government and two from the list the President had submitted yesterday to form an interim government. He was not at all sure, however, about inviting Mikolajczyk. He and

Mr. Harriman and Sir Archibald could discuss with the Poles the question of enlarging the provisional government, and the results of these discussions could then be submitted to their respective governments.

While Molotov was speaking I scribbled the following note to the President: "Mr. President: Not to *enlarge* Lublin but to form a *new* Gov. of some kind."

The Prime Minister declared that we now had reached the crucial point of this great Conference. If we separated still recognizing different Polish Governments, the world would find us wanting. It would be interpreted as a breach between Great Britain and the United States on the one hand and the Soviet Union on the other, with lamentable consequences for the future.

According to the information of the British, the Lublin Government, Churchill charged, did not have the support of the overwhelming mass of the Polish people. There would be an angry outcry in Great Britain, furthermore, if the British Government simply brushed the London Poles aside. Churchill then reminded the Conference of the army of 150,000 Poles who were fighting bravely against the enemy in Italy. If the British Government transferred its support to the Lublin Government it would be regarded by this army as an act of betrayal of Poland.

The Prime Minister added that it would be said anyway that the British Government had given way completely to the Soviet Union on the question of the frontiers. After that, to break altogether with the lawful government of Poland, which had been recognized during all these years of war, would be an act that would bring the most severe criticism at home. Great Britain would be accused of forsaking the cause of Poland, and the debates in Parliament, he warned, would be most painful and most dangerous to continued Allied unity.

If they were to abandon the London Government, he declared, it must be clear that a new start had been made on both sides on equal terms. Before His Majesty's Government would transfer recognition, Churchill warned, it would have to be convinced that a new government, representative of the Polish people, had been created and was pledged to an election based on a secret ballot and universal suffrage with all democratic parties having the right to nominate their candidates. When such elections were held, Great Britain would disregard the London Government and salute the new government. It was frightfully important, concluded Churchill, that the three governments represented there reach a signed agreement on Poland before the Crimean Conference adjourned.

The President said that since all three nations present had agreed on the necessity of free elections, the problem was how Poland was to be governed from now until these elections were held.

Stalin observed that Mr. Churchill had complained that he had no information from within Poland. He could assure the meeting that the leaders of the provisional government were extremely popular. These leaders had not fled Poland but had stayed on and emerged through the underground. The people's sympathies were with the leaders who stayed, the Marshal emphasized, not with those who had fled. The Poles, he declared, were surprised that the London Poles had not participated in the liberation of Poland.

A second fact to remember, he said, was that Poland was liberated by the Red Army. The Poles, in the past, had hated Russia, and with reason, in view of the tsarist participation

Mr. President:

Not to enlarge — Lublin but to form a new Gov. of some kind

The note I passed to the President insisting that we not approve just enlarging the Lublin Government.

in the partitions of Poland. With the advance of the Red Army, however, old resentments were disappearing and good will toward Russia was emerging. Mr. Churchill, Stalin added, was worried that we would leave the Conference without an agreement. Since they had different information about Poland, he suggested that they summon Poles from the different groups and talk face to face with each.

He again emphasized that he could see little difference between the position of De Gaulle and the Polish Provisional Government. Neither had been elected, and yet all three powers had dealt with De Gaulle. Why could we not deal with an enlarged Polish Government? Stalin asked. It would be much better, he insisted, to enlarge the provisional government than to try to establish a new one. It would, of course, be better, he added, if free elections could be held immediately, but up to now the war had prevented this.

The President then asked the Marshal how long it would be before elections could be held in Poland. It might be possible in a month, Stalin answered, provided there were no military reversals. The President then proposed, and it was agreed, that the entire Polish matter be referred to the foreign ministers for further study.

The Prime Minister next proposed that the foreign ministers should meet every three months. After a brief discussion all three leaders agreed not only with this proposal but also with Churchill's desire that the first meeting be held in London. Eden had previously proposed this to me in an informal way and had stated that he was going to urge it upon the Conference. This suggestion of Eden's was the origin of the Council of Foreign Ministers.

At this point Stalin said that he now would like to ask

"THE GLORIES OF FUTURE POSSIBILITIES"

what was holding back the formation of a unified government in Yugoslavia. He would also like to know what was going on in Greece. He was not criticizing the British in Greece, he declared, but merely seeking for information.

Just before the Yalta Conference the British and the Russians had brought the London Yugoslavs and Marshal Tito's Partisans together to form an interim government. Under the new regime Tito was to be Premier and Dr. Ivan Subasitch, of the London Government, was to be Foreign Minister. The agreement signed by Tito and Subasitch also provided for the holding of free and unfettered elections and for the establishment of a government truly representative of the people. Tito was willing to have a regency in place of King Peter, but insisted that the King must not appoint the regents. In a message from Ambassador Winant several weeks prior to Yalta, we had been informed that Mr. Churchill had told King Peter: "The three Great Powers will not lift one finger nor sacrifice one man to put any king back on any throne in Europe." This was an amazing statement in view of Churchill's favorable attitude toward the Italian and Greek monarchies.

The Prime Minister, in his reply to Stalin's question about Yugoslavia, said that King Peter had been persuaded, or even forced, to agree to a regency. Dr. Subasitch was leaving London soon, if he had not already left, for Yugoslavia to appoint the regents and form a government. Churchill observed that Mr. Eden had told him that there were two slight amendments, which Mr. Eden would discuss with Mr. Molotov, to the agreement reached between Dr. Subasitch and Marshal Tito. In regard to the two amendments, if Marshal Stalin said two words to Marshal Tito, Churchill remarked, the matter would be settled.

Stalin replied that Tito was a proud man, and now that he was a popular head of a regime he might resent advice. The Prime Minister answered that he felt that Marshal Stalin could risk this. Stalin observed that he was not afraid to advise Tito.

The Prime Minister then turned to Greece and said that he was hopeful that peace would come. It was doubtful, however, that a government of all parties could be established, since they hated each other too much. Stalin observed that, since the Greeks had not yet become accustomed to discussion, they were following the practice of cutting each other's throats.

The Prime Minister concluded his remarks on Greece by saying that five British trade union leaders had recently visited Greece and had had a difficult time. They were very much obliged to Marshal Stalin, the Prime Minister stated, for not having taken too great an interest in Greek affairs. Stalin repeated that he had no intention of criticizing British actions in Greece, nor, he added, did he have any intention of interfering in that country.

With this remark of Stalin's, the plenary session adjourned to the Russian headquarters at Koreis Villa, where the Russians held a formal dinner for the Conference. Present at the dinner, which included twenty courses, forty-five toasts, and lasted until after midnight were:

THE UNITED STATES	GREAT BRITAIN	THE SOVIET UNION
The President	*The Prime Minister*	*Marshal Stalin*
Mr. Stettinius	*Mr. Eden*	*Mr. Molotov*
Admiral Leahy	*Field Marshal Sir Alan Brooke*	*Mr. Vishinsky*
Justice Byrnes	*Chief Air Marshal Sir Charles Portal*	*Mr. Beria*

"THE GLORIES OF FUTURE POSSIBILITIES"

THE UNITED STATES	GREAT BRITAIN	THE SOVIET UNION
Mr. Harriman	Admiral of the Fleet Sir A. B. Cunningham	Admiral Kuznetsov
Mr. Flynn	Sir Alexander Cadogan	General Antonov
Mrs. Boettiger	Field Marshal Alexander	Air Marshal Khudiakov
Miss Kathleen Harriman	Sir Archibald Clark Kerr	Ambassador Gromyko
Mr. Bohlen	General Sir Hastings Ismay	Ambassador Gusev
	Mrs. Oliver	Mr. Maisky
		Mr. Pavlov

It is interesting to compare the American with the other two delegations. Such military figures as General Marshall and Admiral King were excluded from the dinner, while their counterparts were included in the other two delegations. I greatly resented the fact that those members of the White House staff who had prepared the list of the Americans to be invited had not included Marshall and King. Whatever their reaction, however, these two great men never made known their private feelings over their being excluded.

The atmosphere of the dinner was most cordial, and it proved to be the most important dinner of the Conference. Stalin was in excellent humor and even in high spirits. He offered a toast to the health of the Prime Minister, whom he characterized as the bravest governmental figure in the world. Great Britain, he declared, as a result of Mr. Churchill's courage and staunchness, had fought off Hitlerite Germany when the rest of Europe was falling flat on its face before Hitler. The Marshal concluded by saying that he knew few examples in history where the courage of one man had been so important to the future history of the world.

The Prime Minister replied by toasting Marshal Stalin as the mighty leader of a mighty country which had taken the full shock of the German war machine, had broken its back, and then had driven the tyrants from its soil. He knew that in peace no less than in war, Churchill added, Marshal Stalin would continue to lead his people from success to success.

Stalin next proposed a toast to the health of the President of the United States. He and Mr. Churchill, the Marshal declared, had had relatively simple decisions to make in the war. They had been fighting for their very existence. There was a third man, however, whose country had not been seriously threatened with invasion, but who had perhaps a broader conception of national interests and, even though his country was not directly imperiled, had been the chief forger of the instruments which had led to the mobilization of the world against Hitler. Stalin particularly emphasized Lend-Lease as one of the President's most remarkable and vital achievements in the formation of the anti-Hitler combination.

The President replied to this toast by observing that the atmosphere at the dinner was that of a family, and it was in this way that he liked to characterize the relations among the three countries. Great changes had occurred in the world during the past three years, he noted, and even greater changes were to come. Fifty years ago there were vast areas in the world where people had little opportunity. Although there were still great areas where people had little hope and opportunity, the President remarked, it was their objective here in the Crimea to give to every man, woman, and child on the earth the possibility of security and well-being.

"THE GLORIES OF FUTURE POSSIBILITIES"

Stalin remarked, in a later toast to the alliance among the three powers, that it was not so difficult to keep unity in time of war, since there was the joint aim, clear to everyone, of defeating the common enemy. The difficult task, he warned, would come after the war, when diverse interests would tend to divide the Allies. He was confident, however, that the present alliance would meet this test and that the peacetime relations of the three Great Powers would be as strong as they had been in wartime.

At one point Stalin teased Gusev for always being glum and serious and for never cracking a smile. Stalin carried his jesting almost to the point of extreme ridicule. While the Marshal was plaguing Gusev, I had the opportunity, for the first time at Yalta, to observe L. P. Beria, Commissar of State Security. As the head of the Secret Police (then the NKVD), he was at Yalta for security reasons. I had been informed that he was one of the strong men in the Politburo, and he impressed me that evening as being hard, forceful, and extremely alert.

There were many, many toasts during the evening by practically everyone present. I was immensely impressed, while Churchill was speaking, with the way his attitude had changed on the future of the world. At Malta he had been extremely discouraged and distressed, but in his toasts this evening at Yalta he manifested real hope that there could be a world of happiness, peace, and security.

The dinner party broke up shortly after the Prime Minister had delivered an inspired toast in his incomparable language. We were all standing on the crest of a hill, he said, with the glories of future possibilities stretching before us. In the modern world, he declared, the function of leadership was to lead the people out from the forests into the

221

broad sunlit plains of peace and happiness. This prize, he went on, was nearer our grasp than at any time before in history, and it would be a tragedy for which history would never forgive us if we let this prize slip from our grasp through inertia or carelessness.

CHAPTER 12

The Sixth Day of the Conference

February 9

At the foreign ministers' meeting on February 9, as the presiding officer of the day, I opened the discussion by remarking that I had had a private conference that morning with the President. He had instructed me, I told Molotov and Eden, to explain at the foreign ministers' meeting that one extremely important aspect of the Polish issue had not been sufficiently discussed.

I pointed out that there had been a great debate in the United States over the question of American participation in a world organization for peace and security. The issue of Poland, I declared, was having a tremendous impact on American public opinion, and unless the Polish question was settled in a satisfactory fashion, I warned that it might jeopardize America's participation in a world organization. It was therefore of great and continuing importance, from the standpoint of influencing American participation in the world organization, that the Polish question be settled at the Crimean Conference.

I then said:

"After further consideration, I agree with Mr. Molotov's statement that the question of the creation of a presidential committee should be dropped and am therefore prepared to withdraw our suggestion on that point.

"I believe that, with this change, our three positions are not far apart on the substance of the governmental question. Mr. Molotov spoke of the reorganization of the Polish Government. The British formula suggests the establishment of a fully representative 'Provisional Polish Government' and we speak of the formation of a 'Government of National Unity.' All three agree that only the Poles themselves can definitely decide this. All three agree that this government should be composed of members of the present Polish Provisional Government and in addition representatives of other democratic elements inside Poland and some Polish democratic leaders from abroad.

"The following formula might therefore be considered," I continued:

> "That the present Polish Provisional Government be reorganized into a fully representative government based on all democratic forces in Poland and including democratic leaders from Poland abroad, to be termed 'The Provisional Government of National Unity'; Mr. Molotov, Mr. Harriman and Sir Archibald Clark Kerr to be authorized to consult in the first instance in Moscow with members of the present Provisional Government and other democratic leaders from within Poland and from abroad with a view to the reorganization of the present government along the above lines. This 'Government of National Unity' would be pledged to the holding of free and unfettered elections as soon as practicable on the basis of

THE SIXTH DAY OF THE CONFERENCE

universal suffrage and secret ballot in which all democratic parties would have the right to participate and to put forward candidates.

"*When a 'Polish Government of National Unity' is satisfactorily formed, the three Governments will then proceed to accord it recognition. The Ambassadors of the three powers in Warsaw following such recognition would be charged with the responsibility of observing and reporting to their respective Governments on the carrying out of the pledge in regard to free and unfettered elections.*"

Molotov remarked that he would like to obtain a copy of this statement in the Russian language, as he did not feel prepared to reply to an oral statement.

Eden said that he must frankly tell Mr. Molotov and me of his difficulties on the Polish question. Many people felt that the Poles had been treated harshly by Great Britain's readiness to acquiesce on a frontier along the Curzon Line. He himself had been troubled for some time, he added, that Poland might become a source of difficulty between the Soviet Government and the British.

He might be wrong, he declared, but he thought it was a fact that hardly anyone in Great Britain believed that the Lublin Government was representative of Poland. He thought, too, that this view was widely held in the rest of Europe and in the United States. It was for that reason that the document which he had put forth yesterday had avoided all mention of *adding* to the Lublin Government and had stressed that a *new start* was necessary.

If an agreement were reached at Yalta, he remarked, this would mean transfer of recognition from the London Government to the new government. It would be much easier for the British Government to abandon the London Government if it were made in favor of a new government rather than the existing Lublin Government. Eden also pointed out that the British wanted to include the Polish Army of 150,000 in any settlement. If a fresh start were made on the governmental situation, this task would be made easier.

It had been said, Eden observed, that there was considerable opposition in the Lublin Government to Mikolajczyk. Although he was not convinced of this, in any case the presence of Mikolajczyk in a Polish Government would do more than anything else to add to the authority of that government and to convince the British people of its representative nature.

Molotov told Eden that, while the American document was being translated, he would like to make some comments. Although he could go no further than Marshal Stalin's remarks of yesterday, he recalled that the President had stated that the Polish situation was temporary. From the standpoint of Russian opinion, the most important question was the holding of general elections in Poland as soon as was practicable. These elections would create a permanent government and do away with the present difficulty facing the Allies—that of forming an interim government.

Marshal Stalin, he observed, had referred to the provisional period as lasting possibly one month, while the Prime Minister had mentioned two months. At the present time, however, even though it would be a short interval, it was a question not only of Poland but also of the rear of the Red Army. Even for a short time, therefore, Molotov insisted, it was essential for the three Great Powers to keep this military situation in mind. An impossible situation would result if difficulties arose in the rear of the Red Army. That was why he had recommended yesterday that the reorganization of the Polish Government should be on the basis of the present

THE SIXTH DAY OF THE CONFERENCE

Lublin Government with democratic elements added to it from within and without the country.

It might be a mistake, Molotov added, to say that Mikolajczyk would be unacceptable. The Poles themselves must decide this. Neither the question of Mikolajczyk nor the reorganization of the Polish Government could be cleared up in the Crimea without consulting the Poles. The Moscow Commission, consisting of the American and British ambassadors and himself, would have to discuss this with the Poles and make clear to them the principles reached in the Crimea.

Eden quickly agreed with Molotov on the importance of the Polish elections. The British people, however, would feel that if the elections were controlled by the Lublin Government they would not be free elections truly representing the will of the Polish people. I observed that I was in complete agreement in this respect with Mr. Eden's views.

After a brief pause at this point for Molotov to read the translation of the American proposal, he stated that he would be unable to give a final answer to it until he had consulted with Marshal Stalin. He would like, however, to make a few preliminary comments.

It would be inadvisable to place too much emphasis on any formula for a Polish Government before consulting the Poles. He still believed, he declared, that the new Polish Government should be created on the basis of the Lublin Government. It might be better, furthermore, to leave out the last point about the Allied ambassadors in Warsaw observing and reporting on the elections, since this reference might offend the Poles by its implication that the Poles were under the control of foreign diplomatic representatives. The ambassadors, nevertheless, would observe and report, which was their duty as ambassadors.

Eden stated that the three Allied governments were agreed that a new situation would be created by the complete liberation of Poland by the Red Army. This event, he pointed out, would call for the establishment of a fully representative provisional Polish Government which could be more broadly representative than had been possible before the liberation of Poland. The government should be comprised, he declared, of members of the Lublin Government and other democratic leaders in Poland and abroad. He added that he felt this government should be called the Provisional Government of National Unity.

Molotov, however, continued to advocate the forming of the new government on the basis of the Lublin Government. It would, of course, include other representatives from Poland and from outside the country.

I maintained that it would be preferable to start with an entirely new government and observed that unless the foreign ministers could get away from the words "existing Polish Government," no agreement could be reached. I suggested that Mr. Molotov give consideration to a formula which would state that the Polish Government should be based upon the old *and also* on the democratic leaders who would be brought into it.

Molotov insisted that it was extremely difficult to deal with the Poles and that a serious situation would arise if there were a period during which there was no government in Poland. If the British or the American proposals were adopted, he argued, this period of instability would occur. I interrupted and declared that the present Polish Government would continue to function until the new government had been formed. President Roosevelt, I said, had emphasized this point in our private conversation that morning.

THE SIXTH DAY OF THE CONFERENCE

Molotov, however, replied that the Poles would know negotiations were proceeding on a change in government and that this knowledge might create difficulties for the Red Army. I remarked that Mr. Eden's proposal avoided this situation. Then I said that, under the circumstances, it would be best to report to the plenary session that we had discussed the Polish question on the basis of the American memorandum, and although we had not yet reached an agreement, we had decided to continue the discussions at a later date.

Harriman suggested that Mr. Molotov consider a redraft of the American formula, which would contain the words "based on the old *and also* on other democratic elements from outside and inside Poland." Molotov, however, reacted negatively to this suggestion. He obviously preferred the wording, "based on the old government and with the calling in of representatives . . ."

We then turned to the subject of German reparations. I said I would like to present some counterproposals to the document prepared by Mr. Vishinsky and Mr. Maisky. I had discussed these proposals that morning with President Roosevelt. They were:

> *1. Reparations are to be received in the first instance by those countries which have borne the main burden of the war and have suffered the heaviest losses and have organized victory over the enemy.*
>
> *2. Setting aside for the moment the use of German labor by way of reparations, this question to be considered at a later date, reparations in kind are to be exacted from Germany in the two following forms:*
>
> *(a) Removal in a single payment at the end of the war from the national wealth of Germany located on the territory of Germany herself as well as outside her territory (equipment, machine-tools, ships, rolling stock, German*

investment abroad, shares of industrial transport, shipping and other enterprises in Germany, etc.), these removals to be carried out chiefly for the purpose of military and economic disarmament of Germany.

These removals are to be completed within two years of the end of the war.

Annual deliveries of commodities during ten years after the end of the war.

3. The total of German reparations in the form of removal from her national wealth as well as in the form of annual deliveries of commodities after the end of the war shall be the first subject of study by the Moscow Commission. In this study the Commission will take into consideration the effect of whatever common steps ought to be taken for the elimination or reduction of output of various important German industries, from the standpoint of the total decentralization of Germany. The Commission should take into consideration in its initial studies the Soviet Government's suggested total of twenty billion dollars for all forms of reparation.

Maisky declared that paragraphs 1 and 2 of this proposal were acceptable. Paragraph 3, however, would have to be more fully clarified. He suggested that the Moscow Commission accept twenty billion dollars "as a basis" for its studies. The final figures arrived at by the commission might be a little more or a little less than this figure.

Eden stated that the Prime Minister was strongly opposed to setting a figure in a document on the basic principles of reparations, even as a basis for discussion. I urged that the setting of a figure be left to the commission, although I personally felt that Maisky's figure was reasonable. President Roosevelt had deep convictions that any figure must be used only as a "basis for discussion." It was impossible, he believed, to discuss the amount of reparations in any intelligent fashion until the Allies discovered what was left of Germany after the destruction of war. A great engineering survey would have to take place, he said to me, to find out what amount was practicable to move as reparations. All discussion of an amount now, he emphasized, was purely academic.

Molotov asked whether it would be agreeable to mention only the reparations, to the amount of ten billion dollars, which would go to the Soviet Union. I suggested as a counterproposal that it be stated that fifty per cent of the total sum of reparations collected, a sum not to be specified, would go to the Soviet Union. Molotov did not object to this suggestion, but he still felt that it was important to include a sum in the statement.

Eden observed that his government well understood the extent of the suffering and the need of the Soviet Government and would, therefore, not be parsimonious in the apportionment of reparations to Russia. He felt, however, that the Reparations Commission first should do its research and ascertain the total amount of reparations.

When Molotov replied that the Soviet Union was not endeavoring to supersede the work of the Reparations Commission but only give it guidance, I inquired what price levels the Soviet Union had in mind as a yardstick for measuring the amount of reparations. Molotov answered that reparations should be based on 1938 prices, since the destruction had been measured in terms of prewar values. To a further question of mine, he replied that it was likely that the Soviet Union would add fifteen or twenty per cent to the 1938 prices.

I then asked if the Soviet Union had taken into consideration in their reparations proposal the effect of the partitioning of Germany on the payment of reparations. Maisky replied that they had. Partitioning, he said, would not affect the removals from the national wealth of Germany of equipment located both inside and outside of Germany at the end of the war. It might, however, he admitted, affect the annual payments over the ten-year period.

After some further discussion the Soviet and American delegations agreed that the wording of the third point in the American proposal should read that the Reparations Commission should consider, *as a basis for discussion* (the italics are mine), the Soviet suggestion that the total sum of the reparations in accordance with points (a) and (b) of the preceding paragraph of the American proposal be twenty billion dollars and that fifty per cent of it should go to the Soviet Union. Eden made it clear that he would have to await instructions from his government on this matter.

We then discussed for a short time the form of the invitations to be issued for the San Francisco Conference. I said that it was my understanding that the United States would consult with China and France about including these two countries in the invitations as sponsoring powers before the invitations were issued to other nations. Molotov and Eden agreed that my understanding was correct.

Although we agreed not to include any statement relative to territorial trusteeships in the invitation, we did decide that the five permanent members of the Security Council should consult each other prior to the conference on this matter and prepare recommendations for a discussion of it at San Francisco.

I explained that the United States did not contemplate any detailed discussions of particular islands or territories to be placed under international trusteeship, but that we did wish to establish the right of the world organization to deal with the problem and to create some machinery for a trus-

THE SIXTH DAY OF THE CONFERENCE

teeship system. Molotov and Eden indicated agreement with this suggestion.

The foreign ministers then turned to the question of Yugoslavia, which had been referred to us by the plenary session. Molotov observed that Yugoslavia was in an unstable situation. He therefore could not understand why the British had expressed the desire the day before to supplement the Subasitch-Tito agreement, when steps had not yet been taken to put this original agreement into operation. He proposed, as a result, that the original agreement be executed before any subsequent questions were discussed.

Eden maintained, however, that the amendments suggested by the British Government were reasonable in nature and provided for a more democratic Yugoslavia. He could see no harm, therefore, in their being applied. These amendments recommended that the anti-Fascist Assembly of National Liberation be extended to include members of the last Yugoslav legislature who had not compromised themselves by collaborating with the enemy. The body thus formed would be known as a temporary Parliament. Legislative acts passed by the anti-Fascist Assembly of National Liberation would be subject to subsequent ratification by a Constituent Assembly.

I suggested that representatives of Mr. Molotov and Mr. Eden be appointed to draft a statement on the Yugoslav situation. They both agreed to this step, and Molotov added that it would be desirable to state that it had been agreed at the Crimean Conference that the Subasitch-Tito agreement should be fully executed.

We adjourned after this discussion, and that afternoon at the sixth plenary session I reported on behalf of the foreign ministers. I mentioned that we had discussed the memorandum on the Polish question submitted by the United States delegation. The memorandum, I observed, had dropped our earlier suggestion that a presidential council be created. I also reported that Mr. Molotov had stated that he wished to present to Marshal Stalin certain new considerations in the American memorandum on the question of the Polish Government. I remarked that we, therefore, had not reached agreement on the problem.

Molotov declared that the Soviet delegation was extremely anxious to come to an agreement, and he believed that this could be done with certain amendments to the proposal submitted by Mr. Stettinius that morning.

He suggested that the first sentence in the American proposal be changed to read: "The present Provisional Government of Poland should be reorganized on a wider democratic basis with the inclusion of democratic leaders from Poland itself and from those living abroad, and in this connection this government would be called the National Provisional Government of Poland."

He also suggested that the words "non-Fascist and anti-Fascist" be added to the last sentence of paragraph 1 before the words "democratic parties." He then said that he felt the proposal requiring the ambassadors of the three powers in Warsaw to observe and report on the free elections should be eliminated because it would offend the Poles. It was not a necessary statement, he repeated, since it was the first duty of ambassadors at all times to observe and report.

The Prime Minister remarked that he was glad to see that an advance had been achieved at the foreign ministers' meeting. He continued, however, that in a general atmosphere of agreement we should not put our feet in the stirrups and ride off. It would be a great mistake to hurry this question. It was far better, he urged, to take a few days of latitude than to endanger bringing the ship into port. It was a great mistake to take hurried decisions on these matters, and he felt that he must study the Polish proposals before giving any opinion.

The President then proposed that I finish my report on the meeting and the Conference would then adjourn for half an hour to study Mr. Molotov's amendments to the American memorandum. Both the Prime Minister and the Marshal agreed with this suggestion, and Churchill repeated that the great prize of agreement on Poland should not be imperiled by too much haste. He added that he definitely did not want to leave Yalta without agreement on Poland, which he felt was the most important question before the Conference.

I then reported that in our reparations discussions the American delegation had submitted a proposal on the basic principles of exacting reparations from Germany, for study and recommendation by the Moscow Reparations Commission. We had reached agreement, I told the three leaders, on the first two points of the American proposal, relative to the countries which should receive reparations and to the types of reparations in kind that Germany should pay. The Soviet and American delegations, I said, had reached agreement on the wording of the third and final point of the American proposal, to the effect that the Reparations Commission should consider in its initial studies as a basis for discussion the suggestion of the Soviet Government that the total sum of the reparations, in accordance with points (a) and (b) of the preceding paragraph of the American proposal, should be twenty billion dollars and that fifty per cent of it should go to the Soviet Union. Mr. Eden, I explained, had reserved his position in order to await instructions from his government.

The Soviet delegation, I said, had stated that reparations payments would be based upon 1938 prices with the possibility of increases of fifteen to twenty per cent on the prices of the items delivered.

I then reported that the foreign ministers had agreed that the five governments having permanent seats on the Security Council should consult each other prior to the San Francisco Conference in order to provide machinery in the world charter for dealing with territorial trusteeships and dependent areas.

At this point the Prime Minister exploded. He stated with great vigor that he did not agree with one single word of my report on trusteeships.

The President interrupted and said, "Winston, you have not let Ed finish his sentence."

The Prime Minister continued, however, and declared that he had not been consulted nor had he heard of this subject up to now. Under no circumstances, he declared hotly, would he ever consent to the fumbling fingers of forty or fifty nations prying into the life's existence of the British Empire. As long as he was Prime Minister, he declared, he would never yield one scrap of Britain's heritage.

Cadogan had told us at Malta that he agreed that the subject of dependent areas and territorial trusteeships should be discussed at the United Nations conference, and that it would be most desirable to have preliminary discussion and agreement in principle among the five sponsoring powers before the conference began.[1] We had made it clear that our proposals dealt only with League of Nations mandates established after World War I, territories taken from the enemy during the present war, and any territories which might be

[1] Notes from a meeting aboard H.M.S. *Sirius,* February 1, 1945, at Malta.

THE SIXTH DAY OF THE CONFERENCE

voluntarily placed under trusteeships. Mr. Eden, however, had mentioned that he feared the Prime Minister's reaction.

I am sure that Roosevelt was not astonished at the vehemence with which Churchill attacked the trusteeship proposal. The Prime Minister had announced on November 10, 1942, "I have not become the King's First Minister in order to preside over the liquidation of the British Empire."

On March 17, 1944, when I talked with the President about my proposed mission to London to discuss postwar problems, the President had urged me to raise the trusteeship issue. I wrote in my notes that night:

> The President pointed out he had discussed the question of a trusteeship for French Indo-China with General Chiang Kai-shek at Cairo. . . . The President said the country is worse off than it was a hundred years ago. The white man's rule there is nothing to be proud of. The President said that . . . a trusteeship is the only practical solution. When the President asked Generalissimo Chiang Kai-shek what he thought, the Generalissimo replied that China had no designs on French Indo-China, and that the Chinese did not want that country united with theirs because its people and the country as a whole were completely different from their own. He thought a trusteeship would be an ideal arrangement.
>
> When the President told Churchill that China does not want Indo-China, Churchill replied, "Nonsense." The President had said to him, "Winston, this is something which you are just not able to understand. You have 400 years of acquisitive instinct in your blood and you just don't understand how a country might not want to acquire land somewhere if they can get it. A new period has opened in the world's history, and you will have to adjust yourself to it." The President then said that the British would take land anywhere in the world even if it were only rock or a sand bar.
>
> To make certain about the Chinese position, Mr. Roosevelt asked Generalissimo Chiang Kai-shek again at Cairo whether

237

> they wanted Indo-China, and Chiang assured him again they did not. Then at Teheran the President raised the question with Joseph Stalin, who said that Indo-China should be independent but was not yet ready for self-government. He said that the idea of a trusteeship was excellent. When Churchill objected, the President said, "Now, look here, Winston, you are outvoted three to one."
>
> "But we are still going to have a tough time with the British on this issue," the President said.

The Prime Minister was greatly aroused over the trusteeship statement at the plenary session. After he had finished speaking, he continued to mutter, "Never, never, never." I immediately explained that we did not mean to refer to the British Empire, but that we had in mind the League of Nations mandates and dependent areas such as the Japanese islands in the Pacific to be taken from enemy control.

The Prime Minister quieted down somewhat, but only partially accepted my explanation. He declared that it would be better to specify that the statement did not refer to the British Empire. Great Britain, he added, did not want any territorial aggrandizement, and would not object if trusteeships were to be considered for enemy territory.

He then dramatically turned to Stalin and asked how he would feel if the suggestion were made that the Crimea be internationalized as a summer resort. The Marshal replied that he would be delighted to give the Crimea as a place for meetings of the Big Three.

Fortunately, at this point, there was a short intermission. I asked Hiss to do a quick summary of the State Department's memorandum on the trusteeship issue. Byrnes and I talked it over with the Prime Minister, and I seemed to satisfy him when I showed him the memorandum just written by Hiss. By the time the meeting reconvened, the Prime

THE SIXTH DAY OF THE CONFERENCE

Minister had agreed to our formula although whenever the subject was mentioned thereafter we were never certain that he might not explode again.

The plenary session now turned to the question of Yugoslavia, and I reported that Mr. Molotov and Mr. Eden had appointed representatives to draft a statement on this question. The Prime Minister asked if the Soviet Government had agreed to add the two amendments proposed by Mr. Eden to the Subasitch-Tito agreement.

Molotov declared that amendments meant delay in forming the Yugoslav Government, and that he thought it would be better to discuss the amendments with Marshal Tito and Dr. Subasitch after their agreement had gone into effect. The Prime Minister inquired sharply if it were too much to ask (as one of the amendments required) that legislative acts of the temporary authorities be subject to confirmation by democratic processes. Stalin declared that delays were undesirable and warned that if the British proposed two more amendments the Soviet Government might propose some of their own.

After a brief interchange between the Prime Minister and Stalin as to whether Tito was a dictator or not, Eden remarked that it was not a question of adding the amendments before the agreement went into effect, but rather of a request by the Crimean Conference that the two amendments be adopted.

At this point the Marshal announced that he would agree with the two British amendments, but that he would like the government to be formed first, and then he would favor proposing the amendments to it. Stalin and Churchill finally agreed to urge Tito and Subasitch to put their agreement into effect immediately, and that as soon as the new government had been formed, the adoption of these two amendments would be recommended.

After a half-hour intermission to study Molotov's proposals on Poland, the President declared that they were very near agreement and it was now only a matter of drafting. For those governments which still recognized the London Poles the use of the words "Provisional Government" was somewhat difficult, however, and he felt that the first words of Molotov's amendment might read "The Government now operating in Poland."

It was extremely important, the President declared, that some recognition of the Polish-Americans' desire for free elections be in the final agreement. In the light of this situation, he added, the last sentence, concerning reports by the ambassadors on free elections, was most important. The President concluded by suggesting that the three foreign ministers meet that night and work out the details of the statement.

The Prime Minister said that he wished to emphasize two points. It was desirable first to mention that the new situation, created by the liberation of Poland by the Red Army, required the creation of a government more broadly based than the present one. This might be an ornament, Churchill said, but nevertheless an important ornament. The second point, and a more important one, related to the last sentence of the American draft. ("The Ambassadors of the three powers in Warsaw following such recognition would be charged with the responsibility of observing and reporting to their respective Governments on the carrying out of the pledge in regard to free and unfettered elections.")

He then told Stalin that one of the great difficulties was the lack of accurate information on Poland. The result was

Marshal Stalin and Prime Minister Churchill in good humor between formal sessions of the Conference. (U.S. Army Signal Corps)

Marshal Stalin confers with Mr. Roosevelt in the President's study at Livadia Palace just before a plenary session. (U.S. Army Signal Corps)

that decisions of great responsibility had to be made on the basis of inadequate information. We knew, he added, that there were bitter feelings among the Poles. He understood that the Lublin Government had declared its intention to try members of the Polish Home Army and the underground forces as traitors. These reports, he declared, caused great anxiety and perplexity in Great Britain. He added that he hoped these two points would be considered by Marshal Stalin with his usual patience and kindness.

He personally, the Prime Minister continued, would welcome observers of the three powers wherever they were needed. The last sentence of the American draft, therefore, was most important. He understood, he said, that Tito would have no objections to foreign observers when elections were held in Yugoslavia, and the British would welcome observers from the United States and the Soviet Union when elections were held in Greece and in Italy.

These were not idle requests, Churchill declared. In Egypt, for example, whatever government held the election won. Churchill recalled that for this reason King Farouk had refused to permit Nahas Pasha to hold an election while the latter was Prime Minister.

Stalin remarked that he had heard that in Egyptian elections the greatest politicians spent their time buying each other. Egypt could not be compared with Poland, he contended, since there was a high degree of literacy in Poland.

The Prime Minister observed that he did not mean to compare Poland with Egypt, but the point was that he had to give the House of Commons assurance that free elections would be held in Poland. Would Mr. Mikolajczyk, for instance, he asked, be allowed to take part in the elections? Stalin replied that Mr. Mikolajczyk was a member of the

Peasant party, and since this was not a Fascist party, he certainly could take part in the elections.

When the Prime Minister suggested, as the President had, that the Polish elections be discussed by the foreign ministers that evening, the Marshal observed that this was a matter which should be discussed in the presence of the Poles. The Prime Minister, however, insisted that this was a matter that must be finished at the present Conference and that it was important to assure the House of Commons that free elections would be held in Poland.

The President said that he had one word to add before the foreign ministers met that evening. The elections were the crux of the Polish question, and he would like to have some assurance for the six million Poles in the United States that the elections would be freely held. If such assurances were present, there would be no doubt as to the sincerity of the agreement reached at the Crimean Conference.

The plenary session then directed its attention to the "Declaration on Liberated Europe." The President had decided to submit to the Prime Minister and to Stalin the State Department's draft on this question, but, as has been mentioned in an earlier chapter, he did not submit the State Department's recommendation of a European High Commission, which the Department had expected would implement the Declaration.

The President suggested that the Conference adopt the following text:

> The Premier of the Union of Soviet Socialist Republics, the Prime Minister of the United Kingdom and the President of the United States of America have consulted with each other in the common interests of the peoples of their countries and those of liberated Europe. They jointly declare their mutual

agreement to concert during the temporary period of instability in liberated Europe the policies of their three governments in assisting the peoples liberated from the domination of Nazi Germany and the peoples of the former Axis satellite states of Europe to solve by democratic means their pressing political and economic problems.

The establishment of order in Europe and the rebuilding of national economic life must be achieved by processes which will enable the liberated peoples to destroy the last vestiges of Nazism and Fascism and to create democratic institutions of their own choice. This is a principle of the Atlantic Charter— the right of all peoples to choose the form of government under which they will live—the restoration of sovereign rights and self-government to those peoples who have been forcibly deprived of them by the aggressor nations.

To foster the conditions in which the liberated peoples may exercise these rights, the three governments will jointly assist the people in any European liberated state or former Axis satellite state in Europe where in their judgment conditions require, (a) to establish conditions of internal peace; (b) to carry out emergency measures for the relief of distressed peoples; (c) to form interim governmental authorities broadly representative of all democratic elements in the population and pledged to the earliest possible establishment through free elections of governments responsive to the will of the people; and (d) to facilitate where necessary the holding of such elections.

The three governments will consult the other United Nations and provisional authorities or other governments in Europe when matters of direct interest to them are under consideration.

When, in the opinion of the three governments, conditions in any European liberated state or any former Axis satellite state in Europe make such action necessary, they will immediately establish appropriate machinery for the carrying out of the joint responsibilities set forth in this declaration.

By this declaration we reaffirm our faith in the principles of the Atlantic Charter, our pledge in the Declaration by the United Nations, and our determination to build in cooperation with other peace-loving nations a world order under law, dedicated to peace, security, freedom and general well-being of all mankind.

Stalin suggested one additional sentence to the fourth paragraph of the Declaration: "In this connection, support will be given to the political leaders of those countries who have taken an active part in the struggle against the German invaders."

Stalin mischievously observed that the Prime Minister need have no anxiety that the proposed Russian amendment applied to Greece. The Prime Minister replied that he was not anxious about Greece, and he would welcome a Soviet observer there. The Marshal then remarked that he thought it would have been exceedingly dangerous had the Prime Minister allowed any but British forces to go into Greece. He had, Stalin added, complete confidence in British policy in Greece. The Prime Minister expressed his pleasure with this statement.

The President pointed out that the Declaration would apply not only to Poland but to any areas or countries where it was needed.

The Prime Minister declared that he did not disagree with the President's proposed Declaration as long as it was clearly understood that the reference to the Atlantic Charter did not apply to the British Empire. He declared that he had already made it plain in the House of Commons that, as far as the British Empire was concerned, the principles of the Atlantic Charter already applied. The Prime Minister, a short time after the drafting of the Atlantic Charter, had told the House of Commons: "At the Atlantic meeting, we had in

THE SIXTH DAY OF THE CONFERENCE

mind, primarily, the restoration of the sovereignty, self-government and national life of the States and nations of Europe now under the Nazi yoke, and the principles governing any alterations in the territorial boundaries which may have to be made. So that is quite a separate problem from the progressive evolution of self-governing institutions in the regions and peoples which owe allegiance to the British Crown."

The President then observed that France had been included in an earlier draft of the Declaration but was now dropped because the nation was not represented at Yalta. Stalin remarked that three powers were better than four, but the Prime Minister suggested that it might be possible to ask France to associate itself with the Declaration. The President suggested that this question be considered by the foreign ministers that evening.

The plenary session next turned to the question of war criminals. The Prime Minister observed that he had personally drafted the declaration on German atrocities, issued at the Moscow Conference and dealing with the main criminals whose crimes had no geographical location. It was an egg that he had laid himself, the Prime Minister commented, and he thought that a list of major criminals should be drawn up at Yalta. He added that he thought they should be shot once their identity had been established.

When Stalin asked about Rudolph Hess, whose flight to Great Britain in 1941 had attracted world-wide attention, Churchill replied that events would catch up with Hess, and he thought the war criminals should be given a judicial trial. He then changed his mind about drafting the list of war criminals at Yalta, and added that all they should do at the present Conference was to exchange views on the subject.

The sixth plenary session then closed with a discussion of

the military situation on the western front. When Stalin asked if the expected western offensive had begun, the Prime Minister reported that 100,000 British soldiers had launched an attack on the western front the previous morning. The second wave, consisting of the United States Ninth Army, he said, was to start tomorrow, and the offensive was to continue and grow in intensity.

On January 20 the French First Army had launched an attack against the Germans in the Colmar area. General Eisenhower added an American Army corps to this attack and Colmar fell on February 3. By February 9 the Germans in that region had been driven across the Rhine. On February 4, General Hodges' First Army had launched an attack to take the Roer dams, and captured them within six days. Meanwhile the Canadian Army on February 8 launched its assault. General Simpson's Ninth Army was delayed, however, by floodwaters of the Roer. Their attack was launched on February 23, and in less than a week had captured München-Gladbach. The next few weeks were to see the crossing of the Rhine and the collapse of Germany. At the time of the Yalta Conference, however, the Allied onslaught had only just begun and the news of mounting victories came in the weeks after the Conference had adjourned.

After dinner on February 9, I met with Eden and Molotov to discuss again the Polish question. Eden declared that he had just had a strong cable from the War Cabinet, and unless they could agree to something like his formula submitted on February 8, the day before, there seemed to be little chance of the British Government's approving any proposal on Poland whatever. He then submitted a "British Revised Formula." This proposal pointed out that a new situation had been created by the complete liberation of Poland by the

Red Army. As a result, it was necessary to establish a fully representative provisional Polish Government which was more broadly based than was possible before the recent liberation of western Poland. This government, to be called the Polish Provisional Government of National Unity, should be based upon the provisional government now functioning in Poland and upon other democratic Polish leaders from within Poland and from abroad.

Molotov, Harriman, and Kerr were to be authorized to consult in the first instance in Moscow with members of the present provisional government and with other democratic leaders from within Poland and from abroad in order to reorganize the present government along more representative lines. This "Provisional Government of National Unity" would be pledged to the holding of free and unfettered elections as soon as practicable on the basis of universal suffrage and secret ballot. In these elections all democratic parties would have the right to take part and to put forward candidates.

The final British proposal provided that when a Polish Provisional Government of National Unity had been formed, which the three governments could regard as fully representative of the Polish people, the three governments would accord it recognition. The ambassadors of the three powers in Warsaw, following such recognition, would then be charged with the responsibility of observing and reporting to their respective governments on the carrying out of the pledge in regard to free and unfettered elections.

After a lengthy and grueling discussion of the "British Revised Formula," we all agreed to the following text:

A new situation has been created by the complete liberation of Poland by the Red Army. This calls for the establishment of a provisional Polish government more broadly based than was possible before the recent liberation of western Poland. The provisional government now functioning in Poland should be reorganized on a broader democratic basis with the inclusion of democratic leaders from Poland itself and from those living abroad. This new government will then be called the "Polish Provisional Government of National Unity." Mr. Molotov, Mr. Harriman, and Sir Archibald Clark Kerr, are authorized to consult in the first instance in Moscow with members of the present provisional government and with other democratic leaders from within Poland and from abroad with a view to the reorganization of the present government along the above lines. This "Polish Provisional Government of National Unity" would be pledged to the holding of free and unfettered elections as soon as practicable on the basis of universal suffrage and secret ballot. In these elections all democratic and anti-Nazi parties would have the right to take part and to put forth candidates.

When a "Polish Provisional Government of National Unity" has been properly formed in conformity with the above, the three governments will then accord it recognition.

We were, however, unable to agree on the addition of a further sentence:

The ambassadors of the three powers in Warsaw, following such recognition, would be charged with the responsibility of observing and reporting to their respective governments on the carrying out of the pledge in regard to free and unfettered elections.

Eden and I emphasized the importance of including some such sentence. Molotov insisted, however, that this should be discussed with the Poles by the commission of three in Moscow. The question was finally left for the Prime Minister, the Marshal, and the President to handle at their meeting the next day.

THE SIXTH DAY OF THE CONFERENCE

The second point that we discussed concerned the addition to the "Declaration on Liberated Europe" suggested at the plenary session by Stalin. The Russian proposal read: "And in this connection support should be given to the political leaders of those countries who took an active part in the struggle against the German invaders."

On the basis of a talk I had had with the President just before this meeting, I said that I could not accept this addition and that it was not pertinent to the Declaration. It appeared, I declared, like too much interference in the affairs of liberated countries and involved making decisions on just what peoples had and had not collaborated with the enemy, decisions which we felt should be left to the peoples of these countries themselves. Eden agreed with my views, and it was decided also to refer this problem to the next plenary session of the Conference.

CHAPTER 13

The High Tide of Allied Unity

February 10

On the next to last day of the Yalta Conference the President and I had a morning meeting at which the President agreed to send a letter to Cordell Hull inviting him to be the Senior Delegate and Senior Adviser to the American delegation at the San Francisco Conference.

The President had Poland much in mind, and I went over again the American position on the issue of the Polish Government. We were anxious to reach an agreement with the other two governments that day. We were in full accord that such an agreement must pledge a reorganized government as well as promise free and unfettered elections. On the other hand, we did not wish to prevent a Polish settlement by insisting on the last sentence of our formula, which read: "The Ambassadors of the three powers in Warsaw following such recognition would be charged with the responsibility of observing and reporting to their respective Governments on the carrying out of the pledge in regard to free and unfettered elections."

"If we agree to withdraw this sentence," President Roosevelt said, "it must clearly be understood that we fully expect our ambassador to observe and report on the elections. If the statement of this fact in the agreement irritates the Russians, we can drop the statement, but they must understand our firm determination that the ambassadors will observe and report on the elections in any case."

As a result of these instructions from the President, I announced at the foreign ministers' meeting that the President was prepared to withdraw the last sentence in the American formula for Poland. It must be understood, however, I said, that the President was free to make any statement he felt necessary relative to the fact that the American Ambassador would investigate and report to him about the conduct of the elections in Poland.

When Eden remarked that he was not in agreement with the President in dropping this sentence, I observed that we preferred to have the sentence in the document but that the President was anxious to reach agreement and that to expedite matters he was willing to make this concession.

Molotov then suggested that the last part of the last paragraph of the Polish agreement read: "the Governments of the United States of America and Great Britain will establish diplomatic relations with the Polish Government as has been done by the Soviet Union." I immediately refused to accept this proposed change and Eden concurred. We pointed out that the Polish Government referred to in the formula was a new government and not the present Lublin Government. I remarked that it was vital to adhere to the principle of a new Polish Government.

We next turned to the President's "Declaration on Liberated Europe," and I reported that the President could not accept the amendment proposed the previous day by the Soviet Union calling for Big Three support of the political leaders of occupied countries who had taken active part against the German invaders. Molotov thereupon withdrew his amendment.

He did, however, submit another amendment suggesting that the words "they will immediately establish appropriate machinery for the carrying out of the joint responsibilities set forth in this declaration" be replaced by the words "they will immediately take measures for the carrying out of mutual consultation." Eden and I agreed to this amendment.

Eden then suggested that the three powers express the hope that the provisional government of the French Republic would associate itself with them in this Declaration. I immediately agreed with this proposal, but Molotov recommended that it be left for discussion at the plenary session that afternoon.

On the question of German reparations Eden announced that he favored the establishment of the Reparations Commission as had been agreed upon as soon as possible. He also concurred with the principles contained in the American reparations proposal concerning the immediate withdrawal of property from Germany and the yearly payments. He suggested, however, a redraft of the American proposals. He preferred to see a redraft along the following lines:

(1) A statement that the proportion of reparations allotted the claimant countries be determined in accordance to their respective contributions to the winning of the war and to the degree of material loss which they had suffered.

(2) Reparations should be exacted from Germany in three ways:

(a) Within two years after the surrender of Germany, removals from the national wealth of Germany both from within and outside of her territory. These removals to be made primarily for the purpose of destroying Germany's war potential. Germany's industrial capacity, however, would not be reduced to a point which would endanger the economic existence of the country nor to a point which would endanger the execution of the obligations imposed upon it.

(b) Annual deliveries from current production for a period to be considered.

(c) The use of German labor and lorry service.

(3) In establishing the amount of reparations, account should be taken of arrangements made for the partitioning of Germany, the requirements of the occupying forces, and Germany's need from time to time to acquire sufficient foreign currency from her export trade to pay for her current imports and the prewar claims of the United Nations on Germany.

Eden added that there seemed to be two Russian objectives which were difficult to reconcile. They wanted to deplete German manufacturing capacity, he declared, but at the same time insure German ability to make large payments at a later date.

The British were most anxious, he stated, to avoid a situation in which, as a result of reparations, they would have to finance and feed Germany. Furthermore, the British would like to have France added from the very beginning to the

Reparations Commission. The British also felt that the question of the use of labor should be discussed by the Reparations Commission and that it was inadvisable to name any figure for reparations until the commission had started to function.

Maisky remarked that Mr. Eden's statement was disappointing. He charged that its spirit was to remove as little as possible from Germany. Eden interrupted and said this was not true. The Prime Minister did believe, however, Eden declared, that the Russians would fail to receive anywhere near as much in reparations as they hoped to extract.

Maisky declared that the reparations plan would be adjusted to any partitioning agreement. The amount of annual payments, however, was quite possible after the contemplated removals of property from Germany. The British, he insisted, should accept the American and Russian formula proposed the day before as a basis for discussion and raise the British proposals in the Reparations Commission for further discussion. The use of labor would certainly be discussed by the Reparations Commission. The American and Russian formula, Maisky added, "did not commit the Allies to the exact figure" mentioned in the proposal.

Eden said, however, that the British preferred a period of five years instead of ten for the reparations payments. I pointed out that the ten-year period was merely mentioned as a basis for discussion. I added that neither the American nor the Soviet Government was committing itself to ten years or to twenty billion dollars for the total payment.

Eden then inquired why the ten-year time limit should be included in the formula at all. Maisky replied that it was desired as a basis for discussion. Eden remarked that he would submit an alternative draft for discussion at the plenary session that afternoon.

We next turned to the question of issuing a communiqué on the Conference, and I said that the American delegation was preparing a draft for the consideration of the foreign ministers.

Eden next submitted a report pertaining to the forthcoming world security conference at San Francisco. He suggested that the United States, on behalf of all three powers, be instructed to communicate the decisions on the proposed organization and the plans for the conference to France and China. He also introduced the draft of an invitation to be sent to all nations who were to participate in the conference. Molotov and I agreed to both of Eden's suggestions, and the text of the invitation was later incorporated in the protocol of the Conference.

Eden then submitted a paper on the Austro-Yugoslav frontier and one on the Yugoslav-Italian frontier for a later discussion sometime after the Yalta Conference.

He asked Molotov to review with us the conversations in progress between Yugoslavia and Bulgaria on a treaty of friendship and alliance. The Soviet Government approved this treaty, Molotov replied. The two nations were collaborating against Germany, and as a result, there should be no objection to a treaty.

Eden stated that this treaty raised an important question of principle. The British believed that former enemy states should be prevented from entering into treaty relations with other states while they were under an occupational control and decidedly that they should not make treaties without the concurrence of all the Allies. The British were also anx-

Winston Churchill, wearing a Russian fur cap and holding his big cigar, with Secretary Stettinius after saying good-by to the President when he left Yalta on February 11, 1945. (Sovfoto)

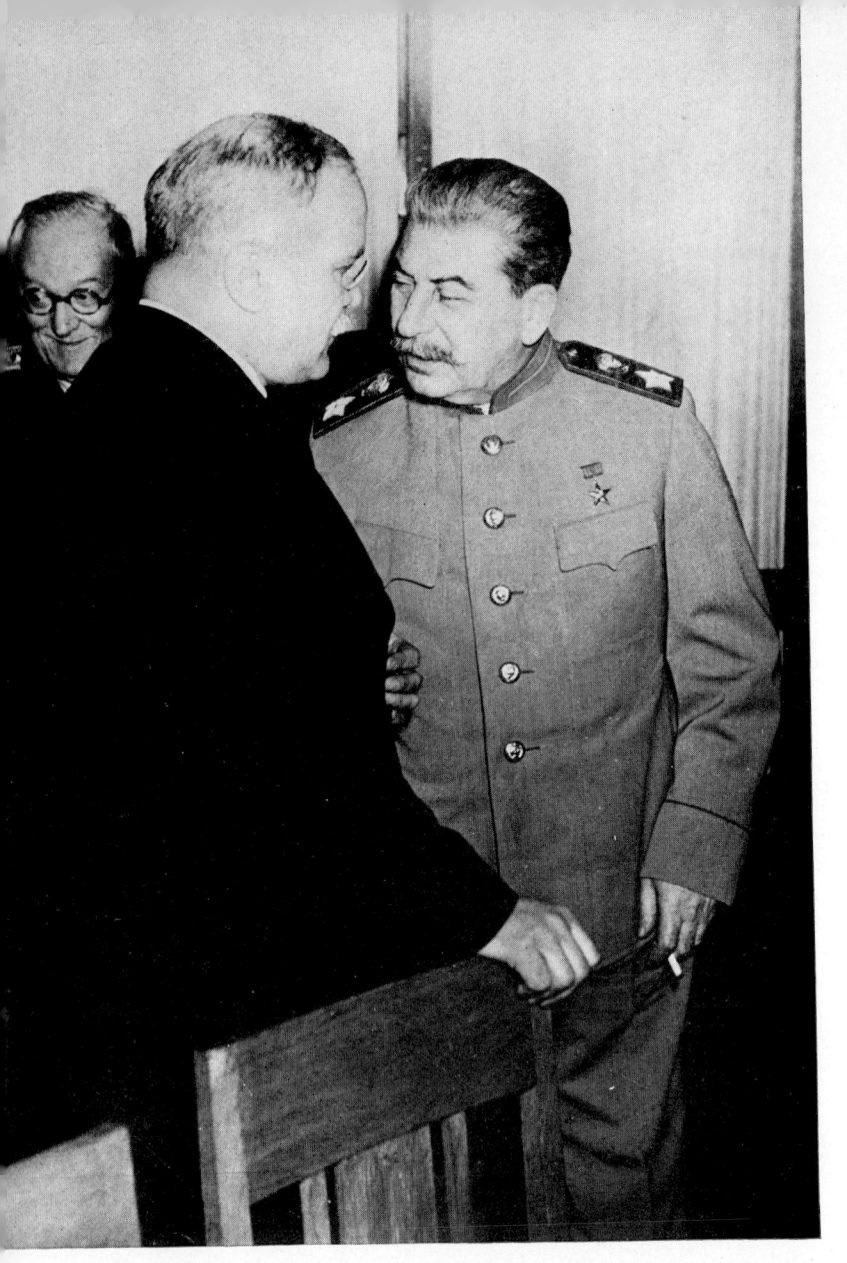

Marshal Stalin and Foreign Minister Molotov confer during an intermission at the Conference. In the background is Deputy Foreign Minister Vishinsky. (U.S. Army Signal Corps)

ious concerning the effect of this treaty on Greek reparations from Bulgaria.

Molotov replied that he had received a note from the British Foreign Office opposing treaty relations of former enemy states under an armistice regime with other enemy states. It was, in this case, however, the question of an ex-enemy and a friendly state. He declared that the British had stated they had no objections to treaties between ex-enemy and friendly states.

Eden questioned this statement. He reiterated that he did not believe that states being administered under an armistice regime should be permitted to make peace treaties without the permission of the other Allies. He added that Great Britain likewise did not favor a Balkan federation either until the armistice period had ended. I stated that I was in accord with Mr. Eden's views on this point.

Eden inquired whether it would not be advisable for Yugoslavia and Bulgaria to wait awhile on their treaty. When Molotov replied that he could not speak for these states, Eden reminded him that Bulgaria had signed an armistice with the Soviet Union and was not free to act on its own volition. I suggested that this question should be discussed promptly in Moscow by Mr. Molotov and Ambassador Harriman and Sir Archibald Clark Kerr.

When Molotov replied that it might be preferable to take the matter up again the next day and endeavor to reach an agreement, I remarked that the President had urged me that morning to do everything humanly possible to speed up the conclusion of the Conference. The President had explained to me that he had pressing problems back in Washington that required his attention; he had already been away too long; and in addition he wished to see Ibn Saud, Haile

Selassie, and King Farouk on his way back. If the Conference continued interminably, however, he would not be able to hold these meetings.

Inasmuch as I could see from the exchange that had just taken place between Eden and Molotov that this complex matter could not be settled at Yalta, I again urged that our ambassadors in Moscow pursue the matter with Mr. Molotov.

We closed our foreign ministers' conference with disagreement on the Iranian question. Eden and I favored the issuing of a document on Iran, and Molotov opposed it. Although we both explained that we attached great importance to the Iranian question, he stated that it was impossible for him to go any further into the question at this time. This was disappointing to both Eden and me.

At the plenary session that Saturday afternoon the President was wheeled into his usual place at the great circular table with his back to the brisk log fire crackling in the fireplace. Both Churchill and Stalin were late for this plenary session. When the Prime Minister arrived he went directly to the President to apologize and told him, "I believe that I have succeeded in retrieving the situation." When Stalin arrived five minutes after the Prime Minister, he too came to the President and apologized for his lateness.

Both Churchill and Stalin were late with good reason. After the close of the foreign ministers' meeting a subcommittee had worked out a wording on the questions of diplomatic recognition of the new Polish Government and observance of the elections which the Prime Minister persuaded Stalin to accept during his call at the Soviet headquarters.

As the plenary session opened the President asked Eden to report on the meeting of the foreign ministers. Eden read the following formula for Poland with one correction made by Molotov:

> A new situation has been created in Poland as a result of her complete liberation by the Red Army. This calls for the establishment of a Polish Provisional Government which can be more broadly based than was possible before the recent liberation of Western Poland. The Provisional Government which is now functioning in Poland should therefore be reorganized on a broader democratic basis with the inclusion of democratic leaders from Poland itself and from Poles abroad. This new Government should then be called the Polish Provisional Government of National Unity.
>
> Mr. Molotov, Mr. Harriman and Sir A. Clark Kerr are authorized to consult in the first instance in Moscow with members of the present Provisional Government and with other Polish democratic leaders from within Poland and from abroad, with a view to the reorganisation of the present Government along the above lines. This Polish Provisional Government of National Unity shall be pledged to the holding of free and unfettered elections as soon as possible on the basis of universal suffrage and secret ballot. In these elections all democratic and anti-Nazi parties shall have the right to take part and to put forward candidates.
>
> When a Polish Provisional Government of National Unity has been properly formed in conformity with the above, the Government of the U.S.S.R., which now maintains diplomatic relations with the present Provisional Government of Poland, and the Government of the United Kingdom and the Government of the U.S.A. will establish diplomatic relations with the new Polish Provisional Government of National Unity, and will exchange Ambassadors by whose reports the respective Governments will be kept informed about the situation in Poland.

The Prime Minister observed that the document made no mention of the Polish boundaries. "We have all agreed on the eastern frontier," he said, and he expressed his belief that Poland should receive compensation in the west. He did not believe, however, that the British War Cabinet would accept the line of the western Neisse. Although there would be some criticism, he thought that the Polish statement should mention something about the territorial settlement.

While Churchill was speaking I scribbled a note to the President informing him that Eden had told me he had just received a "bad" cable from the War Cabinet telling the British delegation that they were going too far on Poland. At the same time, Harry Hopkins wrote the following note to Roosevelt:

> Mr. President:—
> I think you should make clear to Stalin that you *support the eastern boundary but that only a general statement be put in communique saying we are considering essential boundary changes. Might be well to refer exact statement to foreign ministers.*
>
> Harry

The President then told the plenary session that the Polish Government should be consulted before any statement was made about the western frontier.

The Marshal said he agreed with the Prime Minister that some statement should be made on the eastern frontier. Molotov suggested that the statement on the eastern frontier be drafted by the foreign ministers. He added that it was not necessary to be as specific in regard to the western frontier as it was to the eastern frontier.

The Prime Minister remarked that he had already gone on record that Poland would receive a good slice of territory in the north and in the west, but that the opinion of the new Polish Government of National Unity should be ascertained.

> Mr. President:—
>
> I think you should make clear to Stalin that you support the western boundary but that only a general statement be put in communiqué saying we are considering eventual boundary changes. Might be well to refer exact statement to foreign ministers.
>
> Harry

Although the President did not follow Hopkins' advice in this note, and the eastern boundary change was mentioned in the communiqué, the western boundary was left for the Peace Conference.

The President said that he had no objection in principle to such a statement, but that he thought the Prime Minister should draft it. Molotov suggested that it should form a last sentence to the Polish agreement.

Eden, continuing his report of the foreign ministers' meeting, said that the Soviet delegation wished to add to the "Declaration on Liberated Europe" a paragraph to the effect that the three governments should take steps immediately to carry out mutual consultation. Eden also recommended that when the nations issued the Declaration they express the hope that the French Government would associate itself with the agreement. Both of these proposals were accepted.

The President then announced that he had changed his mind about French participation in the German Control Commission. He now agreed with the Prime Minister's view that it would be impossible to give France a zone unless it were a member of the Control Commission. The President's change of mind had not occurred with dramatic suddenness. Freeman Matthews, who had great conviction that the French should be part of the Control Commission, pressed his view on the President and me. Matthews had been counselor at the American Embassy at Vichy under Ambassador Leahy, and he understood the French people and the present French situation as well as any officer of the State Department.

The Marshal replied to the President's announcement with just two words: "I agree." The President never told me just how and when he had persuaded Stalin to make this major concession which was announced so suddenly. Until this moment, whenever this subject had come up both Stalin and Molotov had been adamant in their opposition to French participation on the Control Commission. When Stalin had agreed, Churchill suggested that a telegram be sent to General de Gaulle informing him of these decisions. The President and the Marshal concurred.

Eden stated that the next subject to be reported on was Yugoslavia. He read the draft of a text of a telegram to Marshal Tito and Dr. Subasitch suggesting that their agreement be put into effect as the basis for the formation of a unified Yugoslav Government. The President said that he had not been sure he would be able to join in the Yugoslav statement, but now the telegram seemed satisfactory.

After some disagreement between Stalin and the Prime Minister as to whether the two proposed British amendments should appear both in the telegram and in the joint Yalta Conference communiqué, the Soviet Union gave in to the British and agreed to include the following three points in both the telegram and the communiqué:

(1) that the Tito-Subasitch agreement should go immediately into force,

(2) that the members of the Skupschina (the last Yugoslav Legislature) who had not collaborated with the Germans could be included into the Vetch (the Anti-Fascist Assembly of National Liberation), and

(3) that the actions of the anti-fascist Vetch[1] would be subject to the confirmation by the Constituent Assembly.

In regard to German reparations, the British Government, Eden reported, still had reservations to the Soviet proposals. The Prime Minister interjected that the War Cabinet had taken the position that figures should not be mentioned, and that this question should be left to the Reparations Commission itself to decide.

The President observed that if the word "reparations," and especially if any figures, were mentioned, the American people would believe that actual money was involved. Stalin replied that the monetary sums mentioned were only expressions of the value of reparations in kind—goods or services. The Prime Minister said that he realized no figures would be published in regard to reparations, but that he could not even agree to a definite sum being included in the unpublished agreement.

Stalin, on the question of German reparations, spoke with great emotion, which was in sharp contrast to his usual calm, even manner. On several occasions he arose, stepped behind his chair, and spoke from that position, gesturing to

[1] See *Appendix,* where Vetch is also referred to as Avnoj.

emphasize his point. The terrible German destruction in Russia obviously had moved him deeply. Although he did not orate or even raise his voice, he spoke with intensity.

There should be no confusion in regard to payment in money, he declared, since the Soviet Union's treaties with Finland, Romania, and Hungary specified reparations in kind in terms of monetary value. If the British felt that Russia should receive no reparations, he observed, it would be best that they make their position known now.

The Marshal recommended, however, that the three leaders reach two decisions:

(1) that it was agreed in principle that Germany should pay reparations and

(2) that the Reparations Commission to sit in Moscow should fix the amount and should take into consideration the American-Soviet proposal that there should be twenty billion dollars of reparations, with fifty per cent to the Soviet Union.

When President Roosevelt repeated that he feared the word "reparations" would be understood to mean cash in America, it was suggested that the term "compensation for damages caused by Germany during the war" be substituted.

The Prime Minister continued to insist that the British Government could not commit itself to any figure. Although Churchill spoke at some length during this interchange, I wrote in my notes, "It was always a pleasure to listen to his eloquent sentences. The beautiful phrases just roll out as water in a running stream."

Stalin replied to the Prime Minister that no commitment was involved. The Reparations Commission would merely utilize as a basis for discussion the American-Soviet formula. The Prime Minister thereupon read a telegram from the War

> Mr. President:
>   Gromyko just told me that
> the Marshall thinks you did not
> back up Ed relative to Reparations —
> and that you sided with the British —
> and he is disturbed about it. Perhaps
> you could tell him privately later.
>   Harry

Marshal Stalin at this point seemed to feel that the President was withdrawing from the reparations proposal submitted by me at the foreign ministers' meeting on February 9. At dinner on February 10 the President made it clear that he did not agree with the British idea of not mentioning any figures at all.

> Mr. President:
>   Gromyko just told me that the Marshall thinks you did not back up Ed relative to Reparations—and that you sided with the British—and he is disturbed about it. Perhaps you could tell him privately later.
>   Harry

Cabinet protesting that the twenty-billion figure was too great for Germany's capacity to pay.

Stalin again insisted that there was no commitment on the amount, and that the figure mentioned was to be "used as a basis for discussions—it could be reduced or increased by the Commission in Moscow."

When the President and Eden suggested that the whole matter be left to the Reparations Commission in Moscow, both Molotov and Maisky replied that it was illogical for the Crimean Conference to refer this question to a lesser body.

The Prime Minister again insisted that the British could not agree to a sum being mentioned, and Marshal Stalin gave in and proposed the following formula:

> (1) *that the heads of the Governments had agreed that Germany must pay compensation for the damages caused to the Allied nations as a result of the war and*
>
> (2) *that the Moscow Commission be instructed to consider the amount of reparations.*

The Prime Minister agreed and then said, "How about the United States?"

"The answer is simple," President Roosevelt replied. "Judge Roosevelt approves and the document is accepted."

It should be understood that there was absolutely no commitment at Yalta that the total sum of reparations should be twenty billions and that fifty per cent should go to the Soviet Union. We made it clear that these figures were merely a basis for discussion and that is the way it appears in the protocol printed in the Appendix of this book. In the plenary sessions, as well as at the foreign ministers' meetings, President Roosevelt and I pointed out that we were willing to start with any figure as a basis of discussion, but that we would not agree to an actual amount until after the Reparations Commission had made a thorough investigation of the question. The Russians, after President Roosevelt's death, however, were to claim incorrectly that he had agreed to their figure at Yalta.

At six o'clock there was a fifteen-minute adjournment for tea, which was served as usual in eight-ounce glasses with silver holders. The pace of the Conference was grueling and by this time the President naturally showed fatigue. However, he continued to explain the American position skillfully and distinctly, and he also served as a moderating influence when the discussions became heated.

When the session reconvened, Stalin stated that he would like to say a few words about the Montreux Convention and the Dardanelles. The treaty was now outmoded, he declared. Japan had played a bigger part in drafting that treaty than the Soviet Union, and also the treaty was linked with the League of Nations, which was dead.

Under the Montreux Convention, he observed, the Turks had the right to close the straits not only in time of war but when they felt there was a threat of war. He added that he knew the treaty had been made when British-Russian relations were not perfect, but he did not think that the British now wanted to strangle Russia.

He declared that he did not want to prejudge any discussions to revise the treaty, but he felt that the interests of Russia should be considered. It was impossible, he observed, to accept a situation in which Turkey had a hand on Russia's throat. The revision of the treaty, he added, however, should be done in such a way as not to harm the legitimate interests of Turkey. He concluded by suggesting that the three foreign ministers consider this question at their first meeting after the Crimea Conference.

The President said he did not like fortifications between nations and remarked that he would like to point out that Canada and the United States had had for over a hundred years an unarmed frontier stretching over three thousand miles. It was his hope, he told the Conference, that other frontiers in the world would eventually be without forts or armed forces on any part of their national boundaries.

Roosevelt had a firm conviction that the Soviet Union should have unhampered access to a warm-water port. At Teheran, when the Prime Minister had said that his government believed that the Russian request for a warm-water port was legitimate, the President had suggested that the Russians might have access to the port of Dairen in Manchuria.

The Prime Minister recalled that Marshal Stalin had mentioned the question of the straits to him in Moscow the past autumn. He had said then, Churchill pointed out, that the British were in sympathy with a revision of the treaty. Although the British had suggested that the Soviet Government send a note on the subject, none had as yet been received.

Stalin's proposal that the three foreign ministers discuss the matter was a wise one, Churchill remarked. The British certainly felt that Russia, as a great Black Sea power, should not be dependent on the narrow exit. It might be well, he added, to inform the Turks that the revision of the Montreux Convention would be discussed at the next foreign ministers' meeting.

Eden reminded Churchill that the matter had been mentioned several times to the Turkish Ambassador in London. Churchill observed that, as a result, it might be advisable to give the Turks assurance that their independence and integrity would be guaranteed. Stalin replied that it was impossible to keep anything secret from the Turks and that such an assurance should be made. The President agreed with the other two leaders on this point.

There was considerable banter between Churchill and Stalin after their agreement on this matter. Churchill pointed out that he had tried very hard during World War I to get through the Dardanelles and the Russian Government had made an armed force available to help, but he had not succeeded.

Stalin remarked that the Prime Minister had been in too much of a hurry in withdrawing his troops, since the Germans and the Turks were on the verge of surrender. The Prime Minister reminded Stalin that by that time he had been removed from the government because of the Dardanelles campaign, and thus had had nothing to do with the decision on the withdrawal.

A similar type of good-humored exchange had also taken place between Roosevelt and Churchill. Churchill jollied the President about the phrase "Freedom from want." He said that he had always intended to ask Mr. Roosevelt what he meant by the word "want."

"I suppose," Churchill said, "that it means privation and not desire."

The plenary session closed with another discussion of the Polish question. The President said that he now wished to propose some small amendments to the paragraph regarding frontiers in the Polish statement. While the Polish frontiers were being discussed earlier that afternoon, Harry Hopkins and I had jotted down some notes for the President. Hopkins, who sat just behind the President and me, frequently passed notes, written on ordinary lined paper, to the President. The one on the Polish question was most pertinent and helpful. He warned the President that it was doubtful that he had the constitutional power to commit the United States to a treaty establishing boundaries. The note read:

> Mr. President:
> You get into trouble about your legal powers & what senate will say.
>
> Harry

During one adjournment that afternoon the President asked me to get a lawyer to consult with him over the wording of the Polish boundary statement. I called Alger Hiss and while the two of us were trying to work out a solution for the President, Roosevelt suddenly looked up at us and said, "I've got it."

The President told the Conference that the amendments he was proposing were necessary for American constitutional reasons. He suggested, therefore, that instead of the first words, "The three powers," he would like to substitute, "The three Heads of Government consider." In the second sentence he proposed eliminating the words "three powers," and in the last sentence, the word "feel" instead of "agree" should be used. These changes transformed the statement on boundaries from a governmental commitment to an expression of views in which Roosevelt concurred.

The amendments were accepted and the following text was approved:

> *The three Heads of Government consider that the Eastern frontier of Poland should follow the Curzon Line with digressions from it in some regions of five to eight kilometres in favour of Poland. It is recognized that Poland must receive substantial accessions of territory in the North and West. They feel that the opinion of the new Polish Provisional Government of National Unity should be sought in due course on the extent of these accessions and that the final delimitation of the Western frontier of Poland should thereafter await the Peace Conference.*

Molotov thereupon suggested adding to the second sentence, "with the return to Poland of her ancient frontiers in East Prussia and on the Oder." The President asked how long ago these lands had been Polish, and Molotov replied: "Very long ago."

Such a statement then, the President observed, might lead the British to ask for the return of the United States to Great Britain. Stalin replied that the ocean would prevent this.

The Prime Minister declared that he agreed with the President that the western frontier not be designated at this time. He added that he was not opposed to the line of the Oder in principle if the Poles desired it. Stalin thereupon withdrew Molotov's amendment and left the draft as it was.

The President then announced that he would have to leave Yalta by 3 P.M. the next day. As a result a drafting committee to prepare the Conference's communiqué was appointed and requested to report that evening to the foreign ministers and to the President, the Prime Minister, and the Marshal.

While the communiqué was being drafted, the Prime Minister gave a dinner at the British headquarters. Those present were:

The President	*The Prime Minister*	*Marshal Stalin*
Mr. Stettinius	*Mr. Eden*	*Mr. Molotov*
Mr. Bohlen	*Major Birse*	*Mr. Pavlov*

It was a historic evening and an excellent dinner was served. When President Roosevelt and I arrived, Winston Churchill, with his great sense of showmanship and appreciation of military pomp, had a regimental guard lined up on the steps of the villa. We were shown into a small reception room, beautifully furnished, with a glowing fire in the fireplace. When Stalin and Molotov arrived, we had cocktails and then went in to dinner.

There were many toasts and a great deal of general conversation that evening. At one point Stalin told the Prime Minister that he was dissatisfied with the way the reparations question had been settled at the Conference. He said that he feared to have to go back to the Soviet Union and tell the Soviet people that they were not going to get adequate reparations because the British were opposed. I have always had the feeling that Molotov and Maisky had a private conversation with the Marshal following the plenary session and convinced him that he had conceded too much on the reparations question.

The Prime Minister replied that, on the contrary, he very much hoped that Russia would receive large reparations, but that he remembered the last war, when the Allies had placed the figure at more than the German capacity to pay. Stalin

When the plenary session accepted the President's changes in the wording of the Polish agreement, Harry Hopkins wrote this note:

    Mr. President:
        I think we are through when this discussion is concluded.

                                        Harry

then remarked that he thought it would be a good idea to mention in the communiqué their intention to make Germany pay for the damage it had caused the Allied nations, and also to make some reference to the Reparations Commission. Both the President and the Prime Minister agreed to include these statements in the communiqué. It was also agreed to state in the protocol that the Soviet Union and the United States believed the Reparations Commission should take as a basis of discussion the figure of reparations as twenty billion dollars and fifty per cent of these should go to the Soviet Union, while Great Britain felt that, pending consideration by the Reparations Commission, no figures should be mentioned.

The Prime Minister then proposed a toast to the health of Marshal Stalin. He said that he hoped the Marshal had a warmer feeling for the British than he had had in the past. Churchill added that he felt that the great victories of the Red Army had made the Marshal more mellow and friendly than he had been during the hard times of the war.

Churchill continued by expressing the hope that the Marshal realized that he had good and strong friends in those British and American representatives present. "We all hope," he added, "that the future of Russia will be bright," and he said he knew that he, and he was sure the President, would do all they could to bring this about. He said that he felt that the common danger of war had removed impediments to understanding and that the fires of war had wiped out old animosities. He closed by saying that he envisaged a Russia, which had already been glorious in war, as a happy and smiling nation in times of peace.

I mentioned to Stalin that if we worked together in the postwar years there was no reason why every home in the

Soviet Union could not soon have electricity and plumbing. He nodded his head and remarked, "We have learned much already from the United States."

I then proposed a toast to my predecessor, Mr. Cordell Hull, a great American and a great statesman, who had been an inspiration to all of us in his labors for the creation of a peaceful and orderly world. It was agreed that a message be sent to Hull, and it gave me genuine pleasure, on my return to Livadia Palace, to draft the following radiogram to him:

> We have missed you at our conference and send you our affectionate greetings and wish for you a speedy recovery in order that we may all have the benefit of association with you again.
>
> SIGNED: *Roosevelt, Stalin, Churchill, Molotov, Eden, and Stettinius*

The President said that he recalled an incident involving the Ku Klux Klan, an organization that had hated the Catholics and the Jews. On a visit to a small Southern town, he had been the guest of the president of the local Chamber of Commerce. He had sat next to an Italian on one side and a Jew on the other, and he had asked the president of the Chamber of Commerce whether these two men were members of the Ku Klux Klan. The president had said that they were, but that they were considered to be all right since everyone in the community knew them. This was a good illustration, the President remarked, of how difficult it was to have any prejudices—racial, religious, or otherwise—if you really knew people.

Stalin observed that this was very true. I believe that the whole discussion that evening, as well as the spirit of most of the Conference, furnishes a genuine example to the world that, where objective conditions exist, people with different backgrounds and training can find a basis of understanding.

The President observed that it was his opinion that any leader of a people must take care of their primary needs. The United States, he remembered, when he first became President, was close to revolution because the people lacked food, clothing, and shelter. He had launched a relief and recovery program, he said, and since that time there had been no real problem of social disorder in the United States.

The President remarked that he now desired to propose a toast to the Prime Minister. He personally, he said, had been twenty-eight years old when he entered American politics, but even at that time Mr. Churchill had had long experience in the service of his country. Mr. Churchill had been in and out of the government many, many years, the President continued, and it was difficult to say whether he had been of more service to his country within or outside the government. The President said that he personally felt that Mr. Churchill had been perhaps of even greater service when he was not in the government, since he had forced people to think.

This remark prompted the Prime Minister to observe that he would face difficult elections in the near future, and he did not know what the left would do. Stalin remarked that left and right were now just parliamentary terms. For example, under classical political concepts, Monsieur Daladier, who was a Radical Socialist, was more to the left than Mr. Churchill; yet Monsieur Daladier had dissolved the French trade unions, while Mr. Churchill had never molested them in Britain. Who then, Stalin inquired, could be considered more to the left?

The President recalled that in 1940 there had been eighteen political parties in France and that within one week he had had to deal with three different prime ministers. De Gaulle had told him the summer before, the President added, that he intended to change this situation.

The Prime Minister observed that Marshal Stalin had a much easier political task than the rest of them, since he had only one party to deal with. Stalin replied that experience had shown that one party was a great convenience to the leader of a state.

If he could secure full agreement of all the British people, it would ease his task, commented the Prime Minister. But British activities in the recent Greek crisis for example had cost him some support. The Prime Minister then repeated that he did not know what would be the result of the British elections, but he knew that he and Mr. Eden would continue to support the legitimate interests of, and co-operation with, Russia and the United States, no matter who was in power.

The Prime Minister added that although he had had great difficulty with the one Communist member of the House of Commons, Willie Gallacher, he had nevertheless written him a letter of sympathy when he had lost his two foster children in the war. Churchill observed that he thought the British opposition to Communism was not based on any attachment to private property but on the old question of the individual versus the state.

Marshal Stalin remarked that he did not believe the Labour party would ever form a government in Great Britain. He then asked the President whether there was any labor party, in a political sense, in the United States. The President explained that, although labor was extremely powerful, there was no specific labor party.

The Prime Minister expressed some irritation, at this point, over the President's plan to leave the next day. His irritation was not over the President's plan to visit the kings and emperors but rather that he could not delay the trip another day.[2] He asked Roosevelt to change his plans and remarked, "But, Franklin, you cannot go. We have within reach a very great prize." The President replied in a firm tone, "Winston, I have made commitments, and I must depart tomorrow as planned."

Stalin then remarked that he too thought more time was needed to finish the business of the Conference, but the President replied that he had three kings waiting for him in the Near East. It was clear from what the President had said to me that he felt it was necessary for him to apply such pressure as this in order to prevent the Conference from dragging on for days.

When Stalin asked the President if he intended to make any concessions to Ibn Saud, the President replied that he intended to review the entire Palestine question with the King.

Stalin observed that the Jewish problem was extremely difficult. The Soviet Union had tried to establish a national home for the Jews, but they had stayed only two or three years before returning to the cities. The Jews were natural traders, he added, but much had been accomplished by putting small groups of them in agricultural areas.

When Stalin again expressed concern that the Conference might not complete its work by the next afternoon, the President replied that if necessary he would wait over until Monday.

[2] See Sherwood, op. cit., p. 871. Sherwood quotes a note written by Hopkins stating that Roosevelt flabbergasted Churchill by telling him about his plans to visit the kings for the first time on February 10. In fact, Roosevelt told Churchill about it at Malta on February 2.

CHAPTER 14

The End of the Conference

February 11

President Roosevelt, Prime Minister Churchill, and Marshal Stalin, on the last day of the Yalta Conference, signed the "Agreement on Terms for Entry of the Soviet Union into the War Against Japan." Their final meeting on Sunday morning, February 11, was then devoted to reading and approving the joint communiqué to be issued the next day. The British and Russians had virtually no changes to suggest in the American document prepared principally by Wilder Foote at Steve Early's request. Churchill, who usually enjoyed writing such historic documents himself, proposed only six or seven minor drafting changes. Most of these were to eliminate the word "joint" from the text. The word "joint," he said, meant to him the Sunday family roast of mutton.

After the three leaders had approved the communiqué and ended their last meeting, Eden, Molotov, and I worked on the protocol of the Conference. The communiqué and the protocol, both of which are printed in the Appendix, contained some identical material but the protocol, in addition, included some agreements either not mentioned or only partially developed in the communiqué because of military considerations or the need of further study.

The agreements on Poland and Yugoslavia and the "Declaration on Liberated Europe" were the same in both documents. The fact that the leaders of the three nations agreed on dismemberment of Germany did not appear in the communiqué, however, because it was felt that mention of it might increase enemy resistance.

German reparations were mentioned in the communiqué but not spelled out as in the protocol. It was not spelled out primarily for military reasons, but also because the question had to be referred to the Reparations Commission in Moscow for further study. The voting procedure in the Security Council did not appear in the communiqué because it had to be taken up with France and China before it could be announced. On March 5, as soon as these two nations approved the voting formula, I announced the agreement, in the President's behalf, from Mexico City where I had gone from Yalta to attend the Inter-American Conference. The agreement was also released simultaneously in Washington.

The decision that Great Britain, the Soviet Union, the United States, France, and China would consult prior to the United Nations conference on the question of territorial trusteeships did not appear in the communiqué. Just as in the case of the voting formula in the Security Council, this decision had to be approved by France and China before it could be released.

Mention of such subjects as major war criminals, Yugoslav-Bulgarian relations, the Control Commission in Bulgaria, Iran, and the Montreux Convention and the Turkish straits

THE END OF THE CONFERENCE

was not included in the communiqué since no decisions were reached and all of these questions required further consultations.

The agreement that the United States and Great Britain would support at San Franscisco the proposal to admit the Ukraine and White Russia as original members of the world organization did not appear in the communiqué. I have always felt that it would have been much better for the President, and in the end for the United Nations, if I had been authorized to announce the agreement at the Mexico City Conference when I made the statement on the voting procedure in the Security Council.

The question, however, was not announced because the President wished to have the opportunity of explaining his agreement personally to the congressional leaders, and he also wanted to give the Prime Minister a similar opportunity to decide how to deal with it in the House of Commons. The matter was also kept secret because there was disagreement within the American delegation at Yalta on the issue. Some members of the delegation hoped that the Soviet Union might even be persuaded to withdraw its request. A chance to review the situation with the Soviet Union, however, did not develop. Late in March there was a leak to the press about the American pledge to support the Soviet request at San Francisco. There was widespread criticism of the "deal," and the President authorized a quick announcement confirming the agreement to support the Soviet request.

The criticism of granting the extra votes to the Soviet Union was directed as much to the manner by which it became known as to the arrangement itself. Even those newspapers which considered the extra votes to be unimportant were critical of the fact that this arrangement became known in an inadvertent way. Because the news was a "leak," it gave rise to the charge that there were other "secret agreements" reached at Yalta.

At the time that the President announced American support of the Soviet request he also stated that the United States itself would not ask for two extra votes. The question of extra votes as compensation for the United States had been raised at the Yalta Conference. Ever since the President had agreed to support the request of the Soviet Union at San Francisco for two extra votes in the Assembly, there had been considerable concern over the decision. Justice Byrnes and Edward J. Flynn were particularly disturbed over this question. Both of them probably recalled vividly the way opponents of the League of Nations in 1919 had appealed successfully to anti-British sentiment, particularly among Irish-Americans, over the fact that the British Commonwealth had six votes to one for the United States. They feared a similar reaction now against Russia's having three votes to our one. They urged that some way be found to give the United States the same number of votes as Russia. As it turned out, there was little foundation for these fears. When the facts became known American public opinion condemned any "deal" whereby the United States would get three votes for Russia's three, but there was virtually no opposition to our granting outright the extra votes for Byelorussia and the Ukraine. The matter was scarcely mentioned in the Senate debate on ratification of the Charter. The whole incident was a good example of "Maginot Line" thinking—of preparing for the fight to ratify American participation in the United Nations as if it were the year 1919, not 1945.

The President was persuaded at Yalta by Byrnes and Flynn to write letters on this question to Stalin and Church-

THE END OF THE CONFERENCE

ill explaining that he might face difficulties at home over the fact that the United States was the only one of the Big Three with just one vote in the Assembly of the world organization. If it were necessary for him to ask for additional votes for the United States, Mr. Roosevelt inquired, would the other two leaders support such a proposal?

The Prime Minister replied on February 11 that he would do everything possible to assist in the matter.

> ... Our position is [wrote Churchill], that we maintained the long-established representation of the British Empire and Commonwealth; that the Soviet Government are represented by its chief member, and the two republics of the Ukraine and White Russia; and that the United States should propose the form in which their undisputed equality with every other Member State should be expressed.

Marshal Stalin replied:

> Dear Mr. Roosevelt:
> I have received your letter of February 10. I entirely agree with you that, since the number of votes for the Soviet Union is increased to three in connection with the inclusion of the Soviet Ukraine and Soviet White Russia among the members of the assembly, the number of votes for the USA should also be increased.
> I think that the number of votes for the USA might be increased to three as in the case of the Soviet Union and its two basic Republics. If it is necessary I am prepared officially to support this proposal.
>
> With sincere respects
> (signed) J. Stalin

Roosevelt decided before his death that the United States would not ask for three votes in the Assembly. Although I believe the President's request was a mistake, the letters were another indication of the understanding that existed at this time among Roosevelt, Churchill, and Stalin.

After the Yalta communiqué had been approved at noon on February 11, the State Department staff and I worked throughout the afternoon sending information to Washington on the final agreements at Yalta and also radioing decisions on routine departmental business.

At six o'clock that evening Molotov, Eden, and I signed the protocol of the Conference. By this time the President had left Yalta and was on the first stage of his journey homeward. Since he had told Stalin that he was anxious to see the terrible destruction at Sevastopol, the President drove to that city to spend the night on the American communications ship, the U.S.S. *Catoctin*. When the last word of the protocol had been radioed to Washington, Freeman Matthews said, "Mr. Secretary, our last message has been sent. Can I cut the connections to the ship?" I replied, "Yes," and with the cutting of the communication that had connected us with the U.S.S. *Catoctin*, the work at the Conference came to a close.

After we cut the connection to Washington the State Department staff had a late supper in my room before starting out on our drive to Simferopol. As we reached the crest of the mountains separating Yalta from the western Crimea, we stopped the car for a last view of the site of this historic Conference.

When we reached Simferopol, late at night, we could not find the railroad station. Our NKVD escort got out of the jeep and banged on several doors before he could find anyone to tell him how to reach it. When we reached the station we were shown aboard a train that had been used by the Romanian King and the royal family. We were told that Harry Hopkins and his son Bob were already asleep in the royal car. They had gone ahead of us and after walking up and down the platform for what seemed like hours without anyone offering to help them, they had finally found someone who could speak English and he had put them aboard the train.

The next morning Harry, in his pajamas and bare feet, banged on my door and we talked together at great length over morning coffee. He said: "If I ever see a foreigner on a station platform in America again I'll show him the washroom and then I'll give him a drink."

We had been amused over the description of Harry's plight at the station, but actually he was extremely ill and should not have been exerting himself in this way. All during the Conference Dr. McIntire had kept Harry in bed as much as possible. He had not been allowed, for instance, to attend any of the formal dinners, and it had been a great exertion for him to be present at the plenary sessions.

Our train during the night had moved from Simferopol to Saki. We assembled at the airport and waited until the President arrived from Sevastopol and had boarded the Sacred Cow, with Admiral Leahy, Mrs. Boettiger, and other members of the White House group. Hopkins joined them for the flight to the Middle East where they were to board the *Quincy*, which had been secretly anchored in Great Bitter Lake near the Suez Canal, to await the President's arrival. Immediately after the President took off for the warm sunshine of the Middle East, our party assembled and commenced boarding our C-54, which had remained at Saki throughout the Conference, for a flight to snowbound Moscow.

Our visit to Moscow, although brief, proved to be a useful postscript to the Yalta Conference in a number of matters pertaining to Soviet-American relations. It also enabled me to have some useful private talks with Molotov, Vishinsky, A. I. Mikoyan, Commissar of Foreign Trade, and others.

At lunch I was the guest of the Soviet Foreign Office at their official guesthouse. During the course of the luncheon I talked with Mikoyan and expressed the opinion that peacetime co-operation in economic matters between the Soviet Union and the United States could become a significant factor in maintaining the peace and security of the world.

Vishinsky declared, at one point, that he wished to propose a toast to economics. "We lawyers," he said, "may know nothing of the mechanics of this subject, but we can appreciate the art of it." In wartime, he observed, not only what could be eaten with pleasure was important, but any food at all was important. He said, therefore, that he toasted industry and agriculture and particularly the men who guided and worked in them. He stressed that he wished especially to toast the workers, farmers, and business leaders of the United States, who had created so much that was useful not only to the United States but to other countries as well. He added that the Soviet Union was doing its best to learn from the United States and had already mastered the art of producing many of the things for which America was famous. He hoped, he continued, that the Soviet Union would eventually not only equal but surpass the United States in production. That, he concluded, was the right kind of competition—peaceful economic competition.

That same evening we attended a special command performance of the ballet, which was most beautiful in every respect. During one of the intermissions I discussed with Molotov, who had just arrived from Saki, a question that he had raised at Yalta. He had asked about the possibility of the United States' turning some American cruisers and destroyers over to the Soviet Union. Russian morale, he said, would be increased immensely if ships could be made available to the Soviet Navy before they entered the war against Japan.

I assured Molotov, both at Yalta and Moscow, that I would bring this matter to the President's attention. When I saw the President in Alexandria on February 15, I did raise the Soviet request. After this talk I radioed Molotov from Cairo: "The President wishes the matter to be given urgent attention and requests that it be studied and analyzed by the United States Military Mission in Moscow. Accordingly I would appreciate your pursuing the matter further with Ambassador Harriman." No ships were turned over to the Soviet Union as the result of this Soviet request. After the surrender of Italy in 1943 the Soviet Union had asked for a portion of the Italian fleet. Both the British and American leaders, however, had objected to this, since these ships were valuable to the war effort in the Mediterranean. Furthermore, the Combined Chiefs of Staff took the position that the Italian ships were built for Mediterranean waters and were, as a result, of no use in Northern waters. At Teheran the President and the Prime Minister had agreed, instead of giving one third of the Italian fleet to the Soviet Union, to loan the Russians one obsolete cruiser, the U.S.S. *Milwaukee*, one old British battleship, the H.M.S. *Royal Sovereign*, three submarines, and eight destroyers. These vessels were transferred to the Russians in addition to the normal Lend-Lease transfers of a number of small ships and other craft. Later, however, in the Italian peace treaty, the Soviet Union was allocated one third of the Italian Navy and, in exchange, agreed to return the British and American ships.

We left Moscow early in the morning of February 14. We

drove from the embassy to the airport in pitch-darkness. When we reached the airport we were all surprised to see the field flooded in bright lights. It was below zero and a light snow was falling. Molotov, in a black coat and black fur hat, Vishinsky in his Foreign Office uniform, and other members of the Foreign Office were awaiting us there. As we stepped from our car the band struck up "The Star-Spangled Banner," and we could see the aluminum alloy of the C-54 sparkling in the bright light of the floodlights. Major Richmond and the entire crew were lined up at attention. It was an impressive occasion.

We boarded the plane and in a few minutes were circling Moscow. We flew an agreed air corridor over Turkey to Egypt. Matthews, Hiss, Foote, and I worked most of the day on papers, drafting cables and reports.

At Cairo we stayed at Payne Field, the United States Air Forces base. After dinner I called on Haile Selassie, Emperor of Ethiopia, who was staying, for security reasons, in one of the guest cottages at the field. He was simple and direct in his manner and quick in his understanding.

I told him that the Crimean Conference would result in an organization for peace which we hoped would make it impossible for any aggressor again to attack a small nation as Italy had attacked his country. When I expressed the hope that Ethiopia would send a full delegation to the San Francisco Conference, the Emperor was greatly pleased. He expressed the gratitude of his nation for the aid the United States had already rendered Ethiopia. I replied that I hoped the United States would be able to help Ethiopia develop her natural resources and modernize her agriculture, transportation, and mining.

The next morning I flew to Alexandria to meet the Pres-

After Yalta, President Roosevelt confers with King Farouk of Egypt aboard the U.S.S. Quincy.

(U.S. Army Signal Corps photos)

Ibn Saud of Saudi Arabia and the President meet aboard the U.S.S. Quincy *to discuss Middle Eastern problems.*

Emperor Haile Selassie and the President talk over economic aid to Ethiopia.

Ambassador John G. Winant, Anna Roosevelt Boettiger, and Harry Hopkins aboard the U.S.S. Quincy in Alexandria Harbor after the Yalta Conference. (U.S. Army Signal Corps)

THE END OF THE CONFERENCE

ident. At the Royal Egyptian Yacht Club in Alexandria, where I waited for the *Quincy* to arrive, I met Ambassador Winant, who had just arrived from London by air. Winant had cabled the President at Yalta, expressing regret that he was not present since decisions there would affect his work on the European Advisory Commission. The President, on receipt of Winant's message, remarked that it was not necessary for the Ambassador to Great Britain to be present, but he cabled Winant that he would be happy to see him in Alexandria.

When we saw the *Quincy* coming into the harbor Rear Admiral Polland, the British naval officer in charge, sent us out in his launch to meet the ship. When I reached the *Quincy*, I was taken immediately to the bridge deck where the President was enjoying the view of the harbor. I discussed departmental business with him for half an hour. I secured approval, among other things, of my recommendation of Dr. Isador Lubin to be our representative on the newly created Reparations Commission in Moscow.

The President told me that he would review with me in full in Washington the interesting talks that he had had with Ibn Saud, Haile Selassie, and King Farouk. The President referred to his conversation with Ibn Saud as a memorable one. He told me that he must have a conference with congressional leaders and re-examine our entire policy on Palestine. He was now convinced, he added, that if nature took its course there would be bloodshed between the Arabs and Jews. Some formula, not yet discovered, would have to be evolved to prevent this warfare, he concluded.

On April 5 he wrote the leader of Saudi Arabia,

> Your Majesty will recall that on previous occasions I communicated to you the attitude of the American Government

toward Palestine and made clear our desire that no decision be taken with respect to the basic situation in that country without full consultation with both Arabs and Jews. Your Majesty will also doubtless recall that during our recent conversation I assured you that I would take no action, in my capacity as Chief of the Executive Branch of this Government, which might prove hostile to the Arab people.

After my conference with the President at Alexandria, I flew back to Cairo. Our C-54 took off from Cairo at five-twenty that afternoon, circled the Pyramids, and after a midnight stop at Casablanca we reached Dakar on the southern tip of Cape Verde, the westernmost point of land in the African continent, at noon the next day. After lunch we flew to Liberia, where I was the guest of honor at a reception given by my friend, President William V. S. Tubman. I was greatly impressed that evening with the vision and ability of President Tubman. I had the opportunity too of discussing with Secretary of State Gabriel Dennis the future development of the natural resources of Liberia.

At Alexandria, I had explained to the President that General Marshall, at Secretary Stimson's request, had entrusted me with a special mission to President Vargas in Brazil. After I described my route the President had immediately said that it was vitally important to the United States Government that I pay an official visit, as Secretary of State, to Liberia. The bulge of Africa opposite Brazil, he reminded me he had stated some time before, was of vital interest to the United States. He was determined, he added, to do everything within his power to assist the Liberian people to fulfill their great dream of economic security based upon their own economy.

We left Liberia at 12:35 A.M., February 17, for a night

flight across the South Atlantic. At Rio, I had a successful discussion with President Vargas. Among other things I discussed with him, at his suggestion, the question of Brazil's establishing diplomatic relations with the Soviet Union. In the course of our conversations I emphasized how highly the United States Government regarded the contributions that Brazil had made to the war effort.

On February 19, I left Brazil to fly to Mexico City for the Inter-American Conference at Chapultepec. At this conference the representatives of the American nations produced agreements that reached new heights in inter-American relations. By the time I returned to Washington on March 10, I had been away six weeks, had visited fifteen different countries, and had traveled some twenty-six thousand miles.

The President meanwhile had returned on the *Quincy*. His homeward journey from Alexandria to Norfolk was in some respects sad in comparison with the high spirit and enthusiasm of the outward journey. He was buoyed by his great achievement in the Crimea, but the tragic death at sea of "Pa" Watson, his devoted friend and associate through so many difficult years, caused deep sorrow.

In addition, the President's party had dispersed. Harry Hopkins had flown to North Africa for a brief rest before going to the Mayo Clinic where he was to remain until the President died. The President wanted Hopkins with him to help prepare his message to Congress, and he was annoyed that Harry wished to go ahead by air. In view of Hopkins' utter fatigue and intense suffering, however, his desire to return to the United States as soon as possible was understandable.

Byrnes, Flynn, and Early, also, either went on special missions or returned to Washington ahead of the President. The

President, with his party scattered, sent for his able associate of many years, Judge Samuel I. Rosenman, who was in London on a mission. Rosenman joined the President at Algiers and not only served as his companion aboard ship but also performed a masterful service in helping to prepare the President's memorable message which was delivered to Congress on March 1.

PART THREE

The Balance Sheet

CHAPTER 15

Appeasement or Realism?

The record of the Conference shows clearly that the Soviet Union made greater concessions at Yalta to the United States and Great Britain than were made to the Soviets. The agreements reached among President Roosevelt, Prime Minister Churchill, and Marshal Stalin were, on the whole, a diplomatic triumph for the United States and Great Britain. The real difficulties with the Soviet Union came *after* Yalta when the agreements were not respected.

The main Russian concessions at Yalta were:

(1) *The World Organization.*

(a) The Soviet Union accepted the American formula for voting in the Security Council. John Foster Dulles reported to the American delegation at San Francisco on May 26, 1945, that "Ambassador Gromyko recently had told him the voting formula represented a big compromise from the Russian point of view."

It was clear in the discussions at Yalta that Marshal Stalin was primarily interested in an alliance of Great Britain, the United States, and the Soviet Union. By securing his agreement to the American voting formula, however, President Roosevelt was able to achieve more than an alliance of the Great Powers.

It is absolutely incorrect to state that the permanent members were granted the veto power on most questions only because of Russian insistence. The American delegation, at Dumbarton Oaks and after, favored the big-power veto on matters involving economic and military sanctions. The United States delegation had been advised that the Secretary of War, the Secretary of the Navy, and the Joint Chiefs of Staff were agreed, as a matter of fundamental military policy, that the United States should not join any world organization in which its forces could be used without its consent. The veto was also favored by the members of Congress who were consulted on the plans for the United Nations.

The whole controversy over the veto power of the permanent members of the Security Council overlooks the fact, anyway, that it is not the veto itself but the misuse of power to veto that has impeded the effectiveness of the Security Council.

(b) The Soviet Union withdrew its request for sixteen votes in the face of the adamant position of the United States and Great Britain. The Soviet Union withdrew its request that Great Britain and the United States agree *at Yalta* to invite the Ukraine and White Russia to the San Francisco Conference. The President and the Prime Minister did pledge to support admission of the two, when the San Francisco

Conference voted on this matter. The additional votes in the Assembly were not too significant. They have not been an important factor in the work of the United Nations one way or the other. The effectiveness of the United Nations has been limited by the inability of the Soviet Union, Great Britain, and the United States to work together in an amicable fashion, not because the Soviet Union has three votes in the Assembly.

In view of the many concessions made by the Soviet Union to the American position on world organization, the two additional votes were only a minor concession to the Russians. It was far wiser, President Roosevelt decided, to meet the request of the Soviet Union on this point and to secure its participation in a United Nations conference than possibly to drive them entirely out of participation in a world organization. Whether some people like it or not, we live in an interdependent world. Although the achievement of One World is beset with immense difficulties, Russian participation in the United Nations was and is a necessary step in the right direction.

President Roosevelt expressed this point of view in his message to Congress on March 1, 1945, in the following words:

> *When the conclusions reached with respect to voting are made known I think and I hope that you find them fair—that you will find them a fair solution of this complicated and difficult problem—I might almost say a legislative problem. They are founded in justice, and will go far to insure international co-operation for the maintenance of peace. . . .*
>
> *This time we are not making the mistake of waiting until the end of the war to set up the machinery of peace. . . .*
>
> *The structure of world peace cannot be the work of one man, or one party, or one nation. It cannot be just an American*

peace, or a British peace, or a Russian, French, or a Chinese peace. It cannot be a peace of large nations—or of small nations. It must be a peace which rests on the co-operative effort of the whole world. . . .

(c) The Soviet Union agreed to the American definition of the countries that should be invited to attend the San Francisco Conference. As a result these Associated Nations who declared war by March 1, 1945, were able to participate in the conference as original members. This decision made it possible for a number of Latin-American nations, particularly, to participate in the conference. Here was a substantial concession that Stalin made at the urging of Mr. Roosevelt.

(d) President Roosevelt insisted on the right of full and frank discussions in the world organization. Although the Soviet Union did not like it too well, the President made it clear that all nations had the right to be heard. As a result, the smaller nations have been able to use the United Nations as a forum to present their views to the world.

(2) *Military Co-ordination.*
At President Roosevelt's request Marshal Stalin agreed, for the first time in the war, that there should be real co-ordination of Russian and Western military activities. Stalin also agreed with the President's request that Soviet air bases near Budapest and elsewhere be made available for use by the United States Air Corps.

There was, for the first time as well, a frank statement by the Soviet Union of its future plans for offensive operations.

(3) *The French Zone of Occupation and France's Membership on the German Control Commission.*
Very early in the Conference the Soviet Union withdrew

its objection to the recommendation made by the President and the Prime Minister that the French be assigned a zone of occupation from the British and American zones.

Near the close of the Conference, when President Roosevelt announced that he now agreed with the British that the French should also be on the Control Commission, the Soviet Union withdrew also its vigorous opposition to this proposal. The German zones of occupation were worked out by the European Advisory Commission in London. The zones were drawn before Yalta. I know of no evidence to support the charge that President Roosevelt agreed at Yalta that American troops should not capture Berlin ahead of the Red Army. General Eisenhower has written that the decision that American troops should not push into Berlin was taken in March 1945, solely on military grounds.[1]

(4) German Reparations.

This was one of the most controversial issues at the Conference. Both Great Britain and the United States agreed on the principle of exacting reparations from Germany but we were most anxious to avoid the disastrous experience of reparations after World War I. The British did not wish to agree to the Russian figure of twenty billion. President Roosevelt was willing that the Russian figure be considered by the Reparations Commission *in its initial studies* only as a *basis for discussion* and not as an agreed amount. The Soviet Union accepted the American position.

In July 1946, V. M. Molotov, at a meeting of the foreign ministers, stated that President Roosevelt at Yalta had agreed to ten billion dollars of reparations for the Soviet Union. This was incorrect. The President accepted, purely *as a basis for*

[1] Eisenhower, op. cit., pp. 396, 400, 402.

discussion by the Reparations Commission, the figure of twenty billion dollars, fifty per cent of which was to go to the Soviet Union. Maisky at the foreign ministers' meeting on February 10 at Yalta (and Molotov was present) agreed that the reparations formula "did not commit the Allies to the exact figure." Marshal Stalin at the plenary session that same day stated that no commitment as to figures was involved. The figures mentioned, he explained, would be used merely *as a basis for discussion* by the Reparations Commission.

(5) *The Soviet Union Accepted Two British Amendments to the Agreement on Yugoslavia.*

(6) *The "Declaration on Liberated Europe."*
The American draft was accepted with almost no opposition. When Marshal Stalin realized that President Roosevelt would not accept two amendments proposed by Molotov, the Marshal withdrew them.

(7) *Poland.*
The Polish issue proved to be the most controversial and the most difficult of all the questions considered. While President Roosevelt was meeting with Prime Minister Churchill and Marshal Stalin in the Crimea, American and British troops had just recovered ground lost by the Battle of the Bulge. The Allies had not yet bridged the Rhine. In Italy our advance had bogged down in the Apennines. The Soviet troops, on the other hand, had just swept through almost all of Poland and East Prussia, and had reached at some points the Oder River in Germany. Most of Hungary had been liberated, eastern Czechoslovakia had been cap-

tured, and the Yugoslav Partisans had recaptured Belgrade in November 1944. By February 1945, therefore, Poland and all of eastern Europe, except for most of Czechoslovakia, was in the hands of the Red Army. *As a result of this military situation, it was not a question of what Great Britain and the United States would permit Russia to do in Poland, but what the two countries could persuade the Soviet Union to accept.*

(a) President Roosevelt refused, as did the Prime Minister, to accept the Russian request that the western boundary of Poland be the western Neisse River. Marshal Stalin finally withdrew this demand and agreed to leave the western frontier of Poland to be settled at the peace conference.[2]

(b) The Curzon Line was insisted upon by Marshal Stalin as the eastern frontier of Poland. The Soviet Union considered that the area east of that line had been taken from it by force after World War I. Before the Yalta Conference Churchill had already supported the Curzon Line in the House of Commons.

President Roosevelt suggested that the Soviet Union might consider leaving the Polish city of Lwow and some oil lands to Poland, and the Prime Minister also suggested that some such gesture would be reassuring to the world. Stalin, however, insisted that he could not be "less Russian" than Curzon and Clemenceau, who had first agreed to this frontier line. However, he did later propose minor deviations of from six to eight kilometers in favor of Poland. The United States was in no position at Yalta to change the Russian attitude on the eastern boundary.

[2] Later, at Potsdam, the Oder-Neisse was made the boundary between Poland and the Soviet zone of occupation in Germany, but the final determination of the western boundary continues to await a German peace treaty.

(c) By the time of the Yalta Conference the Soviet Union had established the Lublin Provisional Polish Government. Both President Roosevelt and Prime Minister Churchill adamantly *refused* to recognize this puppet regime. Agreement on the government of Poland proved to be the most difficult and time-consuming question at Yalta. The Soviet Union insisted that all that should be done to the Lublin Government was to *enlarge* it. President Roosevelt and the British insisted that it had to be *reorganized* so as to include democratic leaders from outside Poland.

Stalin finally agreed to the *reorganization* of the Lublin Government by the inclusion of democratic leaders from at home and abroad. He also agreed with the British and American request that free and unfettered elections would be held at an early date. Roosevelt withdrew the phrase from the American formula that "The Ambassadors of the three powers in Warsaw following such recognition would be charged with the responsibility of observing and reporting to their respective Governments on the carrying out of the pledge in regard to free and unfettered elections." Although President Roosevelt did withdraw this wording, he made it clear that the ambassadors *would nonetheless still perform this function*. The sentence was reworded, therefore, to read that the three powers ". . . will exchange Ambassadors [with Poland] by whose reports the respective Governments will be kept informed about the situation in Poland."

It is true, of course, that the decision was not as clear-cut as President Roosevelt had desired. President Truman, in discussing the Polish agreement with me on April 21, 1945, expressed regret that the agreement was not more clear-cut, but added that he realized President Roosevelt had made every effort to make it crystal-clear.

APPEASEMENT OR REALISM?

The agreement on Poland was, under the circumstances, a concession by Marshal Stalin to the Prime Minister and the President. It was not exactly what we wanted, but on the other hand, it was not exactly what the Soviet Union wanted. It was not a "sellout" of democratic Poland, as has been so widely charged, but a pledge from Stalin that he would allow a new government to be organized and that free elections would be held in a country which was entirely at his mercy. The trouble was not the Yalta formula but the fact that the Soviet Union later failed to live up to the terms of the agreement.

President Roosevelt told a joint session of Congress on March 1, 1945: "I am convinced that this agreement on Poland, under the circumstances, is the most hopeful agreement possible for a free, independent, and prosperous Polish State."[3]

The President also pointed out: "The responsibility for political conditions thousands of miles away can no longer be avoided, I think, by this great nation. . . . The United States now exerts a tremendous influence in the cause of peace. . . . The United States will not always have its way 100 per cent—nor will Russia nor Great Britain. We shall not always have ideal solutions to complicated international problems, even though we are determined continuously to strive toward that ideal. But I am sure that—under the agreements reached at Yalta—there will be a more stable political Europe than ever before. . . ."

What did the Soviet Union gain in eastern Europe which she did not already have as the result of the smashing vic-

[3] Although Molotov delayed on inviting Mikolajczyk to Moscow for discussions, Harry Hopkins straightened this out on his trip to Moscow in May 1945. After the Polish elections were held the United States recognized the newly elected government.

tories of the Red Army? Great Britain and the United States secured pledges at Yalta, unfortunately not honored, which did promise free elections and democratic governments.

What, too, with the possible exception of the Kuriles, did the Soviet Union receive at Yalta which she might not have taken without any agreement? If there had been no agreement, the Soviet Union could have swept into North China, and the United States and the Chinese would have been in no real position to prevent it. It must never be forgotten that, while the Crimea Conference was taking place, President Roosevelt had just been told by his military advisers that the surrender of Japan might not occur until 1947, and some predicted even later. The President was told that without Russia it might cost the United States a million casualties to conquer Japan. It must be remembered, too, that at the time of the Yalta Conference it was still uncertain whether the atomic bomb could be perfected and that, since the Battle of the Bulge had set us back in Europe, it was uncertain how long it might take for Germany to crack. There had been immense optimism in the autumn of 1944, as Allied troops raced through France, that the war was nearly over. Then came the Battle of the Bulge, which was more than a military reversal. It cast a deep gloom over the confident expectation that the German war would end soon.[4] In Washington, for instance, the procurement agencies of the armed services immediately began placing new orders on the basis of a longer war in Europe than had been estimated.

With hindsight, it can be said that the widespread pessimism was unwarranted. The significant fact is not, however, this hindsight but the effect of this thinking on the strategy

[4] See Robert E. Merriam, *Dark December; the Full Account of the Battle of the Bulge* (Chicago: Ziff, Davis Co., 1947).

Molotov, Eden, and Stettinius pose after a foreign ministers' meeting. (U.S. Army Signal Corps)

President Roosevelt conferring with Secretary of State Stettinius, with Marshal Stalin as an interested observer. (U.S. Army Signal Corps photos)

The Prime Minister and the President visit aboard the U.S.S. Quincy in Malta Harbor.

and agreements made in the Crimea. It was important to bring the Soviet Union into the united sphere of action. Russian co-operation in the Japanese war ran parallel to their co-operation in the world organization and to united action in Europe. Furthermore, critics of the Far Eastern agreement have tended to overlook the fact that in the agreement the Soviet Union pledged that China was to retain "full sovereignty in Manchuria" and that the Soviet Union would conclude a pact of friendship with the Chinese Nationalist Government. It is my understanding that the American military leaders felt that the war had to be concluded as soon as possible. There was the fear that heavy casualties in Japan or the possible lack of continuous victories would have an unfortunate effect on the attitude of the American people.

President Roosevelt had great faith in his Army and Navy staffs, and he relied wholeheartedly upon them. Their insistent advice was that the Soviet Union had to be brought into the Far Eastern war soon after Germany's collapse. The President, therefore, in signing the Far Eastern agreement, acted upon the advice of his military advisers. He did not approve the agreement from any desire to appease Stalin and the Soviet Union.[5]

It is apparently the belief of some critics of the Yalta Conference that it would have been better to have made no

[5] Admiral Ellis M. Zacharias, formerly Deputy Chief of Naval Intelligence, has written that the Joint Chiefs of Staff persuaded President Roosevelt to make the concessions in order to bring the Soviet Union into the Japanese war on a wholly inaccurate and misleading intelligence report. There was no evidence at Yalta that any intelligence reports other than the one used were in existence. See Zacharias, "The Inside Story of Yalta," *United Nations World*, January 1949, Vol. 3, No. 1, p. 16. The Chinese representative to the United Nations wrote an interesting letter to the New York *Herald Tribune*, January 21, 1949, stressing that President Roosevelt was "ill-informed." He writes, "I was afraid that the American Government, by entertaining an exaggerated opinion of Japan's endurance, might make China pay the price for Soviet military aid. . . ."

agreements with the Soviet Union. Yet if we had made no agreements at Yalta, the Russians still would have been in full possession of the territory in Europe that President Roosevelt is alleged to have given them. The failure to agree would have been a serious blow to the morale of the Allied world, already suffering from five years of war; it would have meant the prolongation of the German and Japanese wars; it would have prevented the establishment of the United Nations; and it would probably have led to other consequences incalculable in their tragedy for the world.

President Roosevelt did not "surrender" anything significant at Yalta which it was within his power to withhold. The agreements, on the other hand, speeded up the end of the war and greatly reduced American casualties. The Yalta Conference, also, made it possible to create the United Nations. Although events since Yalta have made it difficult for the United Nations to operate effectively, I am convinced that the United Nations can still become the greatest achievement of history toward the building of a stable and peaceful world.

On March 15, 1945, after I had returned to Washington from the Chapultepec Conference at Mexico City, I told a bipartisan group of senators that "the atmosphere at Yalta was not one of bickering, that Stalin and his government apparently had made up their minds to take their place among the United Nations. During the talks, the Russians frequently made concessions on a variety of political, economic, and security matters." When Senator Tom Connally said that there was talk that President Roosevelt had given in to Stalin on almost every issue, I emphasized that "at the end of the first day at Yalta it was apparent that we faced a reasonable situation at the Crimea Conference."

I had made a similar statement to President Vargas of Brazil, on February 17, while I was visiting him in Rio. I told Vargas that "I was gratified to be able to report that President Roosevelt had found a high degree of co-operation on the part of Stalin." I also said, "It was apparent within the first forty-eight hours that they would get along and accomplish great results." When President Vargas asked if Stalin "was a very tough man to work with," I replied that "he was very tough but he was also very realistic." I explained to President Vargas that "the President was confident that the Soviet Union had decided to take its place in the United Nations family as a good citizen."

CHAPTER 16

The Breakdown after Yalta

A series of events began soon after the Conference in the Crimea which shattered Anglo-American unity with the Soviet Union. Even before the death of President Roosevelt on April 12, 1945, the tide of unity had begun to ebb. After his death, the defeat of Winston Churchill as Prime Minister in the following July, and bewildering developments within the Soviet Union, a dangerous impasse developed that still exists today.

The high degree of co-operation attained by the three leaders at Yalta began to break down shortly after Yalta. It was the opinion of some of the State Department group who were on President Roosevelt's staff at the Conference that Marshal Stalin had difficulties with the Politburo, when he returned to Moscow, for having been too friendly and for having made too many concessions to the two capitalist nations which could, in dogmatic Marxist eyes, never be really trusted by Communist Russia. Certain members of the

Politburo may well have taken the line that the Soviet Union had been virtually sold out at Yalta.

Ambassador Harriman had cabled the State Department on September 19, 1944, that it seemed clear that powerful elements close to Stalin were unwilling to see the security of the Soviet Union rest solely on an untried world organization. Therefore, Harriman suggested, the Soviet Union might go along with the world organization but, at the same time, build its own sphere of influence. At the San Francisco Conference, Anthony Eden told me that he was convinced that something happened in Moscow after the Yalta Conference, and that the Soviet Union had begun to alter its policy as expressed in the Yalta agreements.

The workings of the Politburo have never been even partially revealed, and I do not pretend to know what took place in Moscow after the Conference. It is possible that Stalin's advisers told him that free elections in eastern Europe would destroy Communist control of the nations in this region. At the Potsdam Conference, I understand, Marshal Stalin actually wanted the United States to recognize the various governments in eastern Europe before the elections provided in the Yalta agreement had been held. Stalin said, "A freely elected government in any of these countries would be anti-Soviet, and that we cannot allow."[1]

It may also be true that President Roosevelt's death strengthened the hand of an anti-American group in the Politburo. It is also possible that the Politburo reviewed its policy after Yalta and decided that the United States was soon going to withdraw from Europe. The emphasis which United States military authorities placed on the Far Eastern

---

[1] See Philip E. Moseley, *Face to Face with Russia* (Foreign Policy Association Headline Series No. 70, p. 23).

THE BREAKDOWN AFTER YALTA

war may have led the Russians to assume that the United States would be so fully committed in a military way in the Pacific that all American troops would be withdrawn from Europe soon after the German surrender. The Politburo may also have been influenced in this line of thinking by President Roosevelt's statement, at the plenary session on February 5, that United States troops probably could not be kept in Europe more than two years after the war.

Whatever the reason, shortly after the Yalta Conference had closed the Soviet Union began to hedge on some of its agreements. The Russians delayed on certain military agreements; they impeded the formation of the German Control Commission; they failed to live up to the "Declaration on Liberated Europe" as applied to Romania; and they greatly impeded execution of the Polish agreement.

The Soviet Union, after allowing Air Corps representatives to survey possible air bases near Budapest, delayed on the granting of the bases. The Air Corps finally dropped the issue because, as a result of the delays, there was no longer need for the bases. At Yalta a military agreement called on each nation to allow the others to send missions behind its lines to deal with its own liberated prisoners. The Soviet Union after Yalta, however, would not allow a United States mission to function behind Soviet lines.

In London the Soviet shift in policy was evident to the American representatives on the European Advisory Commission. One week after Yalta the Soviet member on the commission announced that representatives were coming from Moscow to form with the British and the Americans a nucleus of the Control Commission for Germany. Two weeks after this announcement the Soviet representative stated with great embarrassment that the Russians were not after all sending a group to London. His manner led our representative to believe that a change was taking place in Soviet foreign policy.

In the case of Romania (as well as in the rest of liberated Europe) the "Declaration on Liberated Europe" had pledged the three governments to "jointly assist the people in any European liberated state or former Axis satellite state in Europe . . . to form interim governmental authorities broadly representative of all democratic elements in the population and pledged to the earliest possible establishment through free elections of governments responsive to the will of the people. . . . When, in the opinion of the three governments, conditions in any European liberated state or any former Axis satellite state in Europe make such action necessary, they will immediately consult together on the measures necessary to discharge the joint responsibility set forth in this declaration."

In spite of this pledge of Russian, British, and American joint action, on February 24, 1945, thirteen days after the Yalta meeting adjourned, the Soviet member of the Allied Control Commission for Romania refused to call a meeting of the commission. Three days later Vishinsky arrived in Bucharest and demanded the dismissal of the Radescu government and the formation of a new government. Vishinsky soon forced the King to appoint a government formed by pro-Communist leader Petru Groza. United States protests that the principles of the "Declaration on Liberated Europe" were being ignored were bluntly rejected by the Soviet Union.

Meanwhile the Polish agreement was being jeopardized. Early in March, Ambassador Harriman warned the State Department in Washington that Molotov was insisting that only Polish leaders who were acceptable to the Lublin Government be invited to consult with the commission appointed at Yalta. The Yalta agreement, on this point, read:

> Mr. Molotov, Mr. Harriman and Sir A. Clark Kerr are authorized as a Commission to consult in the first instance in Moscow with members of the present Provisional Government and with other Polish democratic leaders from within Poland and from abroad, with a view to the reorganization of the present Government along the above lines.

The list submitted by Molotov of those Polish leaders who should be invited to come from London to Moscow included only one name that President Roosevelt had suggested, and Molotov specifically refused to invite Mikolajczyk. Molotov also returned to his old thesis that the new government should be little more than an enlarged Lublin Government. The British and American representatives refused to accept this interpretation of the Yalta agreement and pointed out that the agreement had been for a reorganized and not an enlarged Lublin Government.

The Yalta agreement, on this point, was: "The Provisional Government which is now functioning in Poland should therefore be reorganized on a broader democratic basis with the inclusion of democratic leaders from Poland itself and from Poles abroad."

On April 1, President Roosevelt sent an urgent cable on the Polish issue to Marshal Stalin. Both the President and the Prime Minister, late in March, had communicated with each other on the Polish question, and both agreed that the Yalta agreement was in grave danger.

Roosevelt expressed to Stalin his disappointment at "the lack of progress made in the carrying out, which the world expects, of the political decisions which we reached at Yalta, particularly those relating to the Polish question." The President declared that the impasse in Poland arose from the Soviet interpretation of the Yalta agreement that the new government should be little more than an enlarged Lublin Government. The President warned that this could not be reconciled with the agreement and that "any such solution which would result in a thinly disguised continuation of the present government would be entirely unacceptable, and would cause our people to regard the Yalta agreement as a failure."

The President also pointed out that it was essential to settle the Polish question "for the successful development of our program of international collaboration." On the developments in Romania, Roosevelt made it clear that he could not understand why these events did not fall under the "Declaration on Liberated Europe."

On April 7 the Marshal answered and admitted that the Polish question was deadlocked. He charged, however, that this had occurred because the British and American ambassadors had violated the Yalta agreement in insisting upon the complete liquidation of the Lublin Government and the formation of an entirely new government. The Marshal said that only Polish leaders should be invited who would recognize the Yalta agreements, including the decision on the Curzon Line, and leaders who were "really striving to establish friendly relations between Poland and the Soviet Union."

The President died while officers of the Foreign Office and the State Department were drafting parallel replies to Marshal Stalin.

On April 4 and 6, while the difficulties were developing over Romania and Poland, Ambassador Harriman cabled the

Department reports on the Russian situation. He detected three parallel lines of Soviet foreign policy:

(1) *Collaboration with the United States and the United Kingdom in a world organization.*

(2) *Creation of a security ring through domination of the border countries.*

(3) *Penetration of other countries through their Communist parties.*

Harriman recommended that we make sure that the Soviet Union should not be able to play the Western Allies off against each other. We were also to point out to the Soviet Union actual cases where their actions were "intolerable" and demonstrate to the Soviet leaders that they could not continue their present actions except at great cost to Russia.

Before the President died, on April 12, he was greatly irritated by another development in Soviet-American relations. Stalin sent the President a note protesting that negotiations were taking place at Bern between German Army officers and British and American officers for the surrender of the German Army in Italy. The President had advised the Soviet Union before the receipt of Stalin's note that the Germans had requested a meeting, but he had assured Stalin that no negotiations actually had taken place. Stalin's note asserted that the President was not being informed by his own military leaders, since negotiations had been completed and the Germans were allowing the American Army to advance in return for easier peace terms.

The President was angered by this note. He replied sharply that General Eisenhower would not have undertaken negotiations without informing him.[2] Furthermore, the Soviet

[2] See Eisenhower, op. cit., p. 423.

Union had been fully advised as to all the developments. The President remarked that he resented the "vile misrepresentations" of the Marshal's informants and that such information indicated a belief that certain of Stalin's informants desired to destroy friendly relations between the two countries.

Stalin replied that he did not question the President's honesty, but he still believed that he had received accurate information. The tone of Stalin's message, however, was more conciliatory than his previous ones.

Just before he died the President received a message from the Prime Minister asking for advice on what to say to the House of Commons on the Polish question. The day he died the President, at the little White House at Warm Springs, Georgia, sent Churchill the following message:

> *I would minimize the general Soviet problem as much as possible because these problems, in one form or another, seem to arise every day and most of them straighten out as in the case of the Bern meeting.*
> *We must be firm, however, and our course thus far is correct.*

Shortly after President Roosevelt returned from Yalta, he had asked his wise counselor, Bernard M. Baruch, to go to London to discuss a number of peace problems with the Prime Minister. I had a talk with Baruch and asked him to help us win Churchill over to the need for an Economic and Social Council in the world organization. Baruch explored many problems, including the world organization and relations with the Soviet Union, while he was in London. In his report to President Truman on April 20, Baruch wrote on the Russian question:

> *Russia unquestionably is the gravest fear of British officialdom. The Prime Minister was reassured by Mr. Roosevelt's*

last message to Stalin—that we intended to insist that the Russians observe their agreements.

I believe we can get along with the Russians, as I expressed it to many of the British, by doing three things:

    a. Keep our obligations, written or implied, promptly, absolutely and meticulously, making certain the Russians are kept thoroughly posted as to what we are doing and why.

    b. Insist firmly they do the same thing.

    c. Do our homework before going to conferences so that agreements are free of ambiguity and so that we have concise grasp of the policies we wish pursued.

Churchill on April 29, 1945, wrote to Stalin expressing again the Anglo-American attitude on Poland and warning the Soviet leader of the dangerous impasse that would develop unless the Soviet Union agreed to work with the West. Churchill stated:

Side by side with our strong sentiment over the rights of Poland which I believe is shared in at least as strong a degree throughout the United States, there has grown up throughout the English-speaking world a very warm and deep desire to be friends on equal and honorable terms with the mighty Russian Soviet Republic and to work with you, making allowances for our different systems of thought and government, and to work with you for long and bright years for all the world which we three powers can make together.

I who in my years of great responsibility have worked faithfully for this unity, will certainly continue to do so by every means in my power and in particular I can assure you we in Great Britain will not work for or tolerate a Polish Government unfriendly to Russia.

Neither can we recognise a Polish Government that does not truly correspond to the description in our joint declaration at Yalta with proper regard for the rights of the individual as we understand these matters in the Western World. . . .

There is not much comfort in looking into a future where you and the countries you dominate plus the Communist parties in many other states are all drawn up on one side and those who rallied to the English-speaking nations and their associates or dominions are on the other.

It is quite obvious that their quarrel would tear the world to pieces and all of us leading men on either side who had anything to do with that would be shamed before history. Even embarking on a long period of suspicion, of abuse and counter-abuse and of opposing policies would be a disaster hampering the great development of world prosperity for the masses which is attainable only by our trinity. I hope there is no word or phrase in this outpouring of my heart to you, Mr. Stalin, which unwittingly gives offense. If so, let me know but do not, I beg of you, my friend, underrate the divergencies which are opening about matters which you may think are small but which are symbolic of the way the English-speaking democracies look at life.[3]

The misunderstanding that arose between the United States and the Soviet Union over the abrupt ending of the Lend-Lease program—as far as the war in Europe was concerned—to the Soviet Union after V-E Day (May 8), was particularly untimely and did not help Soviet-American relations. The fact that the Soviet Union had pledged itself to enter the Far Eastern war made this order even more incredible and revealed a lack of co-ordination between military and civilian agencies. This order was issued without any warning whatsoever to the Soviet Union and other European countries not involved in the Japanese war, and it caught the State Department completely by surprise. While I was presiding at the San Francisco Conference, Acting Secretary of State Grew phoned me and informed me of the action. I urged him to discuss it with President Truman immediately, which he did, and the President wisely modi-

[3] Winston Churchill divulged this letter to the House of Commons on December 10, 1948.

fied the order. However, psychological damage had been done in our relations with a nation as suspicious as the Soviet Union.

On May 23, Truman sent Hopkins to Moscow to assure Stalin that the death of Mr. Roosevelt would not alter the United States policy of co-operating with the Soviet Union. At a meeting on May 27, Stalin told Hopkins that one of the reasons the Soviet Union believed that the American attitude had cooled toward the Soviet Union was "the manner in which Lend-Lease had been curtailed. He said that if the United States was unable to supply the Soviet Union further under Lend-Lease that was one thing but that the manner in which it had been done had been unfortunate and even brutal. For example, certain ships had been unloaded and while it was true that this order had been cancelled the whole manner in which it had been done had caused concern to the Soviet Government. If the refusal to continue Lend-Lease was designed as pressure on the Russians in order to soften them up then it was a fundamental mistake. He said he must tell Mr. Hopkins frankly that if the Russians were approached frankly on a friendly basis much could be done but that reprisals in any form would bring about the exact opposite effect."[4]

While Hopkins was in Moscow trying to straighten out the Polish question and a number of other issues, the San Francisco Conference reached an impasse that threatened failure in our attempt to build a world organization. On instruction from Molotov, Gromyko insisted at San Francisco that a dispute could not even be discussed by the Security Council without the unanimous vote of the five permanent members unless the situation was one that could be settled by peace-

[4] Sherwood, op. cit., p. 894.

ful means. On June 2, I announced at a meeting of Great Britain, the Soviet Union, the United States, France, and China that it would be utterly impossible for the United States to join a world organization that provided for veto power against the introduction of measures purely for discussion. I advised Gromyko that if the Soviet Union insisted on this view the United States would not join the world organization.

I telephoned President Truman that day and explained that the Soviet Union was insisting that one of the five permanent powers in the Security Council could veto the discussion of a situation, in which that Great Power was not involved, when the discussion was merely for the purpose of enabling the Security Council to explore what action, if any, it should take or recommend.

The President wholeheartedly supported me in my stand against the Russian position and approved my proposal to send a cable to Ambassador Harriman instructing him immediately to discuss the question with Marshal Stalin, accompanied by Hopkins if possible. I sent the message to Harriman that afternoon. I put a key sentence in the cable, saying I was aware that Marshal Stalin, in the past, did not know of "some of the decisions" which had been made and "communicated" to us. I instructed Harriman to describe the gravity of the situation to Stalin, saying that the conference would have to be adjourned unless the Russians withdrew their request.

Hopkins had been in Moscow over a week and had had already a number of conferences with Stalin when my message reached Moscow. He and Harriman, at Hopkins' last meeting with Stalin on June 6, raised the issue in my message with Stalin. It was pointed out to Stalin that the United

THE BREAKDOWN AFTER YALTA

States believed that the Yalta agreement safeguarded freedom of discussion and the right of any member to bring before the Security Council for discussion any situation affecting the peace and security of the world. When Molotov attempted to defend the instructions he had sent to Gromyko, I was told that the Marshal told him not to be ridiculous and that the Soviet Union should accept the American position.

On June 6, while I was presiding at a meeting of the conference in San Francisco, I received a message from Grew that Stalin had accepted the United States position regarding the voting procedure in the Security Council. I immediately talked to Gromyko and advised him of the word we had received from Moscow. His own instructions came in later, and we then proceeded with the final drafting of the Charter.

The entire incident reveals that Stalin could reach a quick decision, even though it meant publicly repudiating the position of his Foreign Minister. If Stalin had adamantly supported Molotov there would have been no United Nations formed at San Francisco. Furthermore, if we had not seized that moment to form the United Nations we would never have succeeded in the trying months that followed the end of the war.

At Yalta, destined to be the last meeting of Roosevelt, Churchill, and Stalin, the President had two main objectives. He desired the speedy and unconditional surrender of the Axis powers, and he desired the establishment of a world organization for peace and security. The Yalta agreements, in spite of the difficulties that followed, made possible the second of these objectives, and probably helped attain the first.

The world is interdependent. We have to make clear, as President Roosevelt did during the war, that we insist on a peaceful world based on tolerance of others, freedom, justice, and increased economic well-being for all peoples, regardless of race, creed, or color. At the same time we have to make sure that the world realizes that we do not countenance aggression on the part of any nation.

From my close association with Franklin D. Roosevelt, I know that he was primarily motivated by the great ideal of friendly co-operation among nations. At the same time he had no illusions about the dangers and difficulties of dealing with the Soviet Union. He emphasized many times that we must keep trying with patience and determination to get the Russians to realize that it was in their own selfish interest to win the confidence of the other countries of the world. We must help them see, he said, that co-operation with other nations was the only way they or we could have a peaceful world. If the Russians could acquire confidence in a world organization, the President was convinced that much could be accomplished. Although he knew that the winning of Russian confidence in a world organization would be difficult, and would take time and patience, peace was too vital a necessity not to make a supreme effort toward achieving this goal.

It was with this in mind that President Roosevelt told Congress on March 1, 1945:

> "... For the second time, in the lives of most of us, this generation is face to face with the objective of preventing wars. To meet that objective, the nations of the world will either have a plan or they will not. The groundwork of a plan has now been furnished and has been submitted to humanity for discussion and decision.

> "No plan is perfect. Whatever is adopted at San Francisco will doubtless have to be amended time and again over the years, just as our own Constitution has been.
>
> "No one can say exactly how long any plan will last. Peace can endure only so long as humanity really insists upon it, and is willing to work for it, and sacrifice for it.
>
> "Twenty-five years ago, American fighting men looked to the statesmen of the world to finish the work of peace for which they fought and suffered. We failed them. We failed them then. We cannot fail them again, and expect the world to survive.
>
> "I think the Crimean Conference was a successful effort by the three leading nations to find a common ground for peace. It spells—and it ought to spell—the end of the system of unilateral action, exclusive alliances and spheres of influence, and balances of power and all the other expedients which have been tried for centuries and have always failed.
>
> "We propose to substitute for all these, a universal organization in which all peace-loving nations will finally have a chance to join.
>
> "I am confident that the Congress and the American people will accept the results of this conference as the beginnings of a permanent structure of peace upon which we can begin to build, under God, that better world in which our children and grandchildren—yours and mine, and the children and grandchildren of the whole world—must live, can live. . . ."

President Roosevelt was well aware of the nature of Soviet society. Its dictatorial and authoritarian aspects were as repugnant to him as to any American. But he also had a strong sense of history. He knew that no society was static, and he believed that the United States could do much, through firmness, patience, and understanding, over a period of time in dealing with the Soviet Union to influence its evolution away from dictatorship and tyranny in the direction of a free, tolerant, and peaceful society.

While this process of evolution was taking place, we could

faithfully support the United Nations Charter over a span of years and use the United Nations in every possible way to keep the world on an even keel and enable it to ride out without disaster the inevitable strains and stresses of the times. This, I believe, was the essence of Roosevelt's policy toward the Soviet Union as expressed at Yalta.

It was essential that Prime Minister Churchill and President Roosevelt make an honest attempt at Yalta to work with the Russians. For the peace of the world, they had to make every effort to test the good faith of the Soviet Union. Until agreements were made and tested, the world could not clearly know of the difficulties of securing Russian compliance with agreements. The Western nations could not follow their present policy toward the Soviet Union unless they had behind them the record of President Roosevelt and Prime Minister Churchill in their joint effort to deal with the Russian leaders in an honest and honorable manner at Yalta.

Appendix

SUMMARY OF THE MAJOR DIPLOMATIC MEETINGS AT THE YALTA CONFERENCE

FEBRUARY 4, 1945
1. Meeting of the President, Marshal Stalin and Mr. Molotov
    Livadia Palace—4:00 PM
       General Discussion
2. 1st Formal Meeting
    Livadia Palace—5:00 PM
       The Military Situation (Europe)
3. President's dinner for the Prime Minister & Marshal Stalin
    Livadia Palace—8:30 PM
       Voice of Smaller Powers in Postwar Peace Organization

FEBRUARY 5, 1945
4. Mr. Molotov's lunch for Mr. Stettinius and Mr. Eden
    Koreis Villa—1:30 PM
       Germany
5. 2nd Formal Meeting
    Livadia Palace—4:00 PM
       Treatment of Germany

FEBRUARY 6, 1945
6. 1st Foreign Secretaries Conference
    Livadia Palace—12:00 Noon
       Press Release
       Dismemberment of Germany

APPENDIX

7. 3rd Formal Meeting
   Livadia Palace—4:00 PM
     World Security Organization
     Polish Question

FEBRUARY 7, 1945

8. 2nd Foreign Secretaries Conference
   Koreis Villa—12:00 Noon
     Dumbarton Oaks
     Dismemberment of Germany
     French Zone of Occupation in Germany and Participation in Control Commission
     Reparations
9. 4th Formal Meeting
   Livadia Palace—4:00 PM
     Dismemberment of Germnay
     Poland
     World Security Organization
     Zone of Occupation in Germany for France and French Participation in Control Commission

FEBRUARY 8, 1945

10. 3rd Foreign Secretaries Conference
   Vorontsov Villa—12:00 Noon
     World Security Organization
     Yugoslavian Frontiers
     Control Commission in Bulgaria and Hungary
     Reparations
     Iran
11. Meeting of the President, Harriman, Stalin and Molotov
   Livadia Palace—3:45 PM
     Use of Airfields and Survey of Bomb Damage in Eastern and Southeastern Europe
12. Meeting of the President, Harriman, Stalin and Molotov
   Livadia Palace—3:47 PM
     Sale of Ships to Soviet Union after the War
     Far East—Political

APPENDIX

13. Meeting of the President, Harriman, Stalin and Molotov
    Livadia Palace—4:00 PM
    Air Bases
14. 5th Formal Meeting
    Livadia Palace—4:15 PM
    Poland
    Declaration on Liberated Areas
15. Marshal Stalin's Dinner for the President, the Prime Minister, etc.
    Koreis—9:00 PM
    General Conversation

FEBRUARY 9, 1945
16. 4th Foreign Secretaries Conference
    Livadia Palace—12:00 Noon
    Poles
    Reparations
    Dumbarton Oaks
    Iran
    Yugoslavia
17. President's lunch for Mr. Churchill
    Livadia Palace—1:00 PM
18. 6th Formal Meeting of Crimean Conference
    Livadia Palace—4:00 PM
    Poland
    Trusteeships and Dependent Territories
    Yugoslavia
    Declaration on Liberated Europe
    War Criminals
19. 5th Foreign Secretaries Conference
    Koreis—10:30 PM
    Poland
    Declaration on Liberated Areas

FEBRUARY 10, 1945
20. 6th Foreign Secretaries Conference
    Vorontsov Villa—12:00 Noon
    The Polish Formula

APPENDIX

      Declaration on Liberated Europe
      Yugoslavia
      Reparations
      Communiqué on the Crimean Conference
      World Organization
      Austro-Yugoslav Frontier
      Yugoslav-Italian Frontier
      Yugoslav-Bulgarian Relations
      Iran

21. Mr. Harriman's meeting with Mr. Molotov
    Koreis—2:00 PM
      Far East—Political
22. 7th Formal Meeting of Crimean Conference
    Livadia Palace—4:00 PM
      Poland
      Declaration on Liberated Europe
      French Participation in Control Commission for Germany
      Yugoslavia
      Dumbarton Oaks: Reparations from Germany, Dardanelles
23. Prime Minister's dinner for Marshal Stalin and the President
    Vorontsov Villa—9:00 PM
      Reparations from Germany
      Communiqué
      British and American Politics
      Jewish Problem

FEBRUARY 11, 1945
24. 8th Formal Meeting of Crimean Conference
    Livadia Palace—12:00 Noon

REPORT OF THE CRIMEA CONFERENCE

For the past eight days, Winston S. Churchill, Prime Minister of Great Britain, Franklin D. Roosevelt, President of the United States of America, and Marshal J. V. Stalin, Chairman of the Council of Peoples' Commissars of the Union of Soviet Socialist Republics have met with the Foreign Secretaries, Chiefs of Staff and other advisors in the Crimea.

In addition to the three heads of Government, the following took part in the Conference:

For the United States of America:
Edward R. Stettinius, Jr., Secretary of State;
Fleet Admiral William D. Leahy, U. S. N., Chief of Staff to the President;
Harry L. Hopkins, Special Assistant to the President;
Justice James F. Byrnes, Director, Office of War Mobilization;
General of the Army George C. Marshall, U. S. A., Chief of Staff, U. S. Army;
Fleet Admiral Ernest J. King, U. S. N., Chief of Naval Operations and Commander in Chief, U. S. Fleet;
Lieutenant General Brehon B. Somervell, Commanding General, Army Service Forces;
Vice Admiral Emory S. Land, War Shipping Administrator;
Major General L. S. Kuter, U. S. A., Staff of Commanding General, U. S. Army Air Forces;

APPENDIX

W. Averell Harriman, Ambassador to the U. S. S. R.;
H. Freeman Matthews, Director of European Affairs, State Department;
Alger Hiss, Deputy Director, Office of Special Political Affairs, Department of State;
Charles E. Bohlen, Assistant to the Secretary of State, together with political, military and technical advisors.

For the United Kingdom:
Anthony Eden, Secretary of State for Foreign Affairs;
Lord Leathers, Minister of War Transport;
Sir A. Clark Kerr, H. M. Ambassador at Moscow;
Sir Alexander Cadogan, Permanent Under Secretary of State for Foreign Affairs;
Sir Edward Bridges, Secretary of the War Cabinet;
Field Marshal Sir Alan Brooke, Chief of the Imperial General Staff;
Marshal of the Royal Air Force Sir Charles Portal, Chief of the Air Staff;
Admiral of the Fleet Sir Andrew Cunningham, First Sea Lord;
General Sir Hastings Ismay, Chief of Staff to the Minister of Defense; together with
Field Marshal Alexander, Supreme Allied Commander, Mediterranean Theatre;
Field Marshal Wilson, Head of the British Joint Staff Mission at Washington;
Admiral Somerville, Joint Staff Mission at Washington, together with military and diplomatic advisors.

For the Soviet Union:
V. M. Molotov, People's Commissar for Foreign Affairs of the USSR;
Admiral Kuznetsov, People's Commissar for the Navy;
Army General Antonov, Deputy Chief of the General Staff of the Red Army;
A. Y. Vishinsky, Deputy People's Commissar for Foreign Affairs of the USSR;

APPENDIX

I. M. Maisky, Deputy People's Commissar for Foreign Affairs of the USSR;
Marshal of Aviation Khudiakov;
F. T. Gusev, Ambassador in Great Britain;
A. A. Gromyko, Ambassador in U. S. A.

The following statement is made by the Prime Minister of Great Britain, the President of the United States of America, and the Chairman of the Council of Peoples' Commissars of the Union of Soviet Socialist Republics on the results of the Crimea Conference:

I. THE DEFEAT OF GERMANY

We have considered and determined the military plans of the three allied powers for the final defeat of the common enemy. The military staffs of the three allied nations have met in daily meetings throughout the Conference. These meetings have been most satisfactory from every point of view and have resulted in closer coordination of the military effort of the three Allies than ever before. The fullest information has been inter-changed. The timing, scope and coordination of new and even more powerful blows to be launched by our armies and air forces into the heart of Germany from the East, West, North and South have been fully agreed and planned in detail.

Our combined military plans will be made known only as we execute them, but we believe that the very close working partnership among the three staffs attained at this Conference will result in shortening the war. Meetings of the three staffs will be continued in the future whenever the need arises.

Nazi Germany is doomed. The German people will only make the cost of their defeat heavier to themselves by attempting to continue a hopeless resistance.

II. THE OCCUPATION AND CONTROL OF GERMANY

We have agreed on common policies and plans for enforcing the unconditional surrender terms which we shall impose to-

APPENDIX

gether on Nazi Germany after German armed resistance has been finally crushed. These terms will not be made known until the final defeat of Germany has been accomplished. Under the agreed plan, the forces of the Three Powers will each occupy a separate zone of Germany. Coordinated administration and control has been provided for under the plan through a central Control Commission consisting of the Supreme Commanders of the Three Powers with headquarters in Berlin. It has been agreed that France should be invited by the Three Powers, if she should so desire, to take over a zone of occupation, and to participate as a fourth member of the Control Commission. The limits of the French zone will be agreed by the four governments concerned through their representatives on the European Advisory Commission.

It is our inflexible purpose to destroy German militarism and Nazism and to ensure that Germany will never again be able to disturb the peace of the world. We are determined to disarm and disband all German armed forces; break up for all time the German General Staff that has repeatedly contrived the resurgence of German militarism; remove or destroy all German military equipment; eliminate or control all German industry that could be used for military production; bring all war criminals to just and swift punishment and exact reparation in kind for the destruction wrought by the Germans; wipe out the Nazi party, Nazi laws, organizations and institutions, remove all Nazi and militarist influences from public office and from the cultural and economic life of the German people; and take in harmony such other measures in Germany as may be necessary to the future peace and safety of the world. It is not our purpose to destroy the people of Germany, but only when Nazism and Militarism have been extirpated will there be hope for a decent life for Germans, and a place for them in the comity of nations.

III. REPARATION BY GERMANY

We have considered the question of the damage caused by Germany to the Allied Nations in this war and recognized it as just that Germany be obliged to make compensation for this damage in kind to the greatest extent possible. A Commission for the Compensation of Damage will be established. The Commission will be instructed to consider the question of the extent and methods for compensating damage caused by Germany to the Allied Countries. The Commission will work in Moscow.

IV. UNITED NATIONS CONFERENCE

We are resolved upon the earliest possible establishment with our allies of a general international organization to maintain peace and security. We believe that this is essential, both to prevent aggression and to remove the political, economic and social causes of war through the close and continuing collaboration of all peace-loving peoples.

The foundations were laid at Dumbarton Oaks. On the important question of voting procedure, however, agreement was not there reached. The present conference has been able to resolve this difficulty.

We have agreed that a Conference of United Nations should be called to meet at San Francisco in the United States on April 25th, 1945, to prepare the charter of such an organization, along the lines proposed in the informal conversations at Dumbarton Oaks.

The Government of China and the Provisional Government of France will be immediately consulted and invited to sponsor invitations to the Conference jointly with the Governments of the United States, Great Britain and the Union of Soviet Socialist Republics. As soon as the consultation with China and France has been completed, the text of the proposals on voting procedure will be made public.

V. DECLARATION ON LIBERATED EUROPE

We have drawn up and subscribed to a Declaration on liberated Europe. This Declaration provides for concerting the policies of the three Powers and for joint action by them in meeting the political and economic problems of liberated Europe in accordance with democratic principles. The text of the Declaration is as follows:

"The Premier of the Union of Soviet Socialist Republics, the

APPENDIX

Prime Minister of the United Kingdom, and the President of the United States of America have consulted with each other in the common interests of the peoples of their countries and those of liberated Europe. They jointly declare their mutual agreement to concert during the temporary period of instability in liberated Europe the policies of their three governments in assisting the peoples liberated from the domination of Nazi Germany and the peoples of the former Axis satellite states of Europe to solve by democratic means their pressing political and economic problems.

"The establishment of order in Europe and the rebuilding of national economic life must be achieved by processes which will enable the liberated peoples to destroy the last vestiges of Nazism and Fascism and to create democratic institutions of their own choice. This is a principle of the Atlantic Charter—the right of all peoples to choose the form of government under which they will live—the restoration of sovereign rights and self government to those peoples who have been forcibly deprived of them by the aggressor nations.

"To foster the conditions in which the liberated peoples may exercise these rights, the three governments will jointly assist the people in any European liberated state or former Axis satellite state in Europe where in their judgment conditions require (a) to establish conditions of internal peace; (b) to carry out emergency measures for the relief of distressed people; (c) to form interim governmental authorities broadly representative of all democratic elements in the population and pledged to the earliest possible establishment through free elections of governments responsive to the will of the people; and (d) to facilitate where necessary the holding of such elections.

"The three governments will consult the other United Nations and provisional authorities or other governments in Europe when matters of direct interest to them are under consideration.

"When, in the opinion of the three governments, conditions in any European liberated state or any former Axis satellite state in Europe make such action necessary, they will immediately consult together on the measures necessary to discharge the joint responsibilities set forth in this declaration.

APPENDIX

"By this Declaration we reaffirm our faith in the principles of the Atlantic Charter, our pledge in the Declaration by the United Nations, and our determination to build in cooperation with other peace-loving nations a world order under law, dedicated to peace, security, freedom and the general well-being of all mankind.

"In issuing this Declaration, the Three Powers express the hope that the Provisional Government of the French Republic may be associated with them in the procedure suggested."

VI. POLAND

We came to the Crimea Conference resolved to settle our differences about Poland. We discussed fully all aspects of the question. We reaffirm our common desire to see established a strong, free, independent and democratic Poland. As a result of our discussions we have agreed on the conditions in which a new Polish Provisional Government of National Unity may be formed in such a manner as to command recognition by the three major powers.

The agreement reached is as follows:

"A new situation has been created in Poland as a result of her complete liberation by the Red Army. This calls for the establishment of a Polish Provisional Government which can be more broadly based than was possible before the recent liberation of western Poland. The Provisional Government which is now functioning in Poland should therefore be reorganized on a broader democratic basis with the inclusion of democratic leaders from Poland itself and from Poles abroad. This new Government should then be called the Polish Provisional Government of National Unity.

"M. Molotov, Mr. Harriman and Sir A. Clark Kerr are authorized as a Commission to consult in the first instance in Moscow with members of the present Provisional Government and with other Polish democratic leaders from within Poland and from abroad, with a view to the reorganization of the present Government along the above lines. This Polish Provisional Government of National Unity shall be pledged to the holding of free and unfettered elections as soon as possible on the basis of universal suffrage and secret ballot. In these elections all democratic

APPENDIX

and anti-Nazi parties shall have the right to take part and to put forward candidates.

"When a Polish Provisional Government of National Unity has been properly formed in conformity with the above, the Government of the U. S. S. R., which now maintains diplomatic relations with the present Provisional Government of Poland, the Government of the United Kingdom and the Government of the United States will establish diplomatic relations with the new Polish Provisional Government of National Unity, and will exchange Ambassadors by whose reports the respective Governments will be kept informed about the situation in Poland.

"The three Heads of Government consider that the eastern frontier of Poland should follow the Curzon Line with digressions from it in some regions of five to eight kilometres in favor of Poland. They recognize that Poland must receive substantial accessions of territory in the north and west. They feel that the opinion of the new Polish Provisional Government of National Unity should be sought in due course on the extent of these accessions and that the final delimitation of the western frontier of Poland should thereafter await the Peace Conference."

VII. YUGOSLAVIA

We have agreed to recommend to Marshal Tito and Dr. Subasitch that the Agreement between them should be put into effect immediately, and that a new Government should be formed on the basis of that agreement.

We also recommend that as soon as the new Government has been formed, it should declare that:

(I) The Anti-fascist Assembly of National Liberation (Avnoj) should be extended to include members of the last Yugoslav Parliament (Skupschina) who have not compromised themselves by collaboration with the enemy, thus forming a body to be known as a temporary Parliament; and (II) legislative acts passed by the Anti-fascist Assembly of National Liberation (Avnoj) will be subject to subsequent ratification by a Constituent Assembly.

There was also a general review of other Balkan questions.

VIII. MEETINGS OF FOREIGN SECRETARIES

Throughout the Conference, besides the daily meetings of the Heads of Governments and the Foreign Secretaries, separate meetings of the three Foreign Secretaries, and their advisors have also been held daily.

These meetings have proved of the utmost value and the Conference agreed that permanent machinery should be set up for regular consultation between the three Foreign Secretaries. They will, therefore, meet as often as may be necessary, probably about every three or four months. These meetings will be held in rotation in the three Capitals, the first meeting being held in London, after the United Nations Conference on world organization.

IX. UNITY FOR PEACE AS FOR WAR

Our meeting here in the Crimea has reaffirmed our common determination to maintain and strengthen in the peace to come that unity of purpose and of action which has made victory possible and certain for the United Nations in this war. We believe that this is a sacred obligation which our Governments owe to our peoples and to all the peoples of the world.

Only with continuing and growing cooperation and understanding among our three countries and among all the peace-loving nations can the highest aspiration of humanity be realized —a secure and lasting peace which will, in the words of the Atlantic Charter, "afford assurance that all the men in all the lands may live out their lives in freedom from fear and want".

Victory in this war and establishment of the proposed international organization will provide the greatest opportunity in all history to create in the years to come the essential conditions of such a peace.

SIGNED
Winston S. Churchill
Franklin D. Roosevelt
J. V. Stalin

February 11, 1945

PROTOCOL OF THE PROCEEDINGS
OF THE CRIMEA CONFERENCE

The Crimea Conference of the Heads of the Governments of the United States of America, the United Kingdom, and the Union of Soviet Socialist Republics which took place from February 4th to 11th came to the following conclusions.

I. WORLD ORGANISATION

It was decided:
(1) that a United Nations Conference on the proposed world organisation should be summoned for Wednesday, 25th April, 1945, and should be held in the United States of America.
(2) the Nations to be invited to this Conference should be:
 (a) the United Nations as they existed on the 8th February, 1945; and
 (b) such of the Associated Nations as have declared war on the common enemy by 1st March, 1945. (For this purpose by the term "Associated Nation" was meant the eight Associated Nations and Turkey). When the Conference on World Organisation is held, the delegates of the United Kingdom and United States of America will support a proposal to admit to original membership two Soviet Socialist Republics, i.e. the Ukraine and White Russia.
(3) that the United States Government on behalf of the Three Powers should consult the Government of China and the

APPENDIX

French Provisional Government in regard to the decisions taken at the present Conference concerning the proposed World Organisation.

(4) that the text of the invitation to be issued to all the nations which would take part in the United Nations Conference should be as follows:

Invitation

"The Government of the United States of America, on behalf of itself and of the Governments of the United Kingdom, the Union of Soviet Socialist Republics, and the Republic of China and of the Provisional Government of the French Republic, invite the Government of _____ to send representatives to a Conference of the United Nations to be held on 25th April, 1945, or soon thereafter, at San Francisco in the United States of America to prepare a Charter for a General International Organisation for the maintenance of international peace and security.

"The above named governments suggest that the Conference consider as affording a basis for such a Charter the Proposals for the Establishment of a General International Organisation, which were made public last October as a result of the Dumbarton Oaks Conference, and which have now been supplemented by the following provisions for Section C of Chapter VI:

"C. VOTING
1. Each member of the Security Council should have one vote.
2. Decisions of the Security Council on procedural matters should be made by an affirmative vote of seven members.
3. Decisions of the Security Council on all other matters should be made by an affirmative vote of seven members including the concurring votes of the permanent members; provided that, in decisions under Chapter VIII, Section A, and under the second sentence of paragraph 1 of Chapter VIII, Section C, a party to a dispute should abstain from voting.

"Further information as to arrangements will be transmitted subsequently.

"In the event that the Government of _____ desires in advance of the Conference to present views or comments concerning the proposals, the Government of the United States of America will be pleased to transmit such views and comments to the other participating Governments."

Territorial Trusteeship

It was agreed that the five Nations which will have permanent seats on the Security Council should consult each other prior to the United Nations Conference on the question of territorial trusteeship.

The acceptance of this recommendation is subject to its being made clear that territorial trusteeship will only apply to (a) existing mandates of the League of Nations; (b) territories detached from the enemy as a result of the present war; (c) any other territory which might voluntarily be placed under trusteeship; and (d) no discussion of actual territories is contemplated at the forthcoming United Nations Conference or in the preliminary consultations, and it will be a matter for subsequent agreement which territories within the above categories will be placed under trusteeship.

II. DECLARATION ON LIBERATED EUROPE

The following declaration has been approved:

The Premier of the Union of Soviet Socialist Republics, the Prime Minister of the United Kingdom and the President of the United States of America have consulted with each other in the common interests of the peoples of their countries and those of liberated Europe. They jointly declare their mutual agreement to concert during the temporary period of instability in liberated Europe the policies of their three governments in assisting the peoples liberated from the domination of Nazi Germany and the peoples of the former Axis satellite states of Europe to solve by democratic means their pressing political and economic problems.

The establishment of order in Europe and the re-building of national economic life must be achieved by processes which will enable the liberated peoples to destroy the last vestiges of Nazism and Fascism and to create democratic institutions of their own choice. This is a principle of the Atlantic Charter—the right of all peoples to choose the form of government under which they will live—the restoration of sovereign rights and self-government to those peoples who have been forcibly deprived of them by the aggressor nations.

To foster the conditions in which the liberated peoples may exercise these rights, the three governments will jointly assist the people in any European liberated state or former Axis satellite state in Europe where in their judgment conditions require (a) to establish conditions of internal peace; (b) to carry out emergency measures for the relief of distressed peoples; (c) to form interim governmental authorities broadly representative of all democratic elements in the population and pledged

APPENDIX

to the earliest possible establishment through free elections of governments responsive to the will of the people; and (d) to facilitate where necessary the holding of such elections.

The three governments will consult the other United Nations and provisional authorities or other governments in Europe when matters of direct interest to them are under consideration.

When, in the opinion of the three governments, conditions in any European liberated state or any former Axis satellite state in Europe make such action necessary, they will immediately consult together on the measures necessary to discharge the joint responsibilities set forth in this declaration.

By this declaration we reaffirm our faith in the principles of the Atlantic Charter, our pledge in the Declaration by the United Nations, and our determination to build in co-operation with other peace-loving nations world order under law, dedicated to peace, security, freedom and general well-being of all mankind.

In issuing this declaration, the Three Powers express the hope that the Provisional Government of the French Republic may be associated with them in the procedure suggested.

III. DISMEMBERMENT OF GERMANY

It was agreed that Article 12 (a) of the Surrender Terms for Germany should be amended to read as follows:

"The United Kingdom, the United States of America and the Union of Soviet Socialist Republics shall possess supreme authority with respect to Germany. In the exercise of such authority they will take such steps, including the complete disarmament, demilitarisation and the dismemberment of Germany as they deem requisite for future peace and security."

The study of the procedure for the dismemberment of Germany was referred to a Committee, consisting of Mr. Eden (Chairman), Mr. Winant and Mr. Gusev. This body would consider the desirability of associating with it a French representative.

IV. ZONE OF OCCUPATION FOR THE FRENCH AND CONTROL COUNCIL FOR GERMANY

It was agreed that a zone in Germany, to be occupied by the French Forces, should be allocated to France. This zone would be formed out of the British and American zones and its extent

APPENDIX

would be settled by the British and Americans in consultation with the French Provisional Government.

It was also agreed that the French Provisional Government should be invited to become a member of the Allied Control Council for Germany.

V. REPARATION

The following protocol has been approved:

1. Germany must pay in kind for the losses caused by her to the Allied nations in the course of the war. Reparations are to be received in the first instance by those countries which have borne the main burden of the war, have suffered the heaviest losses and have organised victory over the enemy.

2. Reparation in kind is to be exacted from Germany in three following forms:

a) Removals within 2 years from the surrender of Germany or the cessation of organized resistance from the national wealth of Germany located on the territory of Germany herself as well as outside her territory (equipment, machine-tools, ships, rolling stock, German investments abroad, shares of industrial, transport and other enterprises in Germany etc.), these removals to be carried out chiefly for purpose of destroying the war potential of Germany.

b) Annual deliveries of goods from current production for a period to be fixed.

c) Use of German labour.

3. For the working out on the above principles of a detailed plan for exaction of reparation from Germany an Allied Reparation Commission will be set up in Moscow. It will consist of three representatives—one from the Union of Soviet Socialist Republics, one from the United Kingdom and one from the United States of America.

4. With regard to the fixing of the total sum of the reparation as well as the distribution of it among the countries which suffered from the German aggression the Soviet and American delegations agreed as follows:

"The Moscow Reparation Commission should take in its

APPENDIX

initial studies as a basis for discussion the suggestion of the Soviet Government that the total sum of the reparation in accordance with the points (a) and (b) of the paragraph 2 should be 20 billion dollars and that 50% of it should go to the Union of Soviet Socialist Republics."

The British delegation was of the opinion that pending consideration of the reparation question by the Moscow Reparation Commission no figures of reparation should be mentioned.

The above Soviet-American proposal has been passed to the Moscow Reparation Commission as one of the proposals to be considered by the Commission.

VI. MAJOR WAR CRIMINALS

The Conference agreed that the question of the major war criminals should be the subject of enquiry by the three Foreign Secretaries for report in due course after the close of the Conference.

VII. POLAND

The following Declaration on Poland was agreed by the Conference:

"A new situation has been created in Poland as a result of her complete liberation by the Red Army. This calls for the establishment of a Polish Provisional Government which can be more broadly based than was possible before the recent liberation of Western part of Poland. The Provisional Government which is now functioning in Poland should therefore be reorganised on a broader democratic basis with the inclusion of democratic leaders from Poland itself and from Poles abroad. This new Government should then be called the Polish Provisional Government of National Unity.

"M. Molotov, Mr. Harriman and Sir A. Clark Kerr are authorised as a commission to consult in the first instance in Moscow with members of the present Provisional Government and with other Polish democratic leaders from within Poland and from abroad, with a view to the reorganization of the present Government along the above lines. This Polish Provisional Government

APPENDIX

of National Unity shall be pledged to the holding of free and unfettered elections as soon as possible on the basis of universal suffrage and secret ballot. In these elections all democratic and anti-Nazi parties shall have the right to take part and to put forward candidates.

"When a Polish Provisional Government of National Unity has been properly formed in conformity with the above, the Government of the U. S. S. R., which now maintains diplomatic relations with the present Provisional Government of Poland, and the Government of the United Kingdom and the Government of the U. S. A. will establish diplomatic relations with the new Polish Provisional Government of National Unity, and will exchange Ambassadors by whose reports the respective Governments will be kept informed about the situation in Poland.

"The three Heads of Government consider that the Eastern frontier of Poland should follow the Curzon Line with digressions from it in some regions of five to eight kilometres in favour of Poland. They recognize that Poland must receive substantial accessions of territory in the North and West. They feel that the opinion of the new Polish Provisional Government of National Unity should be sought in due course on the extent of these accessions and that the final delimitation of the Western frontier of Poland should thereafter await the Peace Conference."

VIII. YUGOSLAVIA

It was agreed to recommend to Marshal Tito and to Dr. Subasitch:

(a) that the Tito-Subasitch Agreement should immediately be put into effect and a new Government formed on the basis of the Agreement.

(b) that as soon as the new Government has been formed it should declare:

(i) that Anti-Fascist Assembly of the National Liberation (AVNOJ) will be extended to include members of the last Yugoslav Skupstina who have not compromised themselves by collaboration with the enemy, thus forming a body to be known as a temporary Parliament and

APPENDIX

(ii) that legislative acts passed by the Anti-Fascist Assembly of National Liberation (AVNOJ) will be subject to subsequent ratification by a Constituent Assembly; and that this statement should be published in the communiqué of the Conference.

IX. ITALO-YUGOSLAV FRONTIER
    ITALO-AUSTRIA FRONTIER

Notes on these subjects were put in by the British delegation and the American and Soviet delegations agreed to consider them and give their views later.

X. YUGOSLAV-BULGARIAN RELATIONS

There was an exchange of views between the Foreign Secretaries on the question of the desirability of a Yugoslav-Bulgarian pact of alliance. The question at issue was whether a state still under an armistice regime could be allowed to enter into a treaty with another state. Mr. Eden suggested that the Bulgarian and Yugoslav Governments should be informed that this could not be approved. Mr. Stettinius suggested that the British and American Ambassadors should discuss the matter further with M. Molotov in Moscow. M. Molotov agreed with the proposal of Mr. Stettinius.

XI. SOUTH EASTERN EUROPE

The British delegation put in notes for the consideration of their colleagues on the following subjects:
(a) the control Commission in Bulgaria.
(b) Greek claims upon Bulgaria, more particularly with reference to reparations.
(c) Oil equipment in Roumania.

XII. IRAN

Mr. Eden, Mr. Stettinius and M. Molotov exchanged views on the situation in Iran. It was agreed that this matter should be pursued through the diplomatic channel.

XIII. MEETINGS OF THE THREE FOREIGN SECRETARIES

The Conference agreed that permanent machinery should be set up for consultation between the three Foreign Secretaries; they should meet as often as necessary, probably about every three or four months.

These meetings will be held in rotation in the three capitals, the first meeting being held in London.

XIV. THE MONTREUX CONVENTION AND THE STRAITS

It was agreed that at the next meeting of the three Foreign Secretaries to be held in London, they should consider proposals which it was understood the Soviet Government would put forward in relation to the Montreux Convention and report to their Governments. The Turkish Government should be informed at the appropriate moment.

The foregoing Protocol was approved and signed by the three Foreign Secretaries at the Crimean Conference, February 11, 1945.

AGREEMENT ON TERMS FOR ENTRY OF THE SOVIET UNION INTO THE WAR AGAINST JAPAN, SIGNED AT YALTA, FEBRUARY 11, 1945, RELEASED SIMULTANEOUSLY IN LONDON, MOSCOW, AND WASHINGTON, FEBRUARY 11, 1946

The leaders of the three Great Powers—the Soviet Union, the United States of America and Great Britain—have agreed that in two or three months after Germany has surrendered and the war in Europe has terminated, the Soviet Union shall enter into the war against Japan on the side of the Allies on condition that:

1. The status quo in Outer-Mongolia (the Mongolian People's Republic) shall be preserved;

2. The former rights of Russia violated by the treacherous attack of Japan in 1904 shall be restored, viz.:

(a) the southern part of Sakhalin as well as all the islands adjacent to it shall be returned to the Soviet Union,

(b) the commercial port of Dairen shall be internationalized, the preeminent interests of the Soviet Union in this port being safeguarded, and the lease of Port Arthur as a naval base of the U. S. S. R. restored,

(c) the Chinese-Eastern Railroad and the South-Manchurian Railroad, which provides an outlet to Dairen, shall be jointly operated by the establishment of a joint Soviet-Chinese Company, it being understood that the preeminent interests of the Soviet Union shall be safeguarded and that China shall retain full sovereignty in Manchuria.

3. The Kurile Islands shall be handed over to the Soviet Union. It is understood that the agreement concerning Outer-Mon-

APPENDIX

golia and the ports and railroads referred to above will require concurrence of Generalissimo Chiang Kai-shek. The President will take measures in order to obtain this concurrence on advice from Marshal Stalin.

The Heads of the three Great Powers have agreed that these claims of the Soviet Union shall be unquestionably fulfilled after Japan has been defeated.

For its part the Soviet Union expresses its readiness to conclude with the National Government of China a pact of friendship and alliance between the U. S. S. R. and China in order to render assistance to China with its armed forces for the purpose of liberating China from the Japanese yoke.

Index

Advisory Council for Italy, 50–51
Aegean Islands, 10
"Agreement on Terms for Entry of the Soviet Union into the War Against Japan," 93–96, 98, 279, 351–52
Albania, 10, 112
Alexander, Sir Harold, 53, 102, 219, 332
Alexandria, Egypt, meeting at, 73, 288–90
Allied Control Commissions: Balkans, 65; Bulgaria, 43, 87; French participation, 129, 139, 163–64, 169–72, 262; Germany, 163, 168, 262, 298–99, 311, 344–45; Hungary, 43, 87; Romania, 43, 87, 312; Roosevelt, 170–72
American Communist party, 113
American formula, for the voting procedure, 54–55, 139, 141–44, 192, 295
American military forces, 18–19, 21
American oil companies, 195
American people, Vishinsky, *quoted* on, 113
Anglo-American co-operation and unity, 8, 309
Antonov, Colonel General, Deputy Chief of the General Staff of the Red Army, 79, 102, 106–7, 219, 332
Arab people, 290
Arciszewski, Miroslaw, Polish diplomat, 155–56
Argentia or Atlantic Conference (1941), 13
Argentina, 113, 199–200
Argonaut (code name), 75, 79–98
Associated Nations, 199–202, 298
Atlantic Charter, 9, 13, 70–71, 244–45, 339
Atlas Mountains, Africa, 35
Atomic bomb, 33–35, 90, 97, 98, 118, 304
Austin, Senator Warren R., 186–87
Australia, 192
Austria, Soviet plans for restoration of (1941), 9
Austro-Italian frontier, 348
Austro-Yugoslav frontier, 256
AVNOJ. *See* Vetch
Axis satellite states, 312
Azores, 32–35

Badoglio, Pietro, 49–50
Balkan Control Commissions, 65
Balkans, 9–12, 61, 97, 257
Baltic area, Soviet plans in, 9, 41
Barkley, Senator Alben William, 5

INDEX

Baruch, Bernard Mannes, 316
"Basic Principles of Exaction of Reparations from Germany," 165–67
Battle of the Bulge, 90, 300, 304
Bavaria, 9, 122
Belgium, 10, 23, 132, 192
Belgrade, Yugoslavia, 301
Beria, Marshal Lavrenty Pavlovitch, 218, 221
Berle, Adolf A., Jr., 50
Berlin, Germany: Allied access to, 37–38; capture, 299
Bermuda, 32
Bern meeting, 315–16
Bevin, Ernest, 72
Bialystok Province, Soviet Union, 154
Bidault, Georges, 56
Bierut, Boleslav, Polish statesman, 156, 158, 210
Birse, Major, British interpreter, 102, 103, 272
Blanchard, Lee, of Crimean Conference secretariat, 31
Bloom, Representative Sol, 186
Boettiger, Mrs. John (Anna Eleanor Roosevelt), 68, 70, 73, 80–82, 134, 219, 285
Bohlen, Charles E.: Naples Conference, 48–49; Soviet Republics (16), right to vote, 21, 55; White House liaison officer, 12; Yalta Conference, 30, 102, 111–13, 116, 196, 219, 272, 332
Bolivia, 193
Bonomi, Ivanoe, Italian statesman, 51
Bowman, Dr. Isaiah, president of Johns Hopkins University, 15–16
Brazil, 193, 290–91
Bremerhaven, Germany, 56, 63
Bridges, Sir Edward, 103, 332
Brooke, Sir Alan Francis, 63, 69, 102, 218, 332
Brown, Admiral Wilson, 69, 134
Bucharest, Romania, Control Commission, 312; Vishinsky's visit (1945), 312
Budapest, Hungary: airfields near, 197, 298, 311
Bulgaria: British attitude toward, 11, 256–57; Control Commission, 49, 87; Soviet attitude toward, 256–58; Soviet influence in, 13; surrender, 23; Yugoslav relations, 348
Bulge, Battle of the, 90, 300, 304

Bullitt, William Christian, *quoted* on Yalta Conference, 5–6
Bundy, Harvey Hollister, 34
Buyak, Polish Professor, 158
Byelorussia, 202–3, 282
Byrnes, James Francis: Malta, 68, 70; Molotov luncheon, 118–19; Russians' request for extra votes, 282–83; trusteeship issue, 238; United Nations conference, San Francisco, 206; Yalta Conference, 82, 87–89, 103, 111, 118–19, 134, 161, 218, 331; Yalta return trip, 291

Cadogan, Sir Alexander: Churchill, 30; German surrender terms, 162; Malta, 59, 63, 67, 236; Roosevelt, 30, 72; Yalta Conference, 102, 219, 332
Cairo, Egypt: Roosevelt-Chiang Kai-shek conference, 237–38; Stettinius, 288, 290
Canada, 192
Casablanca, Morocco, Roosevelt-De Gaulle conversation, 100
Catholic Church, 69, 198
Catoctin (U.S.S.), 27–28, 284
Chapultepec Conference (Mexico City), 280–81, 291, 306
Cherniakhovsky, Russian General, 106
Chiang Kai-shek, Generalissimo, 237–38, 352
Chiang Kai-shek, Madame, 71
Chile, 193, 200
China: "Agreement Regarding Japan," 93–94; America's interest in, 71; Chinese Communists, 20, 44, 66; Dumbarton Oaks, 16–17; French Indo-China, 237; Japanese yoke, 94; Kuomintang-Communist agreement, 87; Manchuria, 93, 98; National Government, 44, 66, 94, 305, 352; San Francisco Conference, 232, 256; Security Council voting, 18; Soviet Union, 94, 304–5, 352; United Nations Declaration, 192
Chinese-Eastern Railroad, 93, 351
Churchill, Winston Leonard Spencer: "Agreement Regarding Japan," 93–95, 279; Allied unity, 274, 283; Argentia Conference, 13; Associated Nations, 200–2; Athens visit, 61; Balkans, 11, 61;

INDEX

British Empire, liquidation of, *quoted* on, 237; British headquarters dinner, Yalta, 272–78; China, America's interest in, 71; Communism, 277; co-operation with Russia, 277; Council of Foreign Ministers, 216; Curzon Line, 301; Dardanelles, 268–69; De Gaulle, 128; "Declaration on Liberated Europe," 242–45; defeat, 72, 309; dispute formula, 22; Economic and Social Council, 17; elections, 114, 241; French participation in German Control Commission, 164, 170–71; German reparations, 131–34, 255, 263–67, 272, 274; Germany, dismemberment of, 121–29, 137–39; good-humored exchange, 269; Greece, 11, 61, 218, 244; Hopkins, 55; India, independence, 188; Italian Government, attitude toward, 49–52, 60–61; Japanese war, Stalin's comment on entry into, 91–92; liberated peoples, 67; Malta, 60–61, 70–71, 74–75; mannerisms, 68, 70, 80, 138; military pomp, 272; Moscow pledge, *quoted*, 15; Moscow visit (1944), 91; peace, 67; pessimism, 68; Polish question, 88, 152–57, 184–86, 209–16, 226, 234–35, 240–42, 258–60, 271, 300–3, 313–14, 316–17; political parties, 277; Quebec Conference (1944), 40; Roosevelt, friendship with, 70–71; Roosevelt, toast to, 276; Russia, test of good will, 324; Russian formal dinner, Yalta, 218–22; Russian request for extra seats in the Assembly, 175–76, 202; Security Council voting, 45–47, 54–55, 87, 115–16, 142–43, 145–50, 172; SHAEF, 74; ships for Russian use, 287; Stalin, attitude toward, 129; Stalin, praise of, 219–20; Stalin conference (1944), 12–13; Teheran Conference, 8, 268; trade unions, 276; trusteeships, 236–39; uniform, 138; United States, extra votes for, 282–83; war criminals, 245; warm-water port for Russia, 268; Washington visit (1942), 13–14; western offensive, 246; world organization, 62; world organization conference, 176–78, 189; world outlook, 67–68, 221–22; world peace, *quoted* on, 24; world problems, grasp of, 30; Yalta Conference, 3, 4, 8, 24, 28–29, 62, 80, 84, 87–88, 91, 93–116, 218–22, 324; Yugoslav problem, 11, 217–18, 239, 262–63

Clemenceau, Georges, French statesman, Curzon Line, 154–55
Cohen, Benjamin Victor, American lawyer, 15
Colombia, 193
Communism: British opposition, 277; China, 20, 44, 66
Compromise, necessity for, 6
Conn, George T., of Crimean Conference secretariat, 31
Connally, Senator Thomas Terry, 5, 186, 306
Control Commissions. *See* Allied Control Commissions
Costa Rica, 192
Council of Foreign Ministers, 216
Crimea, destruction in, 100
Crimean Conference. *See* Yalta Conference
Cripps, Sir Richard Stafford, 55
Cuba, 192
Cunningham, Sir Andrew B., 102, 219, 332
Curzon Line, 9, 41, 86, 151–52, 154–55, 181, 209, 211, 225, 270, 301, 314
Czechoslovakia, 9, 23, 192, 300

Dairen, port, Manchuria, 93, 268, 351
Daladier, Edouard, 276
Damaskinos, Archbishop, ex-Regent of Greece, 61
Danzig, 108, 211
Dardanelles, 44, 267–69, 349
De Gaulle, General Charles: Crimean Conference, 56, 128; *de facto* authority, 101; French participation in German Control Commission, 163, 262; Hopkins, talks with, 56; Moscow visit, 100; Roosevelt relationship, 100–1; Stalin's evaluation, 100; Teheran Conference, 8
Deane, General John R., 91, 95, 98, 102
"Declaration of Iran" (1943), 43–44, 193–94
"Declaration on Liberated Europe," 335–36; 343–44; Churchill, 242–

355

INDEX

45; Eden, 261; Romania, 311–12, 314; Roosevelt, 36, 88, 242–45, 249, 253, 300, 314; Stalin, 242–45, 249, 300
"Declaration on Poland," 346–47
Democratic party, 45
Denmark, 10, 202
Dennis, Dr. Gabriel Lafayette, Liberian Secretary of State, 290
Discussion, freedom of, 141–42
Disputes: American formula for settling, 21–22, 45–47; Security Council, *see* Security Council
Dodecanese Islands, 10
Dominican Republic, 192
Dominion status, 175
Donovan, General William J., 120–21
Dulles, John Foster, American lawyer, 295
Dumbarton Oaks (1944), 16–23, 31; Security Council voting procedure, 140, 146–50, 191; veto power, 296
Dunn, James Clement, American diplomat, 15, 34, 56

E.A.C. *See* European Advisory Commission
Eaker, Lieutenant General Ira C., 49
Early, Stephen Tyree, 68; world security conference, 190; Yalta Conference, 82, 134, 279, 291
East Prussia, 9, 41, 184, 210–11
Eastern Prince (ship), 60
Eaton, Representative Charles A., 186
Economic and Social Council, 16–17, 20, 62, 180–81, 316
Ecuador, 193, 199
Eden, Robert Anthony: "Agreement Regarding Japan," 94–95; Athens visit, 61; Balkan question, 65; British headquarters dinner, 272–78; Bulgaria, 256–57; California, 205; co-operation with Russia, 277; Council of Foreign Ministers, 216; Dardanelles, 268; "Declaration on Liberated Europe," 249, 253, 261; French occupation zone, 129; French participation in German Control Commission, 163–64, 169; German reparations, 167–68, 230–32, 235, 253–56, 263–67; Germany, dismemberment of, 135–37, 162–64, 169; Iranian question, 65–66, 194–95, 258; Italian boundaries, 65; Malta conference, 59, 60, 62–69, 72, 74–75; Molotov luncheon, 118–19; Moscow-Stalin conferences, 9–10; Polish question, 64, 152, 223–29, 246–48, 252, 258–60; protocol, 279–80, 284; Quebec Conference (1944), 40; Russian request for extra Assembly seats, 191, 193, 196–97; San Francisco Conference, 207, 232, 256, 310; Security Council voting procedure, 54–55, 66–67, 115–16, 161–62; Stettinius conference (1944), 16; Teheran Conference, 3; trusteeship, international, 232–33, 237; world organization, 62; 190–91, 197–98; Yalta Conference, 62–63, 80, 102–4, 118–19, 218, 279–80, 284, 310; Yugoslav problem, 217, 233, 239, 256–57, 262
Egypt, 193, 201–2, 241
Eire, 201
Eisenhower, General Dwight David: Berlin capture, 299; Colmar, 246; German Army in Italy, 315–16; Marshall conference at Marseilles, 35; Montgomery, difficulties with, 74; Red Army's winter offensive, 109; Rhine, 108; Soviet commanders, communication with, 99
Embick, General Stanley Dunbar, 18
Emergency High Commission for liberated Europe, 66
Ethiopia, 193
European Advisory Commission: establishment, 88; French participation in German Control Commission, 164, 169–71; German surrender terms, 136; German zones of occupation, 56, 69, 101–2, 169, 299; Germany, dismemberment question, 137, 162–63; Germany, treatment of, 37, 38; Moscow Conference, 36; Soviet policy shift, 311–12; Stalin, 101; success, 88; Winant, 289
European High Commission, 36–37, 85, 88–89

Fairchild, General Muir, 18
Far Eastern agreement, 93–98
Far Eastern war, 8, 91–98
Farouk I, King of Egypt, 72, 241, 258, 289
Fascism, 243

356

INDEX

Fear, freedom from, 71
Finland: reparations, 264; Soviet plans for (1941), 9
Finney, Captain William F., 32fn.
Finnish War (1939), 149
Flynn, Edward J., Democratic party leader, 68–69, 219, 282–83, 291
Foote, Wilder, 30, 36, 83, 103, 137, 279, 288
Foreign ministers' meetings, 118–20, 135–38, 169–70, 190–95, 223–33, 252–58, 327–30
Foreign policy (U.S.), 12
Four Freedoms speech (Roosevelt), 13
Four-Power Declaration (1943), 14
France: British bases in, Stalin's support of (1941), 10; "Declaration on Liberated Europe," 245, 253, 261; devastation, 132; European Advisory Commission, 164; European High Commission, establishment of, 36–37; German Control Commission participation, 126–29, 139, 163–64, 169–71, 262, 298–99; German occupation zone, 63, 89, 101–2, 126–29, 139, 163–64, 169, 298–99, 344–45; German reparations, 133, 254–55; Germany, control of, 163; Germany, plans for treatment of, 37; Lend-Lease, 101; liberation, 23; political parties, 277; Reparations Commission, 254–55; Ruhr, 123; Saar, 123; San Francisco Conference, 232, 256; Security Council, 17; Teheran Conference, 8; United Nations Declaration, 193; world charter conference, 67. *See also* De Gaulle
French Committee of National Liberation, 31, 101
French Indo-China, 237–38

Gallacher, William, member of Parliament, 277
Gaulle, General Charles de. *See* De Gaulle
General Assembly, 16, 31, 173, 174, 188, 194–95, 202, 203, 205, 282, 283, 297
General International Organization, 36
George VI, King of England, 61, 105
German Control Commission, 126–29, 163, 168, 262, 298–99, 311, 344–45
Germany: atrocities, 245; autarchy, 41fn., 86fn.; boundaries, 38, 64–65, 86; casualties, 184; Control Commission for, 163, 168, 262, 298–99, 311–12, 344–45; Crimean destruction, 99–100; decentralization of, 230; defeat in, plans for, 333; disarmament of, 230; dismemberment, 121–29, 135–39, 162–63, 169, 230–31, 254, 280, 344; economic policies, 86; economic treatment of, 38–40; European Advisory Commission, 56, 69, 137, 162; food, 132–33; French occupation zone, 89, 126–29, 139, 163–64, 169, 298–99, 344–45; German-Polish boundary changes, 38, 64–65; industry, 130–31; minorities, 86; Morgenthau plan, 40; national income, 166; occupation and control of, 333–34; occupation zones, 37, 56, 63, 69, 89, 101–2, 123, 299; oil production, 108; peacetime economy, 130; planning for final attack on, 23; Poles, repatriation, 211; Polish boundary problem, 38, 64–65; postwar control of, 36–37; railroad gauge, 106–7; reparations, 10, 40, 119, 122, 130–34, 164–69, 229–32, 235–36, 253–56, 263–67, 272, 274, 280, 299, 334–35, 345–46; Rhineland, Soviet plans for (1941), 9; self-sufficiency, 41, 86; standard of living, 166; submarine warfare, 108; surrender terms, 5, 122, 124, 126, 136, 169; Teheran Conference, 8; treatment, plans for, 37–40, 86; Yalta Conference, 5, 117–34
Gildersleeve, Virginia Crocheron, American educator, 186
Godschalx, Staff Sergeant Raymond J., 32fn.
Grabski, Stanislaw, 153, 155, 158, 210, 212
Graham, Ralph L., 31
Great Britain: acquisitive instinct, 237; Argentina, 200; Balkan difficulties (1944), 11–12; Chinese unity, 66; De Gaulle *de facto* authority, 101; dominions, 175; Dumbarton Oaks talks, 16–17; European High Commission, es-

357

INDEX

tablishment of a, 36–37; Far East, 95; financial policies, 133; German reparations, 130–34; Germany, plans for treatment of, 37; Greece, military responsibility in, 11, 13; Italian Government, attitude toward, 49–53; national structure, 174; Russian request for extra Assembly seats, 187–88; Russian suspicion of, 8–9; secret information, pooling of, 7; Security Council voting, 17, 145–46; Soviet alliance (1942), 10; western European bases, 10; Yalta aftermath, 309; Yalta concessions, 295; Yalta Conference, 3, 4, 6. *See also* Churchill; Eden

Greece: Aegean Islands, Stalin's plan for (1941), 10; British military responsibility in, 11; Bulgarian reparations, 257; Churchill, 11, 61, 218, 244; Dodecanese Islands, 10; elections, 241; liberation, 23; United Nations Declaration, 192; Yalta, 217, 218

Grew, Joseph Clark, 35–36, 83, 318

Gromyko, Andrei A.: Balkan inquiry, 12; Dumbarton Oaks disagreements, 20–22, 148; Economic and Social Council, 20; reparations, 265; San Francisco Conference, 319–21; Security Council voting procedure, 141, 295; Security Council's procedural questions, 17–18; Soviet Republics, additional seats for, 196–98; Yalta Conference, 23–24, 79; 102, 103, 219, 333

Groza, Dr. Petru, Romanian statesman, 312

Guatemala, 192

Gusev, Fedor Tarasovich: foreign secretaries' meeting, 191; Germany, dismemberment of, 162, 163, 169; world security organization, 16; Yalta Conference, 79, 102–3, 219, 221, 333

Hackworth, Judge Green H., 15

Haile Selassie, Emperor of Ethiopia, 72, 257–58, 289

Haiti, 192

Halifax, Lord (Edward Frederick Lindley Wood), Earl of Halifax, 10–11, 54

Hamburg, Germany, 122

Hanover, Germany, 122

Harriman, Miss Kathleen, 82, 134, 219

Harriman, William Averell: Big Three conference, location, 23; Bulgarian armistice, 257; Control Commissions, 43; De Gaulle, 100; Far Eastern agreement, 92–93, 95; Far Eastern question, 91–93; Japanese war, 117; Malta conference, 60, 68–69; Molotov luncheon, 118; Polish question, 210–13, 229, 247, 248, 259; Provisional Polish Government, 182; ships for Russia, 287; Soviet credit, 120; Soviet foreign policy, 314–15; veto power, 320; Yalta Conference, 30, 81, 83, 84, 102, 111, 116, 118, 134, 219, 310, 332

Hepburn, Admiral Arthur Japy, 18

Hess, Rudolf, German politician, 245

Hesse-Darmstadt, 122

Hesse-Kassel, 122

Hiss, Alger, 30–31; Malta conferences, 36; Moscow, 288; Naples meeting, 49; Russian request for extra votes, 196; trusteeship issue, 238; Yalta Conference, 30–31, 83, 84, 103, 137, 138, 270, 332

Hodges, General Courtney H., 246

Holland, devastation, 132

Honduras, 192

Hopkins, Harry Lloyd: Chinese unity, 66; Churchill, 55; De Gaulle, talk with, 56; Far Eastern question, 92–93, 95; German occupation zones, 56; health, 48, 55, 57, 75, 285, 291; Italian question, 52–53; Malta conferences, 66–69; Moscow trip for Truman, 319; Naples conference, 48–49, 52–53; Polish question, 157, 182, 185, 260, 261, 269–71, 273, 303fn., 319; public service record, 48; Quebec Conference (1943), 91; Roosevelt, understanding of, 48, 55; Security Council voting procedure, 54–55, 161; Soviet Republics (16), right each to vote, 55; "T.V.A. note," 178–79; veto power, 320; world security conference, 189; Yalta Conference, 23–24, 82, 83, 92, 95, 103, 118, 138, 284–85, 331

Hornbeck, Dr. Stanley Kuhl, American political scientist, 15

358

INDEX

Hull, Cordell: American delegation, 189; Argentine policy, 199–200; Balkan problem, 11; Halifax, conference with (1944), 10–11; Iran memorandum, 180–81; Italian Government, 50; *Memoirs, quoted,* 9–10; Molotov conference (1942), 8; Moscow Conference (1943), 14–15, 91; Quebec Conference (1944), 40; San Francisco Conference, 251; Teheran Conference, 3; VIPs, acquaintance with, 32; world organization, 16–17; Yalta Conference telegram, 275
Hungary: Control Commission, 43, 87; liberation, 300; reparations, 264; Soviet influence in, 13; Soviet plans for (1941), 9
Hurley, General Patrick Jay, 20, 44

Ibn Saud of Saudi Arabia, 72, 257, 278, 289–90
Iceland, 201
India, 192
Indo-China, 237–38
Inter-American Conference at Chapultepec, 280–81, 291, 306
International co-operation, 14
International Court of Justice, 16
International organization, 14, 15–16, 36, 85
International relations, 47
International trusteeships. *See* Trusteeships
Interpreters, at Yalta, 103
Iran: Allied interference, 194; Allied troops, 44; American oil companies, 195; American troops, 195; "Declaration of Iran" (1943), 43–44, 193–94; Eden, 65–66, 193–94, 258; Lend-Lease, 195; oil concessions, 44, 65, 87, 194–95; Roosevelt, 178, 180–81; Soviet Union, 65; troop withdrawal, 194–95; Yalta protocol, 348–49
Iraq, 193
Ismay, General Sir Hastings, 102, 219, 332
Isolationists, Lend-Lease opposition, 7
Italy: Advisory Council for Italy, 50–51; Churchill's attitude toward Italian Government, 49–53, 60–61; elections, 241; fleet, 287; food rations, 53; frontiers, 348; political and economic situation, 49–53; Yugoslavia, 9–10, 65, 256, 348

Japan, Yalta Conference agreement, 91–98, 279, 351–52
Jebb, Hubert Miles Gladwyn, British diplomat, 196
Jews, in Soviet Union, 278

Kalinin, President Mikhail, 105
Kenneth, Staff Sergeant David T., 32fn.
Kenney, Lieutenant General George C., 32
Kerekes, Master Sergeant Jess J., Jr., 32fn.
Kerr, Sir Archibald John Kerr Clark: Bulgarian armistice, 257; Polish question, 210–13, 224, 247, 248, 259; Provisional Polish Government, 182, 211; Yalta Conference, 219, 332
Khudiakov, Soviet Air Marshal, 79, 102, 219, 333
Kiel Canal, 122
Kilgore, Senator Harley Martin, 5
Kindley Field, Bermuda, 32
King, Admiral Ernest Joseph, Malta, 60, 70; Russian formal dinner, exclusion from, 219; San Francisco for United Nations conference, 205–6; Yalta Conference, 80, 82, 102, 134, 219, 331
Kirk, Alexander Comstock, American diplomat, 49, 52–53
Konev, Marshal Ivan, 106
Königsberg, Germany, 41, 86, 106, 210, 211
Koreis Villa, Yalta, 82, 83, 118, 218
Ku Klux Klan, 275
Kuomintang-Communist agreement, 87
Kurile Islands, 93, 304, 351
Kuter, Major General Laurence S., 102, 331
Kutzeba, Polish Professor, 158
Kuznetsov, Admiral Nikolai Gerasimovich, 79, 102, 219, 332
Kyushu, island, Japan, 97

Lagens Airport, Azores, 32–33
Land, Vice Admiral Emory Scott, 331
Lapham, Roger Dearborn, 207
Latin-American nations, 199–200, 298

359

INDEX

League of Nations: American participation, 19; mandates, 44–45, 236, 238; Soviet Union, 149
Leahy, Admiral William Daniel: France, ambassador to, 262; Malta, 68–70; Yalta Conference, 81, 82, 89, 102, 103, 134, 218, 285, 331
Leathers, Frederick James, Minister of War Transport, 1st Baron Purfleet, 332
Leipzig area, 122
Lend-Lease: cementing force, 7; Free French, 101; Iran, 195; isolationist attitude, 7; Roosevelt, 220; Soviet Union, 7, 120, 318; termination, 318
Lenin, Nikolai, Curzon Line, 154
Liberated countries. *See* "Declaration on Liberated Europe"
Liberia, 193, 290
Life (magazine), *quoted* on Yalta Conference, 5–6
Lippmann, Walter, American author, *quoted* on the Soviet Union, 7
Lithuania, 173
Livadia Palace, Yalta, 28, 81–84, 99, 102, 105, 111, 116, 118, 135, 137, 189–90, 204
London Government. *See* Poland
Lubin, Dr. Isador, American economist, 289
Lublin Government. *See* Poland
Luxembourg, 192
Lwow, Poland, 41, 86, 87, 151, 152, 154

Maisky, Ivan Mikhailovich, Soviet diplomat: German reparations, 130–31, 133, 166, 229–30, 255–56, 266, 272, 300; Yalta Conference, 102, 103, 219, 333
Malta conferences, 28–29, 59–75
Manchuria, 93, 98, 268, 305
Marchionese airfield, Caserta, Italy, 49
Marrakech meetings, French Morocco, 35–48
Marshall, General George Catlett: Azores, 33–35; German zones of occupation, 69; Malta, 60, 63; Russian formal dinner, exclusion from, 219; San Francisco for United Nations conference, 205–6; Smith, Bedell, 73; Vargas mission,

290; Yalta Conference, 80, 82–84, 102, 107–9, 134, 219, 331
Matthews, H. Freeman, American diplomat, 262; German occupation zones, 63; Germany, dismemberment of, 162, 169; Marrakech, 36; Moscow, 288; Naples meeting, 49; Polish-German boundary problem, 65; Yalta Conference, 30, 63, 83, 84, 103, 138, 262, 284, 332
McFarland, General Andrew Jackson, 102
McIntire, Admiral Ross T., 68, 75, 80, 134, 189, 285
McNarney, Lieutenant General Joseph T., 49
Memoirs of Cordell Hull, The (Hull), *quoted,* 9–10
Mexico, 193. *See also* Chapultepec Conference
Mikolajczyk, Stanislaw, 42, 64, 86, 88, 152–53, 155–56, 158, 210, 212, 226, 227, 241–42, 303fn., 313
Mikoyan, Anastas Ivanovich, 286
Military co-ordination, 298
Milwaukee (U.S.S.), 287
Molotov, Viacheslav Mikhailovich: Balkan Control Commissions, 65; British headquarters dinner, 272–78; Bulgaria, 256–58; Chinese Communists, Soviet interest in, 20; Control Commissions, 43, 163–64, 169, 262; cruisers and destroyers, 286–87; "Declaration on Liberated Europe," 253, 300; "Declaration on Poland," 346–47; French occupation zone, 102; French participation in German Control Commission, 163–64, 169, 262; German reparations, 164–70, 231, 272, 299–300; Germany, dismemberment of, 135–38; international trusteeship, 232–33; Iranian question, 194–95, 258; Polish agreement, 312–13, 346–47; Polish problem, 155, 171, 181–82, 184, 209–12, 223–29, 234–35, 240, 246–48, 252, 259, 260, 261, 271, 303fn.; protocol, 79, 284; reparations, 266; Roosevelt conference (1942), 8; Russian request for extra Assembly seats, 173–74, 191–93, 196; San Francisco Bay visit, 205; San Francisco Conference, 206–7, 232, 256; Security Council voting procedure, 141, 144–45,

INDEX

161–62, 172fn.; Soviet credit, 119–20; Stettinius, invitation to, 114; Teheran Conference, 3; veto power, 319, 321; world organization conference, 190–91; Yalta, 79, 80, 81, 83, 84, 93, 99, 102–4, 114–15, 118–19, 218, 266, 288, 332; Yugoslav problem, 217, 239, 256–58
Mongolian People's Republic, 93, 351–52
Montgomery, Field Marshal Sir Bernard Law, 74, 108
Montreux Convention, 44, 267–68, 349
Moral leadership, 46–47
Morgenthau, Henry, Jr., 40, 120
Moscow Conference (1943), 14–15, 36, 88
Moscow Reparations Commission. *See* Reparations Commission
Moscow visit, after Yalta Conference, 285–88
Moseley, Philip Edward, American political scientist, 37, 38fn., 310fn.
Moser, Staff Sergeant Day U., 32fn.
Murphy, Robert Daniel, American diplomat, 50–51
Mustafa el-Nahas Pasha, Egyptian statesman, 241

Nahas Pasha. *See* Mustafa el-Nahas Pasha
Naples meetings, 48–56
National Provisional Government. *See* Poland, Provisional Government
National Socialist party (Nazis), 38, 40, 243
Nationalist Government, China, 44, 66, 94, 305, 352
Nations, smaller, rights of, 112–13, 116, 145, 298
Nazism, 38, 40, 243
Neisse, river, Germany, 155, 184, 210, 260, 301
Netherlands: British bases in, 10; Control Commission, 129; devastation, 132; German reparations, 90, 129; liberation, 23; United Nations Declaration, 192
New York *Herald Tribune*, quoted on Yalta Conference, 4
New York *Times*, quoted on Yalta Conference, 4

New Zealand, 192
Nicaragua, 192
Norway: British bases, 10; devastation, 132; liberation, 23; United Nations Declaration, 192
Notter, Harley, 15

Oder River, 210, 301
Odessa, Soviet Union, 65
Oil: Germany, 108; Iran, 44, 65–66, 87, 194–95
Oliver, Sarah Churchill, 59, 70, 219
Oppeln, district, Silesia, 211
Orion (H.M.S.), 60, 67, 68
Osubka-Morawski, Polish diplomat, 156, 158, 210
Oumansky, Constantine A., 161
Outer-Mongolia, 93, 351–52

Page, Edward, 104, 118–19
Panama, 192
Paraguay, 193, 200
Pasvolsky, Leo, special assistant to Secretary of State, 15, 22, 141
Pavlov, Russian interpreter, 102–3, 219, 272
Payne Field, Cairo, 288
Peace, responsibility for, 111–12
Persia, 180
Peru, 193, 200
Peter II, King of Yugoslavia, 217
Petrov, General Ivan, 106
Philadelphia *Record*, quoted on Yalta Conference, 4
Philippines, 193
Plenary sessions (formal meetings), Yalta Conference, 327–30. *See also* individual subjects discussed; entries for participants in discussions
Poland: agreements, 280; American proposal, 209–10; boundary problem, 5, 8, 9, 38, 41, 64–65, 86–88, 151–55, 168, 181–86, 209–12, 259–61, 269–71, 301, 347; British proposal, 211–12, 246–48; Churchill's attitude, *see* Churchill; Curzon Line, 9, 41, 86, 151–52, 154–55, 181, 209, 211, 225, 270, 301, 314; "Declaration on Poland," 346–47; East Prussia, 9; Eden's attitude, *see* Eden; elections, 64, 86, 210–14, 216, 226–27, 234, 240–42, 251–52, 258–59, 302, 303; Germans, repatriation of, 211; government, 42, 64, 86, 88, 151–59, 168, 171, 181–82, 192,

361

INDEX

210–16, 223–29, 234–35, 240, 242, 246–49, 251, 258–61, 269–70, 302–3, 313–14, 346–47; Harriman's attitude, *see* Harriman; Hopkins, attitude, *see* Hopkins; Kerr, attitude, *see* Kerr; liberation, 23; literacy, 241; London Government, 64, 152–53, 155–56, 210–11, 213–14, 225, 240; Lublin Government, 42, 64, 86, 88, 89, 152, 155–58, 171, 212–15, 225–28, 241, 252, 302, 313–14; Molotov, attitude, *see* Molotov; oil fields, 87; political parties, 42; Provisional Government, 181–82, 210–12, 216, 224–26, 228, 234, 246–49, 259–60; Red Army, 240, 259, 300–1; Red Cross, 89–90; Roosevelt's attitude, *see* Roosevelt; Russian concessions, 300–3; Russian penetration, 300–1; Soviet objectives, 152–54; Stalin's attitude, *see* Stalin; Teheran Conference, 8; treatment plans, 41–42; United Nations Declaration, 192; UNRRA, 89–90; Yalta Conference, 5, 151–59, 337–38
Polish Corridor, 41
Polish-American question, 113
Politburo, 107, 221, 309–11
Political Agenda Group, 15
Polland, Rear Admiral, British naval officer, 289
Pomerania, 41, 64, 86
Port Arthur, 93, 351
Portal, Sir Charles, 102, 218, 332
Portenoy, Lieutenant Norman S., 32fn.
Postwar problems, 8–10. 13
Potsdam Conference, 35, 98, 301fn.
Prisoners, 311
Provisional Government. *See* Poland
Prussia, 9, 41, 122, 184, 210–11

Quebec Conference (1943), 91; (1944), 40
Quincy (U.S.S.), 25, 68–70, 72, 74, 87, 285, 289, 291

Radescu government, 312
Railroad gauges, 106–7
Red Army, 240, 259, 299, 301
Red Cross, 89–90
Reilly, Mike (bodyguard), 80
Reparations. *See* Finland; France; Germany; Great Britain; Greece;
Hungary; Netherlands; Romania; Soviet Union; also participants in discussions such as Churchill; Eden; Molotov; Roosevelt; Stalin
Reparations Commission, 131, 133–34, 164–70, 230–32, 235–36, 254–55, 263, 264–67, 274, 280, 289, 300, 335
Republican party, 45
Rhineland, 9, 56
Richmond, Major William F. (pilot), 32, 35, 288
Riga, Treaty of (1921), 41
Rockefeller, Nelson A., 200
Rokossovsky, Marshal Konstantin, 106
Roman Catholic Church, 69, 198
Romania: Control Commission, 43, 87, 312; "Declaration on Liberated Europe," 311–12, 314; reparations, 264; Soviet military responsibility in, 10–11; surrender, 23
Romer, Tadensz, 153, 158
Roosevelt, Franklin Delano: adventurous spirit, 24; "Agreement on Terms for Entry of the Soviet Union into the War Against Japan," 93–94, 96, 98, 279; Allied Control Commissions, 170–72; Allied unity, 274, 283; Arabs, 289–90; Argentia Conference (1941), 13; Argentina, 113, 199–200; Associated Nations, 199–202, 298; atomic bomb, 33–34; Azores, 33; Balkan proposal of Churchill, 11–12; Bern meeting, 315–16; British headquarters dinner, 272–78; Bullitt, W. C., *quoted* on, 5–6; Churchill, friendship with, 70–71; Churchill, toast to, 276; Congress, joint session of (1945), *quoted,* 303; Crimean destruction, 99–100; De Gaulle, relationship, 100–1; death, 309, 314, 315; Declaration on Liberated Europe," 36–37, 88, 242–45, 249, 253, 300, 314; Dumbarton Oaks, 20–22; Europe, maintaining troops in, 139; European Advisory Commission, 101; European High Commission, establishment of a, 36–37; Far Eastern agreement, 92–93, 305; Farouk, King, 289; foreign policy, 12; Four Freedoms speech, 13; French participation in German Control

362

INDEX

Commission, 170–72; German Army in Italy, surrender of, 315; German Control Commission, 262; German people, *quoted* on, 40; German reparations, 130–34, 167, 229–30, 263–67, 274, 299–300; Germany, attitude toward, 100; Germany, partitioning of, 121–29, 138–39; Germany, zones of occupation, 101–2; good-humored exchange, 269; Haile Selassie, 289; hatred of, 6; health, 5–6, 72–73, 75, 203, 267; Hull, letter to, 251; humor, sense of, 83; hypnotic influence, 25; Ibn Saud, letter to, *quoted*, 289–90; inaugural address, 72, 257, 278, 289–90; Indo-China, problem of, 237–38; international fear, 71; Iranian question, 178, 180–81; Japanese war, 91–96, 117, 304–5; Korea, Russian entry into, 98; Lend-Lease, 220; Malta conference, 68–75; message to Congress (March 1, 1945), 292, 297–98, *quoted*, 322–23; Molotov conference (1942), 85; Moscow pledge, *quoted*, 15; nations, cooperation among, 322; patience and calmness, 22; Persia, 180; personal diplomacy, 25; plans for an enduring peace, 13; Polish boundaries, 87, 151, 168, 181–86, 209–10, 260, 269–71, 301; Polish elections, 240–42, 303; Polish Government, 88, 151–52, 157–59 *quoted*, 168, 171, 181–82, 210–16, 240–42, 302–3, 313–14; political responsibility, 303; postwar planning (1941), 3, 4, 8; prejudices (racial, religious), 275–76; pre-Yalta talks, 62; Quebec Conference (1944), 40; Russian diplomatic relations, 198–99; Russian formal dinner, Yalta, 218–22; Security Council voting procedure, 17–18, 45–47, 54–55, 137–39, 143, 146, 150, 173; Security Council's procedural questions, 17–18; SHAEF difficulties, 74; ships for Russian use, 287; Soviet membership in Assembly, 174–77, 186–88, 191, 193, 195–97, 203, 297; Soviet request for extra seats in the Assembly, 186–88, 191, 193, 195–97, 203, 297; Soviet society, 323; Soviet Union, policy toward, 323–24; Stalin, co-operation, 62, 307; Stalin, praise for, 220–21; Stalin military conference, 195–97; Stalin's attitude toward, 129; Stettinius-Eden conference (1944), 16; Teheran Conference, 8, 146; trusteeships, 236–37; United States, extra votes for, 282–83; vision, 180; world interdependency, 322; world organization, 117–18, 174–80, 188; world peace, 24–26; world problems, grasp of, 30; world security conference, 198–204, 206, 207; Yalta, Big Three conferences, 3, 4, 8, 99–116; Yalta Conference, arrival, 80–83; Yalta Conference, attitude toward, 24–26; Yalta Conference, objectives, 321–22; Yalta Conference, selection of location, 23–24; Yalta trips, 27–30, 80–81, 291–92; Yugoslavian agreement, 262

Rosenman, Judge Samuel Irving, 292
Royal Sovereign (H.M.S.), 287
Ruhr, district, Germany, 56, 122, 123
Rumania. *See* Romania
Russia. *See* Soviet Union
Russian-American relations, 178
Russian-British relations, 178
Russo-Japanese War (1904), 93

Saar River, 122, 123
Sacred Cow (airplane), 80, 285
Sakhalin Island, 93, 351
Saki airfield, Crimea, 28–29, 79–81, 285
Salvador, El, 192
San Francisco Conference: American delegation, 186–87, 189; China, 256; discussion, freedom of, 142fn., 232; Eden, 207, 232, 256, 310; France, 256; Gromyko, 319–21; Hiss, 31; Hull, 251; invitations, 232, 256, 298, 342; Molotov, 256; selection, 203–6
Sapieha, Adam Stephanus, Archbishop of Cracow, 158, 210
Saudi Arabia, 193, 202
Saxony, 122
Secret agreements, 282
Secret information, 7
Security Council: decisions, 342; discussion, freedom of, 141–42, 321; disputes, 45–47, 144, 148, 319; Dumbarton Oaks, 140, 146–50; France, 17; permanent members,

363

INDEX

232, 236; procedural matters, 17–18, 46, 140, 342; sanctions, 19; veto power, 18–19, 21, 296, 320; voting procedure, 5, 17–20, 45–47, 54–55, 61–62, 66–67, 85, 87, 115–16, 137–38, 139–50, 161–62, 171–72, 188, 280–81, 295–96, 319–21, 342
Senate Foreign Relations Committee, 187
Sevastopol, destruction at, 27, 284
Sforza, Count Carlo, 49–52, 61
SHAEF, 74
Shaw, G. Howland, Assistant Secretary of State, 31
Silesia, 41, 211
Simferopol, Russia, 81, 284–85
Simpson, General William H., 246
Sirius (H.M.S), 60, 63, 68, 73
Skupschina (Yugoslav Legislature), 263, 347
Smaller nations, 112–13, 116, 145, 298
Smith, Lieutenant General Walter Bedell, 73–74
Smuts, Field Marshal Jan Christian, 54
Somervell, Lieutenant General Brehon Burke, 60, 331
Somerville, Sir James Fownes, British Admiral, 332
South Africa, 192
South-Manchurian Railroad, 93, 351
Soviet Union: Balkans, 9–12; Brazil, 291; British alliance (1942), 10; China, 93–94, 304–5; Chinese Communists, 20, 44, 66; confidence of other countries, 322; constitution, 192; credits from United States, 119–20; Curzon Line, 9, 41, 86, 151–52, 154–55, 181, 209, 211, 225, 270, 301, 314; De Gaulle *de facto* authority, 101; dictatorship, 323; diplomacy, 96, 198; Dumbarton Oaks talks, 16–22; Economic and Social Council, 16–17, 20; European High Commission, establishment of a, 36–37; extra votes, 117, 186–88, 281–82, 296–97; Far Eastern agreement, 93–98; Finnish War of *1939*, 149; Foreign Office, 286; foreign policy, 314, 315; German reparations, 119, 130–34; Germany, postwar plans for, 37–38; good faith of, 324; international understanding, 6–7; Iran, 43–44, 65, 87, 194–95; Italian fleet, 287; Japanese war, 90–96, 98, 279, 304–5, 351–52; Jews, 278; Kuriles, 93, 304; League of Nations, 149; Lend-Lease, 7, 120, 318; Manchuria, 305; national structure, 174; Poland, 64, 151–59; political power, nature of, 96; postwar claims, 9; reconstruction period, 120; Red Army, 240, 259, 299, 301; Reparations Commission, 133–34; Republics, 192; Romania, military responsibility in, 10–11, 13; secret information, 7; Security Council voting, 18, 55; smaller nations, attitude toward, 112–13; society, 323; suspicion of British and American motives, 8–9, 62; tyranny, 323; United States, attempt at co-operation, 7–8; United States, inaccurate information about, 113; UNRRA, 42–43; veto right, 19; war damages, 121; warm-water port, desire for, 8, 66, 268; winter offensive, 106–7, 109; world organization, 22, 322; Yalta, concessions at, 6, 295–98; Yalta Conference, 3, 4; Yugoslav agreement, British amendments to, 300
Spheres of influence, 11–12, 23, 66, 149
Stalin, Marshal Joseph: Allied unity, 274, 283; appearance, 99; Argentina, 113, 199–200; Bern meeting, 315–16; British headquarters dinner, 272–78; Churchill, attitude toward, 8, 129, 219–20; Churchill conference (1944), 12–13; Churchill letter on Poland (1945), 317–18; Dardanelles, 267–69; De Gaulle, evaluation of, 100; decisions, 25; "Declaration on Liberated Europe," 242–45, 249, 300; dispute formula, 22; Dumbarton Oaks, 21–22; Eden, conference, 9–10; elections, 310; European Advisory Commission, 101; French participation in German Control Commission, 262; German reparations, 130–34, 263–66, 272, 274, 300; Germany, partition of, 121–29, 138; Germany, zones of occupation, 101–2; good-humored exchange, 269; Great

INDEX

Britain and U.S., alliance with, 296; Greek problem, 218, 244; Hess, inquiry about, 245; Hopkins, visit for Truman, 319; Indo-China, problem of, 238; Japanese war, 91–95, 117; Jewish problem, 278; Lend-Lease, 220, 319; mannerisms, 138; military co-ordination, 298; military strategy, 23; Montreux Convention, 267; Moscow pledge, *quoted*, 15; party system, 277; personal habits, 111; Poland, objectives in, 152–54; Polish agreement, 313–14; Polish boundaries, 9, 151–54, 184, 209–10, 258–60, 271, 301; Polish elections, 240–42, 303, Polish Government, 88, 155–56, 182, 186, 210, 214, 216, 226–27, 234, 235, 258–60, 302, 317–18; Potsdam Conference, 310; prejudices (racial, religious), 275–76; Roosevelt, attitude toward, 129; Roosevelt, co-operation, 8, 62, 307; Roosevelt, praise from, 220–21; Roosevelt letter on Poland (Feb. 6), 157–58; Roosevelt military conferences, 195–97; Russia, extra votes for, 187–88, 196, 202–3; Russian formal dinner, Yalta, 218–22; San Francisco Conference, 206–7; Security Council voting procedure, 22, 87, 140–50, 171–72, 321; Stettinius' evaluation, 111; suspicions, 149; Teheran Conference, 8, 91; Turkey, 267–69; "Uncle Joe," 114–15; uniform, 138; United States, extra votes for, 282–83; veto power, 320; western offensive, 246; world organization conference, 178, 198–203; Yalta, Big Three meeting, 3, 4, 99–116; Yalta Conference, aftermath, 309, 310; Yalta Confernece, first plenary dinner, 102–3; Yugoslavia, 217–18, 239, 262

Stassen, Harold E., 186

State Department: American military officials, 52; atomic bomb, 33–35; Balkans, settlements in, 11–12; civilian experts in, 19; European High Commission, 36; Germany, treatment of, 37–40; Lend-Lease, termination, 318; Marrakech discussions, 45–47; military and naval staffs, 18; Political Agenda Group, 15; Soviet loans, 120; United Nations Declaration, 14; White House liaison, 96

Stenographic records, 103

Stevens, Lieutenant Kenneth J. (pilot), 32 fn.

Stimson, Henry Lewis, 34, 40, 96–97, 177, 290

Strong, General George Veazey, 18

Subasitch or Subasic, Dr. Ivan, Yugoslav statesman, 217, 239, 262

Subasitch-Tito agreement, 233, 239

Submarine warfare, 108

Sudetenland, Soviet plans for, 9

Taylor, Myron C., American diplomat, 15

Tedder, Air Marshal Arthur W., 109

Teheran Conference, 15, 105; Churchill, 8; colonial empires, 8; Far Eastern war, 8; France, 8; Germany, partitioning of, 122; Indo-China, problem of, 238; military questions, 4; non-military problems, 3; Polish problem, 151; Roosevelt, 8; ships for Russia, 287; Soviet winter offensive, 109–10; Stalin, 8, 91; warm-water port for Russia, 268

Teheran Declaration, 146, 194

Terceira, island, Azores, 32–33

Territorial trusteeships. *See* Trusteeships

Tito, Marshal Jossip Broz, 65, 217–18, 239, 241, 262–63, 347

Train, Admiral Harold, 18

Truman, Harry S.: Baruch report, 316–17; Hopkins' Moscow trip, 319; Lend-Lease termination, 318–19; Polish agreement, 302; Potsdam Conference, 35; veto power, 320; Yalta Conference, 97

Trusteeships, 44–45, 232–33, 236–38, 343

Tubman, William S., Liberian statesman, 290

Tully, Miss Grace, 22, 30

Turkey: Dardanelles, 44, 267–69, 349; Dodecanese Islands, 10; postwar plans for, 10; Teheran Conference, 8; United Nations Declaration, 193; world organization membership, 200–2; Yalta Conference, 27

Tyson, Major Terence Lloyd, 31

365

INDEX

Ukrainian Republic, 100, 173, 187, 202-3, 281, 282, 296-97
Union of Soviet Socialist Republics. *See* Soviet Union
United Nations, 16-17, 19, 40, 138, 297. *See also* San Francisco Conference; world organization
United Nations Assembly. *See* General Assembly
United Nations Charter, 324
United Nations Conference, 335. *See also* San Francisco Conference
United Nations Declaration (1942), 14, 191-93, 202; Lublin Government, 89; Poland, 89-90; Soviet Union, 42-43
United States: Assembly, 283; Balkan settlements, attitude toward, 11-12; co-operation with Soviet Union, 7; De Gaulle *de facto* authority, 101; diplomatic relations with Russia, 7; Dumbarton Oaks talks, 16-23; European High Commission, establishment of a, 36-37; financial policies, 133; Germany, occupation forces in, 127; Germany, plans for treatment of, 37; Italian Government, attitude toward, 49-53; national structure, 174; Reparations Commission, 133-34; Russian suspicion of, 8-9; secret information, pooling of, 7; Security Council voting, 18; Yalta aftermath, 309; Yalta concessions, 295; Yalta Conference, 3, 4, 6; western offensive, 246. *See also* Roosevelt; Truman
UNRRA, 42-43, 89-90
Upper Silesia, 41, 210
Uruguay, 193, 200

Valletta, Malta, capital, 59, 60
Vandenberg, Senator Arthur Hendrick, 5, 186-87
Vargas, Dr. Getulio Dornelles, 290-91, 307
Venezuela, 193, 200
Vetch (Anti-Fascist Assembly), 263, 348
Veto power, 135-50, 296, 320
Victor Emmanuel III, King of Italy, 49-51
Vishinsky or Vyshinsky, Dr. Andrei Yanuarievich: Bucharest, 312; competition, *quoted* on, 286; economics, 286; German reparations, 229; Germany, dismemberment of, 162, 169; Yalta Conference, 79, 102, 103, 112-13, 218, 288, 332
Vorontsov Villa, 82, 190
Voting procedure, problems of. *See* Security Council

War criminals, 245, 346
Watson, General Edwin M., 68, 80, 82, 291
West Coast, Soviet intelligence activity, 34
Westphalia, 122-23
White, Senator Wallace H., Jr., 5
White Russia, 173, 187, 202, 281, 296-97
Wilhelmina, Queen, 90
Willson, Admiral Russell, 18
Wilson, Edwin Carleton, 31
Wilson, Lord (Henry Maitland), British Field Marshal, 332
Winant, John Gilbert, 37, 56, 162-63, 169, 191, 217, 289
Witos, Vincente, Polish statesman, 158, 210, 212
World organization, 8-9, 13, 14, 23, 24; American participation, 223-24; American proposals on, 16-17; Assembly membership, 173; Churchill, 62, 176-78; conference sites, 117-18; discussions on, 19; Dumbarton Oaks, 16; international trusteeships, 44-45, 232-33; members, 197-98; Roosevelt, 139, 174-80, 188; Russian concessions, 295-98; Soviet participation, 22, 148-49, 173-74, 187-88, 310; Soviet Republics, 17, 20, 55; Stettinius, 137-39, 142; Yalta, 116, 186
World peace, 24-26

Yalta Conference, Crimea (1945), 79-351; American participants, 30-31, 35, 331-32; Soviet Union participants, 332-33; United Kingdom participants, 332
Yugoslavia, 347-48; agreements, 280; Austro-Yugoslav frontier, 256; British amendments, 300; British influence, 13; -Bulgarian relations, 348; Churchill, 11, 217-18, 239, 262-63; Eden, 217, 233, 239, 256-57, 262; elections, 217, 241; government, 239-40, 262-63;

Italian boundaries, 65, 256, 348; Italy, Stalin's plan for (1941), 9–10; liberation, 23; Molotov, 217, 233, 239, 256–57; restoration, Soviet plans for (1941), 9–10; Roosevelt, 262; Russian influence in, 13; Stalin, 217–18; United Nations Declaration, 192; war settlements, 11; Yalta, 217–18, 338–39

Zacharias, Admiral Ellis M. (formerly Deputy Chief of Naval Intelligence), 305 fn.

Zhukov, Marshal Gregory, 106